The English Connection

The English Connection

A Text for Speakers of English as a Second Language

Gail Fingado   *Columbia University*

Leslie J. Freeman   *New York Institute of Technology*

Mary Reinbold Jerome   *Columbia University*

Catherine Vaden Summers   *Columbia University*

(Coauthors in alphabetical order)

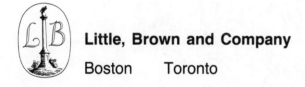

Little, Brown and Company

Boston   Toronto

Library of Congress Cataloging in Publication Data

Main entry under title:

The English connection.

Includes index.
1. English language—Text-books for foreigners.
I. Fingado, Gail
PE1128.E543   428.2′4   82–14807
ISBN 0–316–28312–6

Cover, interior design, and illustrations by Robert & Marilyn Dustin

Library of Congress Catalog Card No. 82–14807

ISBN 0-673-39261-9

15 14 13 12 11

KPF

Printed in the United States of America

For

Kenny Brawner
Joel Brodkin
Eva Linnell Jerome
Jerry Leff

Brief Contents

1 The Present Continuous   2

2 Going To and Will   14

3 The Simple Past Tense   28

4 The Simple Present Tense   48

5 There + Be; Count and Non-Count Nouns   70

6 Verb + Infinitive, Verb + Object + Infinitive, Verb + Gerund   90

7 Time Clauses and the Real Conditional   108

8 Can, Could, Be Able To   122

9 The Past Continuous Tense   132

10 Comparison of Adjectives, Adverbs, and Nouns   144

11 The Superlative of Adjectives and Nouns   166

12 Have To and Must   180

13 May, Might, Must, and Could   194

14 Should, Ought To, Had Better, Would Rather, and Supposed To   214

15 Too, Enough, So, and Such   236

16 The Simple Present Perfect Tense   258

17 The Present Perfect Continuous and the Simple Present Perfect Tenses   276

18 The Past Perfect Tense, Past Perfect Continuous Tense, and the Future Perfect Tense   292

19 Modal Perfects   310

20 Simple Passive: Present, Past, and Future   328

21 Perfect Passives, Continuous Passives, Modal Passives   344

22 Present Unreal Conditional and Wish Clauses   364

23 Past Unreal Conditional and Wish Clauses   384

24 Causative   400

25 Noun Clauses in Object Position: Indirect Questions   422

26 Adjective Clauses   436

27 Final Integration of Verb Tenses: Active and Passive and Modal Auxiliaries   456

Appendix: Irregular Verbs in English   462

Index   467

Contents

• Chapter	• Grammatical Focus	• Theme	• Dialogue Situation	• Page
1	• Present continuous	• Dating	• Jack and Arnold discuss dating and meet two women	2
2	• The future: *going to* and *will*	• Dating customs	• Molly and Yolanda talk about their first date with Jack and Arnold	14
3	• Simple past, used to	• Space travel	• Molly, Jack, Arnold, and Yolanda discuss the space shot to Jupiter	28
4	• Simple present; adverbs of frequency	• Energy and conservation	• Jack and Arnold discuss the energy crisis and the oil companies	48
5	• There is/are, there was/were; count nouns; non-count nouns	• Native Americans and immigrants	• Arnold, Yolanda, Jack, and Molly talk about their backgrounds	70
6	• Verb + infinitive; verb + object + infinitive; verb + gerund	• Rock and Roll and the generation gap	• Arnold and his father argue about Arnold's future career as a rock musician	90
7	• Time clauses and real conditional	• Physical fitness and sports	• Yolanda and Molly are jogging in Central Park to get in shape	108
8	• Can, could, be able to	• More sports	• Arnold and Jack discuss the Yankees at a baseball game	122
9	• Past continuous	• UFO's and other unexplained phenomena	• Jack and Molly talk about a man who claims he saw creatures from another planet	132
10	• Comparative adjectives, adverbs, and nouns	• Cities	• Arnold, Jack, Yolanda, and Molly talk about different cities in the United States	144
11	• Superlative of adjectives and nouns	• Astonishing facts	• Yolanda and Arnold talk about their day at the circus	166

12	• Have to and must	• The military	• Jack, Arnold, Yolanda, and Molly discuss military spending	180
13	• May, might, must, could	• Leisure time	• Yolanda and Jack talk about Molly, who is in Vermont	194
14	• Should, ought to, had better, would rather, supposed to	• Personal problems	• Molly and Yolanda discuss whether Molly should move out of her mother's home	214
15	• Too, enough, so, and such	• Exploration and achievement	• Yolanda, Molly, Jack, and Arnold are packing for a camping trip	236
16	• The present perfect: questions with ever, how many times; already/yet; unstated past	• Love and marriage	• Yolanda and her sister Sandra talk about Sandra's plan to marry Jeff	258
17	• The present perfect and the present perfect continuous with how long	• Changes	• Yolanda, Jack, and Arnold discuss the change in Molly since she got her own apartment	276
18	• Past perfect, past perfect continuous, future perfect	• Medicine	• Arnold and Yolanda talk about some amazing changes in the field of medical science	292
19	• Modal perfects	• Disasters	• Jack tells Molly and Yolanda about his friend's experience skydiving	310
20	• Simple passive: present, past, and future	• Government	• Jack and Yolanda discuss inflation and taxes	328
21	• Perfect passives, continuous passives, modal passives	• Education	• Molly tells Yolanda that she is going to apply to medical school	344
22	• Present unreal conditional and wish clauses	• Inflation	• Molly and Yolanda are discussing Yolanda's party and the high cost of living	364
23	• Past unreal conditional and wish clauses	• The Civil War	• Jack, Arnold, Yolanda, and Molly talk about slavery	384

24	• Causatives	• Television	• Arnold and Yolanda talk about television	400
25	• Noun clauses	• Famous Americans	• Molly tells Jack about an article she read on Albert Einstein	422
26	• Adjective clauses	• National parks	• Jack, Molly, Yolanda, and Arnold talk about national parks they are going to see on their trip West	436
27	• Grammar Integration			456
	• Appendix of irregular verbs			462
	• Index			467

Intended for intermediate students of English as a second language, this grammar text uses topics of current interest to provide a context for the explanation and illustration of the structures it presents. Although intermediate students have already had some exposure to many of the major structures of English, they need additional practice to attain mastery of these structures. At the same time, they need to be challenged by adult content. We have therefore focused on social, economic, interpersonal, and political questions. It is expected that this material will not only be absorbing and informative, but will also provoke stimulating discussions. Four characters are used throughout the text in the dialogues, examples, and exercises. They meet, interact, develop, and to some extent provide a model for discussing the issues and ideas that are presented. Throughout the book, students are encouraged to draw on their own experience and to share their opinions and feelings with one another.

The text is divided into twenty-six primary chapters. Each has a specific grammatical and thematic focus, and each includes a wide range of exercises, some controlled, some free, providing practice of the structures taught in the chapter. Students can use this text independently at home or in a classroom situation. While the chapters are arranged in order of increasing complexity, there is no reason why the students cannot study the structures in a different sequence. It is our hope that this grammar text will provide the student of English as a second language with fresh and exciting material as well as clear and concise explanations of the language.

To the Teacher

This book can be used for both the introduction and review of English structures. It is assumed that the student has some familiarity with the basic patterns of English but needs additional work to master the structures presented here and to achieve fluency with them.

Format of Each Chapter

Each chapter opens with a dialogue in which the target structures are illustrated in natural spoken English. A grammar explanation follows, along with examples in which the new structures are highlighted in a context thematically related to the whole chapter. Exercises of varying levels of control provide an opportunity for practice, mastery, and testing of the grammar. Every chapter concludes with a series of questions which invite the students to use their personal perceptions and experiences in expressing ideas and opinions evoked by the material presented in the chapter. While each chapter builds to some degree on preceding chapters, there is no reason why chapters cannot be used in a different sequence. Neither is there any reason why the dialogue must introduce the chapter; it is equally possible to use the dialogue for an integration at the conclusion of the lesson.

How to Use Each Chapter: Suggestions

While this text lends itself to many different teaching approaches, here are some suggestions that you may find useful.

The Dialogue

Each dialogue involves two or more of the four characters who reappear throughout the book. You might begin by having the students read the dialogue silently and notice the grammar structures in bold type as a preview to the chapter. Alternatively you might begin by using the dialogue as a listening comprehension exercise. Here you might start by describing the situation of the dialogue and directing the students to listen to the conversation and answer questions about the content—"Why was Arnold so angry?"—and questions about the grammatical focus of the dialogue— "What do you think was the grammatical focus of this dialogue?" Students might then open their books and read the dialogue silently. Another way to use the dialogue is to break the class up into small groups and direct them to read and practice the dialogue as a preparation for role-play or improvisation. You can move around the room to help the students with the dialogue and to correct pronunciation. The students can also be asked to use their imaginations and continue the conversation in the dialogue in either written or spoken form. You can expand on the vocabulary and idiomatic expressions in the dialogue by suggesting other ways to express similar emotions. If a dialogue involves an argument, for example, you can provide other expressions used in arguments, and then have the students role-play other types of arguments. After completing the dialogue, students often want to react to and comment on the issues raised in the conversation.

Grammar Explanations and Examples

The examples can be used as either short reading selections or listening comprehension passages. We have found that students enjoy listening to the examples and then answering questions or asking questions of each other about the content. Grammar practice often flows naturally from the situations we have provided.

Exercises

The exercises can be done as homework and collected by the teacher or can be corrected in class either in small groups or by the teacher. Many exercises can be used as readings or listening comprehension passages before students are asked to fill in answers at home. Many exercises are meant to provoke discussions which lead to compositions.

Expressing Your Ideas

Each chapter concludes with a series of questions about the issues raised in the chapter. These questions help the students use the grammar and the vocabulary of the chapter in a freer context. They also allow the students to draw on their own experience and background and to make comparisons between their own countries and the United States.

To the Student

We have written this book to give you a review of the important structures of English as well as information about the United States and the world that we believe will capture your interest. Many people think grammar has to be boring. On the contrary, we believe grammar can be fascinating if it is taught in a relevant context. For this reason we have selected topics that are frequently controversial. We have used four main characters throughout the book in the dialogues and examples and have tried to make them as human as possible. We address this book to you as adult learners to whom issues of social, economic, and political significance are of interest. We hope that you will find it an interesting and challenging way to review and learn English structure.

Acknowledgments

We would like to express our appreciation to the following people who have assisted us with this book:

To our students and colleagues at the American Language Program of Columbia University, especially Lou Levi, Dick Faust, Henrietta Dunham, Frank Horowitz, Thad Ferguson, Linda Lane, and Arley Gray;

To Joel Brodkin, Sheila Fields, and the students of the New York Institute of Technology;

To our families and friends, especially Kenny Brawner, Jim Jerome, Bill Jerome, Ann Raimes, and Teri Phillips.

The English Connection

The Present Continuous

Hearts and Flowers

Dating Service Questionnaire

Name _____

Address _____

Age _____ Height _____ Weight _____ Color of Eyes _____

Color of Hair _____ Present Job _____

Educational Background_____

Where have you lived in the United States? _____

Have you traveled abroad? Where? _____

Do you speak other languages? Which ones? _____

What do you like to do in your spare time? List your specific interests or hobbies.

_____

What kind of books do you like to read? _____

What kind of movies do you like to go to? _____

Are you athletic? What sports do you enjoy? _____

Do you want to get married? ____ Do you want to have children? ____ How many? ____

Where do you want to live, in a small town or in a large city?_____

What is your astrological sign? _____

Which of these qualities describe you best? Check the appropriate boxes.

☐ romantic   ☐ impulsive   ☐ warm
☐ jealous   ☐ cautious   ☐ dependent
☐ artistic   ☐ tense   ☐ independent
☐ shy   ☐ relaxed   ☐ distant
☐ outgoing   ☐ practical-minded   ☐ hot-tempered
☐ competitive   ☐ spontaneous   ☐ affectionate

What qualities do you look for in a man or in a woman? List the following qualities
in the order of importance to you, beginning with the most important.

kindness	social status	good looks
intelligence	creativity	age
openness	taste in clothes	good conversational ability

Theme: Dating

Grammar: The Present Continuous

Dialogue

(ARNOLD and JACK are sitting in a bar having a drink and discussing their love life.)

JACK: Hey, Arnold, how **are** things **going** with you and Susan?

ARNOLD: Don't ask. Things **aren't working** out at all. We **aren't seeing** each other much anymore.

JACK: That's too bad.

ARNOLD: Yeah. She**'s going** out with someone else now. I have rotten luck with women.

JACK: Well, I guess we're in the same boat[1] now. I**'m trying** to meet someone too.

ARNOLD: It's really tough to meet people.

JACK: What about a computer dating service?

ARNOLD: **Are** you **kidding**? That's not going to work.

JACK: How do you know? It's worth a try.[2]

ARNOLD: Hey, Jack. Look at those two girls.

JACK: What girls?

ARNOLD: They**'re sitting** at the next table.

JACK: Arnold, you**'re staring** at them.

ARNOLD: That's okay. They**'re staring** at us.

JACK: Hey, the girl with the dark hair **is waving** to us.

ARNOLD: I think she**'s inviting** us to their table. (He gets up and starts walking toward the other table.)

JACK: Wait a minute. What **are** you **doing**? Where **are** you **going**?

ARNOLD: Come on. What **are** you **waiting** for? Let's go.

---

1. *We're in the same boat:* We have the same problem.
2. *It's worth a try:* There's a chance you will succeed.

The present continuous tense is used in three ways:

1. to talk about an action that is happening now;
2. to talk about an action in the extended present; and
3. to talk about an action in the future.

STATEMENTS

$$\text{Subject} + \begin{array}{c} am \\ is \\ are \end{array} + \text{(not)} + \text{base form}[3] + ing$$

A girl is waving to Arnold.

QUESTIONS

1. (Question word) $+ \begin{array}{c} am \\ is \\ are \end{array} +$ subject + base form + ing?
   What
   Who(m)
   Where
   Why
   How

What is Arnold doing?

Short answers: Yes, subject $+ \left\{ \begin{array}{l} am \\ is \\ are \end{array} \right.$

No, subject $+ \left\{ \begin{array}{l} am + not \\ isn't \\ aren't \end{array} \right.$

NOTE: We do not use contractions with affirmative short answers.

2. Negative questions:

$$(\text{Question word}) \left\{ \begin{array}{l} + \ aren't \ + \left\{ \begin{array}{l} I \\ you \\ we \\ they \end{array} \right. \\ \\ + \ isn't \ + \left\{ \begin{array}{l} he \\ she \\ it \end{array} \right. \end{array} \right. + \text{base form} + ing?$$

---

3. *base form*: the form of the verb without any marking for tense or person. This is the form of the verb you find in the dictionary.

Part 1   The Present Continuous: The Present Moment

Many languages use only one present tense. English has two. We use the present continuous to talk about an action that is happening now (at the present moment).

You are reading about the present continuous now.

Part 2   The Present Continuous: The Extended Present

We often use the present continuous to talk about an action that is happening in the extended present. By the extended present we mean "these days" or "nowadays." When we use the present continuous in this way, we are often talking about changes.

Dating customs are changing these days in the United States.

Examples

EXTENDED PRESENT
These days many single people **are complaining** that it is very difficult to meet people. More and more singles **are turning** to special services that help people meet each other. Computer dating services **are becoming** more popular.

PRESENT MOMENT
A reporter for television station WKJB is doing a special report on computer dating services.

REPORTER: I'm **standing** in the office of Hearts and Flowers Computer Dating Service. As you can see, they **are doing** a good business in here today. By the way, if my wife **is watching** this show, I'd like to say: Honey, I'm **not looking** for anyone new. I'm just **reporting** on the singles scene[4] here in this city.

These people **are filling** out questionnaires. They're **answering** questions about their age, their interests, their hobbies, and the qualities they prefer in a man or a woman.

Here's the computer, Big Mac. Right now Mac **is processing** applications and **is matching** men and women with similar interests.

Here's a happy looking man. Sir, what **are** you **doing** here?

---

4. *singles scene:* the different places single people go to meet each other.

MR. X: I'm **talking** to this very nice woman.
REPORTER: Oh, aren't you lucky. Did the computer match you two?
MR. X: No, we met right here in the office. Forget the computer. We're on our way to lunch together.

Part 3   Present Continuous: Future Meaning

When we have a definite plan for the future, we can sometimes use the present continuous to talk about this plan.

Examples

REPORTER: **Are** you **leaving**, miss? Did you have much luck here?
MISS Y: Yes, this place is great. I'm **meeting** a new date *this weekend*, and I'm **bringing** my girl friend here *tomorrow*.
REPORTER: Well, that's all, folks. *Tomorrow* I'm **reporting** on video dating services. Tune in then.

Part 4   Questions with <u>Who</u> and <u>What</u> When They Are the Subject of the Sentence

Explanation

When *Who* and *What* are the subject of the verb in a question, notice these things:

1. The verb is always in the singular, even when the answer is plural.
2. Begin the question with *Who* or *What* and follow the normal word order.
3. These rules are true for all tenses.

$$\begin{matrix} Who \\ What \end{matrix} \; + \; is \; + \; \text{base form} \; + \; ing?$$

Short answer: singular subject + *is*.
plural subject + *are*.

Look at these questions about the scene in the computer dating office:

Who's asking questions about the dating service?
   A reporter **is**.
Who's leaving to have lunch?
   Two customers **are**.
What television station **is** broadcasting this report?
   WKJB **is**.

Notice the difference between *Who/What* subject questions and *Who/What* object questions (the reporter is talking to Mr. Peterson, the owner of the Computer Dating Service):

Who's *talking* to Mr. Peterson?
  The reporter is.
Who is the reporter talking **to**?
  He's talking **to Mr. Peterson**.

NOTE: Notice that the question word *Whom* as the object in the question is the correct form, but in conversational English we rarely use it. We usually say *Who*.

Part 5   Spelling Problems for the Present Continuous Tense

A. Double Consonants

When you see this pattern in one-syllable words:

consonant   vowel[5]   consonant

the final consonant almost always doubles.

sit → sitting
cut → cutting
rob → robbing
swim → swimming
shop → shopping

With words of more than one syllable, the rules are difficult to follow. Use your dictionary. We do.

B. Final e

Drop the final *e* of the base form when you add *ing*. Do not double the consonant.

write → writing
smoke → smoking
take → taking
change → changing

C. Final ie

When the base form ends in *ie*, change the *ie* to *y* and add *ing*.

die → dying
lie → lying
tie → tying

---

5. a, e, i, o, u.

If the base form ends in y, keep the y and add *ing.*

$$carry \rightarrow carrying$$
$$hurry \rightarrow hurrying$$

Exercise 1   Present Continuous: Present Moment
and Extended Present

Directions
Fill in the correct form of the present continuous tense.

REPORTER: Tonight I *'m reporting* to you from a video dating
                          (report)

service. The owner, Mr. Peterson, _____ next to
                                                        (stand)

me. Mr. Peterson, this is a very unusual service. How

_____ your business _____?
                                                (do)

MR. PETERSON: Business _____. New people _____
                                      (boom)   (come)

in every day. Our list of customers _____ by
                                                        (grow)

leaps and bounds.[6]

REPORTER: Mr. Peterson, please tell our viewers about your unique

service.

MR. PETERSON: In this room Miss Quinn _____ a videotape.
                                                    (make)

The gentleman next to her is one of my employees. He

_____ her.
        (interview)

REPORTER: What about the people in this room? What _____
                                                                        (do)

they _____?

---

6. *by leaps and bounds:* rapidly.

MR. PETERSON: These customers _____ our library of video-
(view)

tapes and _____ about which people they would
(think)

like to date.

REPORTER: Then what happens?

MR. PETERSON: Well, for example, if Miss Quinn chooses Mr. Dirkson's tape,

then Mr. Dirkson comes into the office to see Miss Quinn's

tape. If he likes her tape, then we arrange a date for them.

REPORTER: Oh, here's Miss Quinn. _____ all this

_____ you nervous?
(negative, make)

MISS QUINN: Yes, _____. Look at my hands. They
(short answer)

_____. What _____ you
(shake)   (do)

_____ here? _____ you
                                   (make)

_____ a videotape, too?

REPORTER: No, _____. I'm with WKJB Television News.
(short answer, negative)

Millions of people _____ this program right now.
(watch)

MISS QUINN: Millions! Oh, no! That _____ me even more
(make)

nervous.

REPORTER: Tell me something, Miss Quinn. _____ people

_____ each other in traditional ways anymore?
(negative, meet)

MISS QUINN: Sure, _____. People these days _____
(short answer)   (meet)

still _____ in churches and in schools and at

parties.

REPORTER: Why then _____ people _____ out
(seek)

services such as video dating?

MISS QUINN: Well, I think it's the isolation in big cities. Many people

_____ to church anymore, and they're out of
(negative, go)

school. So more and more people _____ for new
(look)

ways to make friends.

REPORTER: Thank you very much, Miss Quinn. We _____
(break)

now for a commercial.

Exercise 2 Present Continuous with Future Meaning

REPORTER: Today I am reporting to you from the offices of Club Med. Club

Med has resorts all over the world. Many of these resorts are

extremely popular with singles. Sir, *are you taking* a Club
(take)

Med vacation?

MR. FRANK: Yes. I _____ to Martinique tomorrow.
(fly)

REPORTER: _____ you _____ alone?
(go)

MR. FRANK: Yes, I _____.
(short answer)

REPORTER: How long _____ you _____?
(stay)

MR. FRANK: I _____ for a week.
(go)

REPORTER: I guess you _____ your heavy winter coat.
(negative, take)

MR. FRANK: No, I _____. I _____ the whole day
(short answer)   (spend)

on the beach tomorrow.

REPORTER: It sounds like a great vacation. Have a wonderful time.

Exercise 3   Questions

A. Directions
Write questions with *Who* about the subject of these sentences. Look at the answer first. This is a continuation of the scene in the opening dialogue.

1. Arnold is talking to Jack.

    QUESTION: Who *is talking to Jack* ?

    ANSWER: Arnold is.

2. Molly and Yolanda are looking at Arnold and Jack.

    QUESTION: Who_____?

    ANSWER: Molly and Yolanda are.

3. The waiter is taking Molly's order.

    QUESTION: Who_____?

    ANSWER: The waiter is.

4. Arnold and Jack are walking toward Molly and Yolanda's table.

    QUESTION: Who_____?

    ANSWER: Arnold and Jack are.

B. Directions
Write questions with Who(m) about the object of the sentence.

1. Arnold is talking to Jack.

    QUESTION: Who *is Arnold talking to* ?

    ANSWER: To Jack.

2. Molly and Yolanda are looking at Jack and Arnold.

    QUESTION: Who_____?

    ANSWER: At Jack and Arnold.

C. Directions

Write *Who* subject or object questions. Look at the answer first to decide if the question is about the object or the subject.

1. Yolanda is introducing Molly to Jack and Arnold.

   QUESTION: Who *is introducing Molly to Jack and Arnold*?

   ANSWER: Yolanda is.

2. Molly and Jack are shaking hands.

   QUESTION: Who_____?

   ANSWER: Molly and Jack are.

3. The bartender is pouring beer for their table.

   QUESTION: Who_____?

   ANSWER: The bartender is.

4. Jack is paying the waiter.

   QUESTION: Who_____?

   ANSWER: The waiter.

5. The bill is wrong. Jack is complaining to the manager.

   QUESTION: Who_____?

   ANSWER: To the manager.

Expressing Your Ideas: Speaking and Writing

1. Are matchmaking services such as computers, newspapers, and television shows becoming popular in your country? What is your opinion of these services?
2. Are dating customs changing in your country? If so, how?

3. Imagine you are in a discotheque watching what is going on around you. There are many different people here. Write about what each person is doing. For example:

A tall man with dark sunglasses is playing a saxophone.

2

Going To and Will

YOLANDA

ARNOLD

MOLLY

JACK

Theme: *Dating*

Grammar: *Going to; Will (For Making Promises, Making Requests, Offering Help, and Making Predictions)*

Dialogue

(Tonight MOLLY and YOLANDA are going to go out with JACK and ARNOLD for the first time. In this dialogue YOLANDA and MOLLY are talking on the telephone.)

YOLANDA: Hello?

MOLLY: Hi, Yolanda. This is Molly.

YOLANDA: Hi, Molly, What's up?[1]

MOLLY: I'm really nervous about this date tonight. **I'm going to need** your help.

YOLANDA: What's the matter?

MOLLY: It's my first date with Jack. What **am I going to do?** What **am I going to say** to him?

YOLANDA: Wait a minute, Molly. Things **will work** out.

MOLLY: Okay. But I'm really nervous. I can't think straight.[2] **Are** you **going to offer** to pay for your ticket?

YOLANDA: Yes, I am. A lot of women are paying for themselves these days.

MOLLY: Yeah, that's true. What time **are** they **going to pick** us **up?**[3]

YOLANDA: They **aren't**. We**'re going to meet** them at eight o'clock sharp[4] in front of the theater. Be sure to be there on time.

MOLLY: What? **Aren't** they **going to pick** us **up?**

YOLANDA: No. They want to meet us at the movie.

MOLLY: I don't want to go alone.

YOLANDA: **I'll pick** you **up** on my way to the theater. **Will** you **meet** me downstairs?

MOLLY: All right. But don't forget to call me before you leave your house.

YOLANDA: All right. **I won't**.

MOLLY: Yolanda, there's another question on my mind. **Are** you **going to go** up to Arnold's apartment after the movie?

YOLANDA: Mmm. . . . I don't know, Molly. It's only our first date. **I'm going to play** it by ear.[5]

MOLLY: I'm so nervous! I know **I'm going to do** something stupid and **put my foot in my mouth.**[6] This **isn't going to be** an easy evening for me. I can feel it.

---

1. *What's up?*: What's new? What's going on?
2. *think straight*: think clearly.
3. *pick someone up*: meet someone at his or her home to go out on a date.
4. *sharp*: precisely.
5. *play it by ear*: leave plans indefinite and decide later.
6. *put your foot in your mouth*: say something stupid or embarrassing.

Part 1 Going To

Explanation

When we talk about our plans or intentions for the future, we usually use the *going to* form for the future. Use this form:

> Subject + *be (am, is, are)* + *going to* + base form
>
> *They are going to meet at 8:00.*

Here are some time expressions that we frequently use to talk about the future:

tomorrow	next week	a few minutes from now
the day after tomorrow	next month	in a second
tonight	next year	in a minute
this weekend		in a week
this afternoon		in a little while
this evening		
in the future		
in the near future		
in the distant future		

Examples

(In this dialogue YOLANDA, ARNOLD, JACK, and MOLLY are standing in line in front of the movie theater.)

ARNOLD: Look at that line! It's a mile long. I'**m going to have** a cigarette. Who has a match?

YOLANDA: I have some, but I'**m not going to give** them to you. Cigarettes are really bad for you.

ARNOLD: Come on, Yolanda. Have a heart. Give me the matches.

YOLANDA: Well . . . I don't know.

MOLLY: Wait, I have a match right here. (She opens her pocketbook and drops it. Ten candy bars fall out.)

JACK: Molly! **What are you going to do** with all of those candy bars? **Are you going to eat** them all yourself?

YOLANDA: (Laughs). I'm so jumpy. First dates are really hard for everyone, aren't they? I'**m going to bite** my fingernails in the movie. Molly'**s** probably **going to eat** too much. And Arnold's probably **going to smoke** too much. What's your nervous habit, Jack?

JACK: Who's nervous?

Exercise 1

Directions

Read the following situations. Write questions about what you think is going to happen. Then write answers to your questions. Include at least one negative sentence.

A.   Jack is sitting in front of a pile of books, holding his head. He is reaching for a bottle of aspirin. He says, "I have a terrible headache."

   1.   What _is he going to do_ ?
   _____(do)_____

   2.   _Is he going to study_ any more tonight?
   _____(study)_____

   Story: *Jack is going to take a break. He isn't going to study anymore tonight. He's going to take some aspirin and then he's going to take a walk.*

B.   Arnold is looking down in surprise at a hundred dollar bill on the sidewalk. A policeman is walking toward him.

   1.   _____ ?
   (pick up)

   2.   _____ to the policeman?
   (give)

   3.   How much _____ on a date with Yolanda?
   (spend)

   4.   What _____ with the money?
   (do)

   Story:

C. Jack is sitting on a bench with a "WET PAINT" sign on it. Molly is
    covering her mouth in horror and pointing at the sign.

    1. What _____ ?
                        (Molly/do)
    2. What _____ ?
                        (Jack/do)
    3. _____ on the bench?
                    (Molly/sit)
    4. What _____ with his pants?
                    (Jack/do)
    Story:

D. Arnold and Yolanda are standing on a corner in formal clothes under
    an umbrella. There is an enormous puddle of water in front of them. A
    maniacal cab driver is just about to drive into a puddle of water.

    1. What _____ ?
                        (happen)
    2. Who _____ ?
                        (get wet)
    3. How _____ ?
                        (look)
    4. How _____ ?
                        (feel)
    5. _____ the cleaning bill?
                (the cab driver/pay)
    6. _____ their clothes?
                        (change)
    Story:

A. <u>Will</u> of Promise

Explanation

In general, *going to* is used in more situations than *will*. In some situations you can use *will* or *going to* for the same meaning. However, there is one situation where we almost always use *will*: when we make a promise or offer our help. We also use *will* in questions when we make a request for help.

I
you
he, she, it ⎬ + *will* + base form
we
they

Things will work out, Molly. I promise.

Contractions:
I
you
he, she, it ⎬ + *'ll* + base form
we
they

I'll pick you up.

Examples

(ARNOLD, JACK, YOLANDA, and MOLLY are leaving the movie theater and are deciding what to do.)

YOLANDA:	That was a great movie. What are we going to do now?
JACK:	Let's go to my place. It's just two blocks from here.
ARNOLD:	Do you have any wine?
JACK:	No.
ARNOLD:	**I'll get** some. Oh, no! I don't have any more money.
YOLANDA:	That's okay. You paid for the movie. Molly and I **will buy** the wine.
JACK:	**I'll go** back and straighten up[7] my apartment. **Will** you **get** some bread and cheese too?
YOLANDA:	Sure, we **will**.
JACK:	Here's some money.
YOLANDA:	No, it's okay. We**'ll get** some cheese, and we**'ll see** you in a few minutes.

---

7. *straighten up*: put things in order.

B. Negative of Will: <u>Won't</u>

Explanation
Won't is the negative form of *will*. Here are three different meanings of won't:

1. when we promise not to do something;
2. when we refuse to do something; and
3. when something is broken and isn't working.

Subject + *will* + *not* + base form
Contraction:

        won't + base form

Yolanda won't forget to pick Molly up.

Example
(In JACK'S apartment an hour later.)

YOLANDA: Jack, your place is really nice.

JACK: Thank you. Oh, no. There's a pair of my socks under the sofa!

YOLANDA: Who cares? We **won't look** under the sofa. We promise.

MOLLY: Jack, please don't give me any more wine. I'm really high.

JACK: Okay, I **won't**. Say, Arnold, what about that new guitar you saw? Are you going to buy it?

ARNOLD: No, my father **won't lend** me the money, and I don't have enough myself.

JACK: That's too bad.

YOLANDA: Jack, will you come here for a **minute**? Where is your bread knife? This old knife **won't cut** anything.

JACK: I'll be right there.

C. <u>Will</u> of Prediction

Explanation
When we want to make a prediction about the future, we frequently use *will*.

Example

ARNOLD: I never have any money. I'm tired of being poor.

YOLANDA: A musician's life is really hard sometimes. Be patient. You**'ll be** famous someday. Then you**'ll be** rich.

ARNOLD: I hope you're right. But when **will** it **happen**?

Exercise 2   *Will* of Promise

Your boy friend or girl friend is afraid of marriage. You are proposing.
Make promises about how wonderful married life will be. You can role play
this situation in class or do it for homework.

AFFIRMATIVE STATEMENTS:

1.   We _____ very happy together.
          (be)

2.   I _____ forever.
          (love)

3.   I _____ everything you want.
          (give)

4.   We _____ beautiful children.
          (have)

Now make more promises about your house, your children, a job, and your
standard of living.

5.   _____.

6.   _____.

7.   _____.

8.   _____.

9.   _____.

10. _____.

Now make promises about what will *not* happen.

11. I _____ anyone but you.
          (love)

12. We _____ about anything.
          (argue)

13. I _____ you until the day I die.
          (leave)

Exercise 3   Negative of <u>Will</u> (Refusal)

Write negative statements to mean *refuse to.* Use *won't.*

Example

Read the following situation. Then write a negative statement.

A politician and a reporter are talking. The reporter says, "Is it true that United Oil Company gave you $1 million dollars for your campaign?" The politician answers, "No comment."

The politician **won't answer** the reporter's question.
                     (answer)

1. Molly and Jack are in a room. Molly is struggling to remove a cork from a wine bottle. Jack is struggling to open a window.

   Molly is trying to open the wine bottle, but the cork _____.
                                            (come out)

   Jack is trying to open the window, but it's stuck. It _____.
                                            (open)

2. Yolanda and her landlord are in Yolanda's apartment. Yolanda looks very angry. Yolanda says, "Will you please paint this place, fix the ceiling, and give me a new refrigerator?" The landlord answers, "No!"

   The landlord _____ her apartment.
                          (paint)

   The landlord _____ the ceiling.
                          (fix)

   The landlord _____ a new refrigerator for her.
                          (buy)

Exercise 4   <u>Will</u> of Prediction

The world is changing very fast nowadays. Nobody knows what changes the future will bring or how fast they will happen. Write predictions about the year 2030 using *will.* You can write about transportation, family life, communication, food, or space travel.

Example

Everyone will have a computer in his home.

Exercise 5   Integration: <u>Going To</u> and <u>Will</u>

Directions

Fill in the blanks with *going to* or *will*. Remember we usually use *going to* to state an intention or plan and *will* to make a promise or to offer help. (Either *going to* or *will* is correct in some examples. However, a native speaker usually follows the rules we gave in this chapter.)

1.   (JACK and MOLLY are in a restaurant.)

> MOLLY: What's the matter, Jack?
>
> JACK: There's a fly in my soup! I can't believe it. I *'m going to*
> _____ *complain* to the manager.
> (complain)
>
> MOLLY: I _____ the waiter for you.
> (call)
>
> JACK: I _____ sick.
> (be)
>
> WAITER: Oh, I'm sorry, sir. I _____ another bowl of soup
> (bring)
> for you. Please sit right there. Don't leave.
>
> JACK: Okay, I _____ .
> (negative)
>
> WAITER: Here's your soup, sir. We _____ you anything.
> (negative, charge)

2.   (Now JACK is at ARNOLD'S apartment.)

> ARNOLD: Jack, what's the matter with you? You look uptight.[8]
>
> JACK: I am. My parents _____ into Manhattan tonight
> (come)
> and _____ me out to dinner. In a few minutes I
> (take)
> _____ Molly and invite her to go with us, but I'm
> (call)
> not sure if my parents _____ her.
> (like)

---

8. *uptight:* anxious and uncomfortable.

ARNOLD: You need a drink, Jack. I have a bottle of wine in my refriger-

ator. I _____ you some. It _____ you
            (get)   (calm)

down.

JACK: Thanks.

ARNOLD: Here's your wine. Relax. But don't drink too much before you

call Molly.

JACK: I _____ .
            (negative)

ARNOLD: And don't worry about tonight.

JACK: You're right. I _____ . This wine is making me
                            (negative)

feel better already.

Exercise 6   Future Predictions

MADAME WIZ: ROLE PLAYING

Madame Wiz knows everything. She sees into the future and reads minds.
She is a famous fortune teller. She has a crystal ball that gives her amazing
powers.

You are Madame Wiz, and you have her amazing power. People come to
see you, and you look into your crystal ball and you know everything. Tell
the future of each of the following people. (You can use the questions as a
guide). Role play this in class.

A.   Molly is sitting in front of you and asking you a lot of questions. Answer
her questions and tell her fortune. Molly's questions:

When will Jack ask me out again?
When will we get married?
Am I going to leave home this year?
Am I going to get my own apartment?
When am I going to get a job?
Will I ever get rich?
Will Jack and I be happy together?

B. You are the president of the United States. You are very worried about the future. You are asking Madame Wiz a lot of questions about your future, your country's future, and the future of the world. Your partner is Madame Wiz and will answer your questions.

C. Choose a name for yourself and choose a new career that you are starting. Ask Madame Wiz about your future. She will answer you.

Exercise 7   *Grammar Integration: Present Continuous and Future*

Directions

You are the minister of economic development in your country. A journalist is interviewing you about your country's future.

INTERVIEWER: What problems is your country facing nowadays?

YOU: _____

INTERVIEWER: Will these problems become more serious in the future, in

your opinion?

YOU: _____

INTERVIEWER: What is the population of your country?

YOU: _____

INTERVIEWER: According to sociologists, is it going to increase?

YOU: _____

INTERVIEWER: What do you think your country's population will be in twenty

years?

YOU: _____

INTERVIEWER: Is overpopulation a problem? What is your government doing

about it now? What is your government going to do about this

problem in the future?

YOU: _____

INTERVIEWER: What are the main industries of your country?

YOU: _____

INTERVIEWER: What industries do you think your country will develop in the next twenty years?

YOU: _____

INTERVIEWER: What products will your country export and import because of these new industries?

YOU: _____

INTERVIEWER: Is unemployment a problem at the present time? Is the government doing anything about this problem now?

YOU: _____

INTERVIEWER: Do you think unemployment is going to increase or decrease in the next decade?

YOU: _____

INTERVIEWER: In your opinion, what role is your country going to play in the world?

YOU: _____

Expressing Your Ideas: Speaking and Writing

1. Sociologists say that the relationship between men and women is changing rapidly nowadays. Dating customs are changing. More women are working. Family life is changing. Men are helping more in the home. At the same time, the divorce rate is rising. More and more single parents are raising children nowadays.

What changes are taking place in your country nowadays? Discuss these changes.

What are your predictions for the future? What changes in behavior will become acceptable in the future? Will more women work? Will divorce become more common? Will the size of the average family change? What things won't change?

2. Look at exercise 7. Choose one area to discuss at length. For example, unemployment, overpopulation, industrial growth. Write about what is happening at the present time and predict what will happen in the future.

The Simple Past Tense

Man walking on the moon.

Theme: *The Space Program*

Grammar: *The Simple Past Tense; Used to*

Dialogue

(JACK, ARNOLD, YOLANDA, and MOLLY are sitting in a cafe and having a cup of coffee together.)

YOLANDA: Where **did** you and Jack **meet**, Arnold?

ARNOLD: We **were** classmates at City University, but I **dropped** out[1] a year ago to play music.

YOLANDA: When are you going to finish your degree, Jack?

JACK: In two years.

YOLANDA: Astronomy is an unusual field. What are you going to do with your degree—teach?

JACK: Yes, I think so.

MOLLY: I think astronomy is fascinating. **Did** you **watch** the news on television last night? They **had** a program on the space shot to the planet Jupiter. It **was** really interesting.

YOLANDA: Oh, what time **was** it on? I **didn't see** it.

MOLLY: It **was** on the six o'clock news.

JACK: I **saw** it. It **was** an amazing program. The spacecraft **came** within 278,000 kilometers of Jupiter.

YOLANDA: **Did** it **send** back a lot of pictures? **Were** they interesting?

MOLLY: Oh, yes. The photographs **were** fantastic.

JACK: Scientists **discovered** that Jupiter has rings.

YOLANDA: **Did** everything **go** okay when the spacecraft **landed?**

JACK: It **didn't land**. It **circled** Jupiter for thirty-nine hours and then **headed out** toward Saturn.

YOLANDA: It's too bad that I **missed** the news last night. I'm sorry that I **didn't see** those photographs.

---

1. *drop out*: leave school before graduation.

Part 1   The Simple Past Tense: Regular and Irregular Verbs

Explanation

Use the simple past tense when you want to talk about something that happened at a specific time in the past. Here are some time expressions that we use with the simple past:

yesterday	last night	(_____) ago
the day before yesterday	last week	a minute ago
	last month	two hours ago
	last year	a few days ago

A. Affirmative Statements

1. REGULAR VERBS: In English there are both regular and irregular verbs. Most verbs are regular. To form the simple past tense of a regular verb, add *d* or *ed* to the base form.

Examples

In October 1957 the Soviet Union launch**ed** the world's first satellite, Sputnik I. The success of Sputnik I shock**ed** Americans. After the Soviet success, the United States push**ed** ahead rapidly with its own space program.

2. IRREGULAR VERBS: Many common verbs have a completely different form in the simple past tense. They do not add *ed* or *d* to the base form to form the simple past. Turn to the Appendix for a list of the most common irregular verbs.

Examples

On April 12, 1961, the Soviet Union **sent** the first man, Yuri Gagarin, into space. Soon after, President John F. Kennedy **gave** his complete support to the United States space program. The space budget soon **grew** to $5.25 billion. Finally, on July 15, 1969, *Apollo 11* **took** off. This was the first space-craft which carried men to the moon. Millions of people **saw** the takeoff on television. On July 20, 1969, the spacecraft landed on the surface of the moon.

B. Negative Statements: Regular and Irregular Verbs

Use *did not* (*didn't*) and the base form of the verb.

Examples

In the early years of the United States space program, some launchings **didn't go** smoothly. Some rocketships **didn't** even **leave** the ground. Scientists solved most of these problems, but years later other problems came up on the *Apollo 11* moon shot. Some equipment **didn't work** properly. For example, the lunar module **didn't connect** perfectly with the command ship. Fortunately the astronauts corrected their error, and they **didn't get** hurt.

C. Past Tense Chart: Affirmative and Negative Statements

Subject	Verb				
	Helping Verb	Not	Base Form	Past	
President Kennedy				gave	support to the space program.
President Eisenhower	did	n't	give		much support to the space program.

D. Questions

1. QUESTION WORD ORDER: REGULAR AND IRREGULAR VERBS

(Question word) + did (n't) + subject + base form?

Examples
Did the Soviet Union **send** a woman astronaut into space?

Yes, it *sent* Valentina Tereshkova into space.
Did the United States **launch** the world's first satellite?
No, it **didn't.**
Did the astronauts **leave** footprints on the moon?
Yes, they **did.**
What else **did** the astronauts **leave** on the moon?
They *left* an American flag.
Where **did** *Apollo 11* **splash** down?
It *splashed* down in the Pacific Ocean.

2. QUESTIONS WITH WHO AND WHAT

Explanation A
When *who* or *what* is the SUBJECT of the verb, do not use *did* in questions. Use the simple past form of the verb. Note that the short answer is: subject + did.

Examples
Who **walked** on the moon in 1969?
Armstrong and Aldrin **did.**
Who **sent** the first woman astronaut into space?
The Soviet Union **did.**
What **protected** the astronauts from the extreme temperatures on the moon?
Their spacesuits **did.**

Explanation B

In questions when *who* or *what* is the OBJECT of the verb, use *did* and the base form of the verb.

Examples

Who **did** Armstrong and Aldrin **leave** in the command ship when they walked on the moon?

They left Mike Collins in the command ship.

Who **did** the astronauts **talk** to from the moon?

They talked to President Nixon.

What **did** the astronauts **eat** on the *Apollo 11* flight?

They ate freeze-dried food such as steak and eggs out of plastic bags.

NOTES:

1. In more formal English, we use *whom* when the question is about the object of the verb. However, to many Americans this sounds too formal for conversational English.

2. Notice that we frequently use a short answer with *did* for the *Who* subject question. It is impossible to do this for a *Who* object question.

3. WHAT HAPPENED?

Explanation

This is another kind of question where you do not use *did* and the base form.

Example

What happened when the astronauts splashed down?

They went into isolation and doctors examined them carefully.

E. Question Review Chart: Simple Past Tense

Wh- Questions	Helping Verb	Subject	Base Form	
	Did	the U.S.S.R.	send	a woman into outer space?
Where	did	*Apollo 11*	splash	down?
Why	did	the astronauts	go	into isolation?
What	did	the astronauts	eat	on the flight?
Who(m)	did	the astronauts	talk	to from the moon?

	Wh- Questions as Subject	Past Form	
	Who	walked	on the moon in 1969?
	What	protected	the astronauts from the extreme temperatures on the moon?

F. Spelling Problems for the Simple Past Tense

1. When you add *ed* or *d* to many regular verbs, you need to double the final consonant. See part 5 of chapter 1 and read the rules for doubling the consonant when you add *ing*. The rules are the same when you add *ed* or *d*.

stop	→	stopped
rob	→	robbed
omit	→	omitted
admit	→	admitted
rip	→	ripped

2. When a verb ends with a consonant and *y*, change the *y* to *i* when you add *ed*.

hurry	→	hurried
try	→	tried
apply	→	applied

3. When a verb ends with a vowel followed by *y*, you don't change *y* to *i*.

stay	→	stayed
obey	→	obeyed
play	→	played

G. Pronunciation of Regular Verbs in the Simple Past Tense

/ɨd/	/d/	/t/
Pronounce *ed* as /ɨd/ only with verbs that end with a /t/ or /d/ sound. **Examples:** operate → operated 　　　　　　　/ɨd/ wait　　　hand visit　　　provide demand　collect land	Pronounce *ed* as /d/ with— a. verbs than end with these consonants: *b, g, j, l, m, n, r, v, z.* **Examples:** grab → grabbed 　　　　　　/d/ hug　　　stare call　　　starve dim　　　buzz open b. with verbs that end with vowel sounds. **Examples:** stay → stayed 　　　　　　/d/ cry　　　allow veto　　　agree argue　　review	Pronounce *ed* as /t/ with these consonants: *c, ch, f, k, p, s, sh, x.* **Examples:** kiss → kissed 　　　　　　/t/ slice　　　hope watch　　wash fluff　　　fix talk

Exercise 1　Neil Armstrong: The First Man on the Moon

Directions

Fill in the blanks with the simple past form of the verb under the line.

Neil Armstrong *grew up* in Ohio. He was a very bright student.
　　　　　　　　　(grow up)

In the first grade he _____ ninety books. He _____
　　　　　　　　　　　　(read)　　　　　　　　　　　　　　　　　(negative, attend)

the second grade because he already _____ on a fifth-grade
　　　　　　　　　　　　　　　　　　　　　(read)

level. In high school he _____ in science and mathematics. He
　　　　　　　　　　　　　(excel)

even _____ these subjects for a while when his science teacher
　　　　(teach)

was sick. In high school he was very studious. He _____ very

much. According to his brother, he _____ many dates.
(negative, have)

   Neil Armstrong _____ interested in flying at a young age.
(become)

When he was six years old, he _____ in a plane for the first
(fly)

time. His hobby was building model airplanes. He _____
(build)

hundreds of them. When he was a teenager, he _____ at a
(work)

small airport in his home town. He _____ his pilot's license
(get)

before he _____ his driver's license. He _____ his
(get)   (start)

professional flying career after college when he _____ a pilot
(become)

for the Navy.

Note: The "(negative, socialize)" label appears under the first blank in the first line.

Exercise 2   *Question Formation in the Past Tense*

A. Ask questions about Neil Armstrong. The verb is under the line. Then answer the questions. Practice this exercise in pairs orally. Then write it.

Example

1. Where *did Neil Armstrong grow up* ?
(grow up)
Neil Armstrong *grew up in Ohio* .

2. _____ many books in the first grade?
(read)

_____

3. What _____ in high school?
(study)

_____

4. _____ in high school?
(teach)

_____

5. _____ many dates in high school?
      (have)

_____

6. _____ in a plane when he was young?
      (fly)

_____

7. _____ a hobby?
      (have)

_____

8. What _____ ?
      (do)

_____

9. _____ when he was a teenager?
      (work)

_____

10. When _____ his driver's license?
      (get)

_____

B. You are a reporter. You are going to interview Neil Armstrong about his trip to the moon. Write five questions that you want to ask him.

C. Interview a classmate about his or her past. You can ask the same questions that you asked about Neil Armstrong in Exercise A and you can add other questions, too.

1. Where _did you grow up_ ?
   I _grew up in a small town_.

Exercise 3   *Past Tense: Affirmative and Negative Statements*

Directions
Fill in the blanks with the past tense of the verb under the line. Some verbs are in the affirmative, and others are in the negative. Use the helping verb *did* for a short statement.

1. In the early days of the space program, American spaceships

   <u>*splashed down*</u> in the ocean. They <u>*didn't land*</u> on solid
   (splash down)   (negative, land)

   ground. Soviet spaceships ___ *did* ___ .

2. The Soviets _____ the first man into space. They
                             (send)

   _____ the first man to the moon. The Americans _____ .
   (negative, send)

3. The Soviets _____ a woman into space. The Americans
                             (send)

   _____ .
   (negative)

4. A *Viking* spacecraft _____ to Mars. It _____
                                 (go)   (negative, go)

   to the moon. The *Apollo 11* _____ .

5. The *Viking* spacecraft _____ equipment on Mars. It
                                 (leave)

   _____ men. Only the *Apollo* flights _____ .
   (negative, carry)

Exercise 4   *Past Tense: Negative Questions*

Directions
Ask questions in the negative using the simple past tense.

Example

1. Armstrong and Aldrin walked on the moon.

   (go) <u>*Didn't*</u> the third astronaut ___ *go* ___ with
   them?
   No, he didn't. He stayed in the command module.

2. President Kennedy gave more support to the space program than any
   other president did before him.

   (give)   Why _____ other presidents before Kennedy

   _____ as much support as he did?
   Because the United States didn't realize that Soviet space technology was more advanced in this area.

3. Two astronauts walked on the moon on the *Apollo 11* spaceshot.

    (walk)   Why _____ the third astronaut _____
             on the moon, too?
    Because someone had to be in the command ship.

4. On the *Apollo 11* flight the astronauts walked on the moon.

    (ride)   _____ they _____ in a moon vehicle,
             too?
    Yes, they did.

5. The lunar module and the command ship almost missed each other on
    the *Apollo 11* flight.

    (connect)   Why _____ they _____ at first?
    Because the equipment didn't function properly.

6. The first woman to travel in space was Valentina Tereshkova, a Soviet.

    (have)   _____ the Americans _____ women
             in their Apollo program?
    No, they didn't.

Exercise 5   *Who* and *What* Subject and Object Questions

A. *WHO/WHAT SUBJECT QUESTIONS:* Ask questions about these sentences
with *Who* or *What* in the subject position.

Example

1. A French author wrote *Voyage to the Moon.*

    Who wrote Voyage to the Moon ?

2. Two Americans flew the first airplane on December 17, 1903.

    _____

3. An American made the first flight from New York to Paris on May 21,
    1927.

    _____

4. A special rocket lifted *Apollo 11* into space.

    _____

5. Something slowed down the space capsule before it splashed down in the ocean.

_____

Answers:

1. Jules Verne did.
2. The Wright brothers did.
3. Charles Lindbergh did.
4. A *Saturn* rocket did.
5. A giant parachute did.

B. WHO/WHAT OBJECT QUESTIONS: Ask questions with *Who* or *What* about the object of the sentence.

Example

1. The Soviets sent the first man into space.

   Who did the Soviets send into space?

2. King Ferdinand and Queen Isabella of Spain sent a famous explorer on a long voyage in 1492.

   _____

3. The Italian Amerigo Vespucci mapped part of a continent.

   _____

4. The Church persecuted a famous scientist because he believed the earth moved around the sun.

   _____

5. Thomas Edison invented many important things.

   _____

Answers:

1. Yuri Gagarin.
2. Christopher Columbus.
3. Part of the Americas.
4. Galileo.
5. The first successful phonograph, for example.

C. INTEGRATION: <u>WHO/WHAT</u> QUESTIONS IN SUBJECT AND OBJECT POSITION: Read the sentence. Then write a question about it with *Who* or *What* in the subject or object position. Look at the correct answer to the question first and write the correct question for the answer.

Example

1. Homer, a Greek poet, wote *The Odyssey*.

    a. ___*Who wrote the Odyssey*___?
       Homer did.

    b. ___*What did Homer write*___?
       The Odyssey.

2. Ptolemy, a famous ancient astronomer, believed that the earth was the center of the universe.

    a. _____?
       Ptolemy did.

    b. _____?
       That the earth was the center of the universe.

3. Stanley Kubrick, an American filmmaker, made a famous film, *2001, A Space Odyssey*.

    a. _____?
       2001, A Space Odyssey.

    b. _____?
       Stanley Kubrick did.

4. An apple fell from a tree. It hit Isaac Newton on the head.

    a. _____?
       An apple did.

    b. _____?
       It hit Isaac Newton.

5. Albert Einstein won the Nobel Prize for Physics in 1921.

    a. _____?
       Albert Einstein did.

    b. _____?
       The Nobel Prize for Physics.

D. CLASSROOM ACTIVITY: Test your classmates on their knowledge of history. Think of famous writers, artists, generals, inventors, and scientists. Ask subject or object questions beginning with *Who* and *What*.

Examples
Who invented the telephone?
Who painted the *Mona Lisa*?
Who did Romeo love?
What famous battle did Napoleon lose?

Part 2 Was and Were: Past Tense of Verb To Be

A. Statements

1. AFFIRMATIVE STATEMENTS: With *I, he, she, it,* use *was.*
   With *you, we, they,* use *were.*
2. NEGATIVE STATMENTS: *was + not = wasn't.*
   were + not = weren't.

Examples
American astronauts **were** the first men on the moon, but Americans **weren't** always in first place in the "space race." The first two men in space **were** Soviets. John Glenn **was** the first American in space. On February 20, 1962, he circled the earth three times.

B. Questions

Put *was* or *were* before the subject.

Examples
Was John Glenn alone in the space capsule?
  Yes, he was.
How long **was** he in space?
  He was there for four hours and 56 minutes.
Were Americans proud on this day?
  They certainly were.

C. Questions with Who

When *who* is the subject of the verb, it is always singular.

Examples
Who **was** the first man in space?
  Yuri Gagarin **was**.
Who **was** in control of his spacecraft?
  Soviet scientists on the ground **were**.

Exercise 6   <u>Was</u> and <u>Were</u>

Directions

Complete the following dialogue by filling in the blanks. Use *was* or *were*.

Arnold and his father argue about almost everything. In this dialogue they are arguing about the moon shot.

ARNOLD: Remember the moon shot?

FATHER: I remember. Three Americans landed on the moon.

        __*Wasn't*__ that exciting?
          (negative)

ARNOLD: Only two landed on the moon. One stayed in the capsule.

FATHER: Oh, yes, that's right.

ARNOLD: How long _____ they on the moon? Do you remember

exactly?

FATHER: I think they _____ there a couple of days.

ARNOLD: No, that's impossible. They _____ there only a few

hours.

FATHER: Oh, well, I guess you're right. Where _____

Armstrong when he spoke to President Johnson? _____

he on the moon or back in the capsule?

ARNOLD: Johnson? Johnson _____ president then. Nixon
                               (negative)

_____ .

FATHER: All right, Mr. Know-it-all, how do you know so much?

ARNOLD: I _____ in a bar with friends. We _____

there for hours. We watched the broadcast on TV there. And

where _____ you?

FATHER: I don't remember where I _____ .

Exercise 7   Scrambled Sentences

Directions

Use the words in the correct sentence word order and use the past tense. When you finish, you will have a short paragraph about the life of John F. Kennedy. In general, use this word order in your sentences:

a.   subject + verb + object + place + time
b.   subject + (to be) + (adjective or noun) + place + time

Example

1.   (be) (president) (John F. Kennedy)   (during the first great expansion of the space program)

   John F. Kennedy was president during the first great expansion of the space program.

2.   (be) (he) (as a writer) (successful) (also)

   _____

3.   (be) (Massachusetts) (his home state)

   _____

4.   (grow up) (Kennedy) (there) (and) (Harvard University) (attend) (later)

   _____

5.   (write) (at Harvard) (he) (*Why England Slept*)

   _____

6.   (be) (before World War II) (about England) (this book)

   _____

7.   (experience) (fifteen years later) (Kennedy) (severe back pain)

   _____

8.   (be) (he) (for many months) (in the hospital)

   _____

9. (write) (he) (another book) (at this time)

   _____

10. (describe) (famous Americans) (in this book, *Profiles in Courage*)
    (he)

   _____

11. (win) (in 1956) (it) (for literature) (the Pulitzer Prize)

   _____

Exercise 8   *"Moon Walk": Integration of the Simple Past and Present Continuous*

VOICE COMMUNICATION: SUNDAY, JULY 20, 1969, 10:56 P.M.
(In this dialogue Neil Armstrong is already on the moon. Aldrin is still in the lunar module. He is getting ready to join Armstrong on the moon. They are talking to Ground Control in Houston, Texas.

ARMSTRONG: I *am standing* on the moon. I _____
            (stand)   (look)
            up at the windows of the lunar module.

GROUND CONTROL: We _____ a picture on the TV now. You
                     (get)

                  _____ upside down in the picture.
                     (stand)

ARMSTRONG: I'm not upside down here. Look, I _____
                                                  (make)
            footprints in sand. Beautiful view here.

ALDRIN: (from the lunar module) Ready for me?

ARMSTRONG: Roger.[2] Take it easy now. You _____ my
                                                (see)
            difficulties when I _____ down before.
                                  (step)

ALDRIN: I _____ on the top step now.
            (stand)

_____

2. *Roger:* That's right. Yes.

ARMSTRONG: OK. I _____ down the steps very slowly. I
(come)

_____ . That _____ comfortable
(hop)   (be)

for me.

ALDRIN: Good. I _____ down now too. Here I
(come)

_____ . It _____ beautiful!
(be)   (be)

ARMSTRONG: You _____ down easily. _____
(come)   (negative, be)

it fun?

ALDRIN: It sure _____ . I _____ any
(be)   (negative, have)

trouble. Hey, you _____ around like a
(jump)

kangaroo!

ARMSTRONG: I _____ almost _____ !
(float)

ALDRIN: Hey, what _____ ? Why _____
(happen)

you _____ ? _____ you
(stop)   (find)

something?

ARMSTRONG: Yes, I _____ a purple rock. Look at it!
(find)

GROUND CONTROL: Bring it back!

Part 3   Used To

Explanation

When we want to talk about an action that we did repeatedly in the past but that we don't do anymore, we use the expression *used to.*

STATEMENTS: Subject + *used to* + base form

Subject + *didn't use to* + base form

QUESTIONS: *Did* (n't) + subject + *use to* + base form?

Examples

People **used to believe** the earth was the center of the universe. They **used to think** the sun revolved around the earth.

NOTE: Sometimes when we want to emphasize that something that happened repeatedly in the past continues in the present, this is how we express it:

> The ancient Egyptians **used to tell** time by a sundial, and in some parts of of the world, people **still do.**

When we want to show that something happened repeatedly in the past and we want to emphasize that it no longer happens in the present, we express this idea in this way:

> People **used to think** that an eclipse of the sun meant the end of the world, but they **don't anymore.**

Exercise 9 Used To

Directions
Write sentences with *used to. Answer the following questions.*

1. What are some things people used to believe about the universe that they no longer believe? (Write five sentences.)

Example
People used to believe the earth was flat.

2. Write five sentences about things that you don't do anymore, but that you used to do either in your country, when you were a child, or when you lived with your parents.

3. Pretend you are a reporter interviewing a two-hundred-year-old man. Ask him questions about how the world used to be a hundred years ago, and how it is different today. Write both the questions and the answers.

Example

REPORTER: In your youth, how did you use to get around?
OLD MAN: I used to walk everywhere or I rode around in a horse and carriage. People don't walk enough anymore. They don't get enough exercise.

Expressing Your Ideas: Speaking and Writing

1. What do you remember about man's first walk on the moon? How old were you in 1969? Where were you? Did you watch it on television? How did you feel about it? How did people in your country react?

2. You just returned from a space flight to Mars. Write a report on your expedition. Here is some vocabulary you might want to use:

to blast off	command ship
to orbit a planet	countdown
to land	space capsule
to make a soft landing	spacesuit
to travel through space	to set up scientific instruments
to collect rock samples	to see canals on Mars
to see signs of life	to communicate with ground control
to splash down in the ocean	to see other galaxies
Martians	to feel dizzy
vegetation	to experience weightlessness
spaceship	to travel into outer space

3. From the 1950s to the early 1970s the Soviet Union and the United States spent billions of dollars on their space programs. Why was the space race so important to these two countries? Was competition for power and prestige the main reason for the space programs? Was exploration of the new frontier the main reason? What's your opinion?

4. How did people benefit from the space program? What new advances in technology resulted from the program? How did it change our lives? In your opinion, was the space program valuable?

5. Did the United States and the Soviet Union spend too much money on the space program? Did they neglect social programs because of the space program? Was it worthwhile to put a man on the moon? Should we continue to spend money on the space program?

The Simple Present Tense

The cooling towers of the John Amos nuclear power plant near Charlestown, West Virginia.

Theme: Energy

Grammar: The Simple Present Tense; Frequency Adverbs;
Stative Verbs

Dialogue

ARNOLD: Can you believe it? There's another oil spill[1] off the coast of California! Why **don't** oil companies **find** another way to transport oil?

JACK: We **don't have** the technology to transport it any other way.

ARNOLD: But oil spills from tankers are a serious threat to the environment. They **kill** birds and fish and **ruin** the beaches.

JACK: It **doesn't happen** that often. And besides, **don't** we **need** the oil? This country **depends** on oil imports. Even plastics **come** from oil.

ARNOLD: Sure we **need** the oil. But the big oil companies are destroying the environment. They **don't care** about anything but money.

JACK: You're exaggerating. Look, the oil companies **make** big profits, but they **use** the money to search for more oil.

ARNOLD: Wait a minute, Jack! How often **do** you **read** the newspaper?

JACK: What **do** you **mean?** I **read** it every day.

ARNOLD: Did you see that article in the *Times*[2] this morning?

JACK: What article?

ARNOLD: That one about the oil companies and the president. Even the president **wants** to limit their profits. He **doesn't want** the oil companies to take advantage of[3] the energy shortage.

JACK: Okay, give it to me, but I **don't think** we're ever going to agree about this.

---

1. *oil spill:* When a tanker carrying oil has an accident and the oil escapes into the ocean, we call this an oil spill.
2. *Times:* The New York Times.
3. *to take advantage of:* to profit from.

Part 1 Introduction to the Simple Present Tense

Use the simple present tense when you want to talk about:

1. an action that you do every day: Yolanda gets up early every morning; Arnold smokes a lot.
2. an action that is a fact or general truth: Water boils at 212°F or 100°C.

A. Affirmative Statements

I you we they	+ base form			he she it	+ base form +	s es

Plastics come from oil. America depends on oil imports.

Examples

There are many sources of energy in the world today. Oil and coal **come** from under the ground. We **burn** coal and oil to make heat. We also **mine** uranium, a radioactive mineral, to make nuclear energy. Solar energy **comes** from the heat of the sun. The sun **supplies** an enormous amount of energy. Wind also **produces** energy, and the ocean **does** too.

B. Negative Statements

I you we they	+ do not + base form

Oil spills don't happen that often.

he she it	+ does not + base form

America doesn't import all its oil.

Contractions: do + not = don't
does + not = doesn't

Examples

The supply of oil on earth is limited. Oil **doesn't exist** in infinite amounts. Most countries **don't produce** enough oil for their energy needs, so they import oil from other countries. The OPEC countries have the capacity to produce more oil, but they **don't want** to use up their oil too rapidly. For this reason, they limit their production.

C. Questions

(Question word) + do + $\begin{matrix} I \\ you \\ we \\ they \end{matrix}$ + base form?

How often do you read the newspaper?

(Question word) + does + $\begin{matrix} he \\ she \\ it \end{matrix}$ + base form?

How often does Jack read the newspaper?

Examples

Do American oil companies **drill** for oil only in the United States?
　No, they don't. They drill for oil all over the world.
Does the United States **use** other sources of energy besides oil?
　Yes, it does. It uses coal, gas, nuclear, and solar energy.
Do the big oil companies also **own** a lot of coal and uranium mines?
　Yes, they do. They own more than 1 billion tons of coal and a lot of the uranium in the U.S.
Where **do** the big oil companies **get** crude oil?
　They get it from Alaska, Norway, Venezuela, Nigeria, Mexico, the Middle East and the continental United States.
What **does** an oil refinery **do**?
　It takes crude oil and makes it into heating oil and gasoline.

D. Who/What Questions

Explanation

When Who or What is the subject of the verb in the question, the verb is always singular. When Who or What is the object of the verb, the question formation is the same as all other wh- questions. In formal English, we use Whom for the object questions.

Examples: Subject Questions

Who **mines** uranium?
　A lot of the big oil companies **do.**
Who **regulates** the production of nuclear energy?
　The government **does.**
What **powers** most modern submarines?
　Nuclear reactors **do.**
　NOTE: When you follow What with a plural noun, the verb is plural:
What kind of companies operate nuclear power plants?
　Utility companies **do.**

Examples: Object Questions

Who **do** the OPEC countries **sell** their oil to?
  They sell it to countries all over the world.
Who **does** Mexico **sell** most of its oil to?
  It sells it to the United States.

E. Simple Present Tense Charts

AFFIRMATIVE AND NEGATIVE STATEMENTS

Subject	Verb				
	Helping Verb Do/Does	Not	Base Form	s/es	
Oil			come	s	from under the ground.
The big oil companies			own		a lot of coal and uranium.
Oil	does	not	exist		in an infinite supply.
The OPEC countries	do	not	want		to use up their oil.

QUESTIONS

Wh- Question Word	Helping Verb Do/Does	Subject	Base Form	
	Does	the U.S.	use	nuclear power?
What	does	an oil refinery	do	?
Who	does	Mexico	sell	most of its oil to?
		Wh- Questions as Subject	Third-Person Singular	
		Who	mines	uranium?

NOTES:

1. When the base form of a verb ends in ss, sh, ch, x, z, or o, you add es for the third-person singular (he, she, it): pass = passes; fix = fixes; go = goes; do = does.

2. I, you, we, they + have
   he, she, it   + has

Exercise 1　Simple Present

A.　Fill in the blanks with the correct form of the simple present tense.

Coal is a major source of energy in the United States. A lot of coal

mining ___*takes*___ place in the Appalachian Mountains in the
　　　　　(take)
eastern part of the country.

A coal miner usually _____ long hard hours. He
　　　　　　　　　　　　　　(work)

_____ into the mines when it is still dark, often before six
　　(go)
in the morning. He _____ a hat with a bright light on it so
　　　　　　　　　　　(wear)
he can see. He _____ heavy tools with him when he
　　　　　　　　(carry)

_____ down in the mine. He _____ these tools
　　(go)　　　　　　　　　　　　　　　(use)
to break off pieces of coal. Sometimes he _____ explosives
　　　　　　　　　　　　　　　　　(use)
to break up the coal. Then he _____ the coal onto railroad
　　　　　　　　　　　　　(load)
cars. These railroad cars _____ the coal up out of the
　　　　　　　　　　　(carry)
mine. When the coal miner _____ work and _____
　　　　　　　　　　　(finish)　　　　　　　(come)
back out of the mine, he is covered with black coal dust.

Coal mining is a dangerous occupation. One of the dangers is the

black coal dust which the miners _____. The dust some-
　　　　　　　　　　　　　　(breathe)
times _____ black lung disease. Coal miners often
　　　(cause)

_____ trouble with their lungs as well as other health
　　(have)
problems.

B.　Now write a paragraph about your daily routine.
C.　Write a paragraph about someone you know who has an interesting
　　(boring, dangerous, etc.) job.

Exercise 2   More Simple Present

Directions

Fill in the blanks with the correct form of the simple present tense.

All power plants _**produce**_ heat. The process _____
(produce)   (start)

in different ways. Some plants _____ oil, and others
(burn)

_____ coal or uranium. When these fuels _____,
(use)   (burn)

they _____ a lot of heat. This heat _____ water
(give off)   (boil)

and _____ steam. The steam then _____ a turbine,
(create)   (spin)

and this _____ electricity.
(generate)

The fuels that _____ from under the ground—oil, coal,
(come)

natural gas, uranium—_____ most of the energy we
(supply)

_____ in our daily lives. But there are other sources that
(use)

_____ energy.
(provide)

Every day the earth _____ 10,000 times more energy from
(receive)

the sun than mankind _____ from all other kinds of fuel
(get)

together. Many countries _____ solar energy. In the United
(use)

States, for example, 30,000 homes _____ solar heat. In Israel
(use)

200,000 homes _____ solar water heaters. In Japan over two
(have)

million buildings _____ their heat from solar water heaters,
(get)

and in Australia the law _____ solar water heaters on all new
(require)

buildings. A disadvantage of solar energy is that it _____ a
(take)

very large area to collect solar heat for use by a small number of people. An

advantage of solar energy is that it is very clean and plentiful.

Exercise 3   Negative Statements

Directions
Look at the underlined part of the sentence. Change the underlined part of the sentence to the negative so it fits the blank space in the following sentence.

(The utility company, Con Elec, turned off YOLANDA'S electricity this morning. YOLANDA is talking to an official of the utility company in this dialogue.)

YOLANDA: Why did you turn off my electricity? <u>You have my payment.</u>

OFFICIAL: I'm sorry. We _don't have your payment_.

   We have <u>half</u> your payment.

YOLANDA: That's not true! You're wrong. Con Elec always <u>overcharges</u> me.

OFFICIAL: Con Elec _doesn't overcharge anybody_, Miss.

   You probably <u>have three or four air conditioners</u> in your house.

YOLANDA: That's ridiculous! I_____.

   I have only one air conditioner.

OFFICIAL: Well, you probably <u>leave it on all day.</u>

YOLANDA: What are you talking about! I _____.

   It doesn't even work.

OFFICIAL: Well, you use something, Miss. You <u>probably have a lot of other</u>

   <u>electrical appliances.</u>

YOLANDA: That's outrageous! I _____.

   All I have is <u>one</u> electric typewriter.

OFFICIAL: Well, I don't know what to say to you. <u>Con Elec tries to be fair.</u>

YOLANDA: _____!

Con Elec raises its rates for no reason. Con Elec <u>makes a fortune!</u>

OFFICIAL: No, we _____.

Con Elec <u>loses money</u> because of people like you.

YOLANDA: Con Elec _____.

Con Elec makes money. All I can say is, turn my electricity back

on. I paid my bill.

Exercise 4   Questions

Directions

Write the correct question for the answer.

(You are a reporter writing an article about solar energy. You are interviewing a producer of solar heaters.)

(produce)   REPORTER: *Does your company produce* solar energy?

PRODUCER: Yes, we do. We make solar water heaters.

(cost)   REPORTER: _____ solar energy _____ a

lot of money?

PRODUCER: Yes, it does at the present time.

(negative,   REPORTER: Why _____ the government
help)

_____ your company?

PRODUCER: It helps us a little. But solar energy isn't very

profitable yet. The technology isn't very developed.

(require)   REPORTER: _____ some countries _____

                                         solar water heaters in new homes and office

                                         buildings?

          PRODUCER: Yes, they do. They require them in new buildings in

                                           Australia.

(heat)   REPORTER: _____ a solar water heater

                                     _____ a house after the sun goes down?

          PRODUCER: Yes, it does.

(do)   REPORTER: What _____ a solar heater

(operate)   _____ ? How _____ it

                                     _____ ?

          PRODUCER: It collects solar heat during the day and stores it so

                                       that you have heat when there is no sun.

Exercise 5   Questions with <u>Who</u>

Directions

Write two different questions beginning with *Who*. Write one about the subject of the sentence and one about the object. Remember that the *Who* subject question is always singular. Look at the answer first.

Example

1. The United States buys oil from the Middle East producers of oil every

   day.

   Who buys oil from the Middle East producers?

   The United States does.

   Who does the United States buy oil from ?

   It buys oil from the Middle East producers of oil.

2. The president often asks the American public for cooperation in conserving energy.

_____?

The president does.

_____?

He asks the American public.

3. Congressmen sometimes disagree with the president about his energy policies.

_____?

Congressmen do.

_____?

They disagree with the president.

4. Congress often funds groups interested in protecting the environment.

_____?

Congress does.

_____?

They fund groups interested in protecting the environment.

Part 2   Frequency Adverbs

Explanation

Frequency adverbs are often used with the simple present tense to indicate how often or how many times we do something. They are used with other tenses also, but here we are talking about their use with the simple present. Frequency adverbs occur in different positions in the sentence.

A. Middle-Position Frequency Adverbs

always	rarely
almost always	hardly ever
usually	almost never
often	never
seldom	

AFFIRMATIVE STATEMENTS: These frequency adverbs usually go after the verb *be* and before other verbs.

Examples

a.   The Verb *Be*

Many oil companies such as Exxon, BP, and Arco are exploring Alaska for oil. They **are** *always* interested in new sources of energy. The oil in Alaska **is** *often* offshore and deep under the sea.

b.   Other Verbs

U.S. oil companies *often* **import** crude oil and refine it for fuel. They also drill oil wells all over the world in Alaska, Europe, Africa, South America, and Indonesia. The Phillips Company *usually* **produces** 19,500 barrels of oil a day from the North Slope of Alaska. The big oil companies *almost always* **make** good profits.

NEGATIVE STATEMENTS: In negative statements we usually place *always*, *almost always*, *usually*, and *often* after *not*. This is true of *be* and other verbs.

Examples

The production of oil does**n't** *always* increase from year to year. When companies drill for new oil wells, they do**n't** *always* find oil.

B. Frequency Adverbs in Initial or Middle Position

Sometimes, *occasionally*, and *frequently* can go at the beginning or in the middle of a sentence.

C. Frequency Adverbs in Middle or Final Position

The following expressions usually come at the end of the sentence. Sometimes they come in the middle.

once a day	every day	every now and then
twice a week	every year	every once in a while
three times a year	every summer	from time to time
five times a week	all the time	

Examples

The energy producers and environmentalists[4] disagree about nuclear energy *all the time.* Environmentalists say nuclear plants give off small but dangerous amounts of radiation *from time to time.* Energy producers say they check radiation levels *every day,* and there is no danger.

D. Questions and Short Answers

1. POSITION OF FREQUENCY ADVERBS

All the frequency adverbs in sections A and B usually go after the subject in *yes/no* questions. In a short answer, they also usually go after the subject.

Examples

Are American homes and office buildings often overheated and over-airconditioned?
  Yes, they *often* **are.**
Do American drivers frequently waste gasoline?
  Yes, they *frequently* **do.**

2. QUESTIONS WITH EVER

Explanation

We often use *ever* in *yes/no* questions when we want to ask about frequency. *Ever* means at any time. Don't use *ever* in the main clause of an affirmative statement. Use a frequency adverb to answer a question with *ever.*

Examples

Do people *ever* use solar energy to heat their homes?
  Yes, they *sometimes* do. About 20,000 American homes use solar heat.
Do people *ever* use windmills for energy in their homes?
  Yes, they *sometimes* do.

3. QUESTIONS WITH HOW OFTEN

Explanation

We also use *how often* in questions when we want to ask about frequency.

Examples

How often **do** American utility companies send out bills to their customers?
  They send them out *once a month.*
How often **does** a new model of an American car come out on the market?
  A new model comes out *every year.*

---

4. *environmentalists:* people who work to protect the environment.

Part 3   Stative Verbs and Verbs of Perception

A. Stative Verbs in the Present Tense

Explanation

Certain verbs are rarely used in the present continuous (*-ing*) tense even when they have a now meaning. These verbs are called "stative verbs," or verbs of perception: *know, want, like, love, need, feel, cost, forget, remember, hear, prefer, understand, exist, believe, belong, own.*

Examples

(JACK, MOLLY, YOLANDA, and ARNOLD are driving to YOLANDA's house to listen to the president's speech on energy on television.)

YOLANDA: Let's hurry. I **want** to hear the president's speech. It starts in fifteen minutes.

JACK: Oh, no! My gas gauge is on empty. Sorry, Yolanda, but I **need** gas.

MOLLY: There's a station on the corner. Why don't you pull over there?

JACK: My car is falling apart. It's so old.

MOLLY: Oh, I **like** it. It has character.

YOLANDA: Come on, let's go. You know we **need** to hurry.

B. Verbs that Change Meaning

Explanation

Certain verbs have one meaning when used in the simple present and another meaning in the present continuous. These verbs are: *think, look, have, taste, feel, smell, see.* When they are used in the present continuous, they describe an action that is happening *now*. When they are used in the simple present, they describe a quality (*feel, taste, smell, look*) or an opinion (*think*) or possession (*have*).

Examples

(At YOLANDA's house and watching the president on television)

JACK: The president **looks** very tired. Maybe he has a cold.

MOLLY: Yeah, he does. Why **is** he **looking** at something over the camera?

JACK: I **think** he's reading his speech from a screen.

ARNOLD: Jack, you're frowning. What **are** you **thinking** about?

JACK: I**'m thinking** about all the money I spend on gasoline, and prices are going up again.

ARNOLD: Why **do** you **have** a big car?

JACK: I bought it second hand[5] a long time ago.

YOLANDA: Please stop talking. I**'m having** a hard time hearing anything. I **think** this is an important speech.

---

5. *second hand:* A second-hand car is a used car.

Exercise 6 Frequency Adverbs

A. Here is a paragraph about the climate of Alaska. To make it accurate, you need to add frequency adverbs. First read the paragraph.

A lot of oil comes from Alaska. The climate of Alaska varies in different parts of the state and affects the lives of the oil workers. The Panhandle is an area in the southeastern part of the state next to Canada. [1]Winters there are mild. [2]It rains in the winter, [3]but it doesn't snow. The interior of Alaska has very different weather conditions. [4]The winters there are extremely cold. [5]The temperature reaches −40°C. [6]In this same area, however, the summers are very hot, but short. The northern coast of Alaska is the area where oil was discovered. [7]This area isn't free of ice. [8]The ground there doesn't thaw; it is permanently frozen. With its different climates and types of terrain, Alaska is a land [9]where travel is a problem. Oil workers do not move about easily in the winter months. If they make a trip, [10]it is by air. Air travel is still the easiest form of travel in this state.

B. Rewrite the paragraph (use a separate sheet of paper) and put the following frequency adverbs in the correct position in the sentence or part of the sentence that has the number in front of it. The first sentence is written for you as an example. Continue rewriting the paragraph, adding the frequency adverbs.

1. usually
2. often
3. seldom (remember that *seldom* is already negative, so you must change the verb to the affirmative for this sentence.)
4. always
5. sometimes
6. almost always
7. rarely (remember to change the verb to the affirmative)
8. never (remember to change to the affirmative)
9. frequently
10. often

1. *Winters there are usually mild.*

C. Write some yes/no questions about the paragraph on the climate of Alaska. Put the frequency adverb in the correct position in the question. Then write a short answer using a frequency adverb.

Example

(Look at 1.)   1. *Are winters usually mild in the Panhandle?*
Yes, they usually are.

(Look at 2.)   2. _____

_____

(Look at 5.)   3. _____?

_____

(Look at 8. Use   4. _____?
ever in this
question.)   _____

(Look at 10.)   5. _____?

_____

D.   Now write a paragraph (on a separate sheet of paper) about a season
     in a place in your country. Follow the example about Alaska and use
     frequency adverbs.

Exercise 7   More Frequency Adverbs

Every person feels differently about the morning. Some people are in a bad
mood and are very slow in the morning; others are happy and full of energy.
Some do exercises. Some only need fifteen or twenty minutes to get ready
for work or school; others need an hour or more. Some people are late every
morning. Some people don't talk in the morning. Some need a cup of black
coffee right away. Some eat a big breakfast; others eat nothing.

A.   Write a short composition about how you feel and what you do in the
     morning. Use a lot of frequency adverbs (*always, almost always, usually,
     frequently, often, sometimes, seldom, rarely, hardly ever, almost never,
     never, one/twice/three times a* _____, *every morning, etc.*)

B.   Write about a person who does the opposite of what you do in the
     morning. Now you will write in the third-person singular.

Exercise 8   *How Often*

A.   This is an imaginary meeting. The Nuclear Regulatory Commission
     (NRC) is interested in the safety of nuclear power plants. The NRC
     wants to know how often accidents happen, how often the company
     does a safety check on equipment, and so forth.
        Write questions for the NRC to find out information. Write some
     questions with *how often* and some *yes/no* questions. Ask about how

often the workers have accidents, how often the plant changes the uranium, how often it removes the old uranium, how often it checks for radiation, how often it checks workers for exposure to radiation, how often it is dangerous to go into the plant, how often they wash down the plant. Then answer the questions.

You may want to use some of this vocabulary in your questions or answers:

wash down: clean the surfaces of the plant with water

nuclear power plant: a factory where uranium is used to produce electricity

radioactivity: rays of energy that are dangerous to people

accident: something goes wrong in some part of the plant

overheated: when the uranium isn't cool enough and becomes dangerous

shutdown: when the plant closes down because of safety problems

routine shutdown: when the plant closes on a regular schedule

exposure: when someone gets near the dangerous rays of energy; when these rays get absorbed by the body, we say the person has been exposed to radiation.

CHAIRMAN OF THE NRC: *How often do you have accidents in the plant?*

OFFICIAL OF NUCLEAR POWER PLANT: *We almost never do.*

CHAIRMAN: *How often do the workers go for medical checkups?*

OFFICIAL: *They see our doctors almost every three months.*

CHAIRMAN: _____

OFFICIAL: _____

NRC: _____

OFFICIAL: _____

NRC: _____

OFFICIAL: _____

B.   Person A is an official of a nuclear power plant. Person B is an environ-
      mentalist asking questions about this nuclear plant. Role play a meeting
      between these two people. Ask *how often* and *yes/no* questions.

C.   Person A is a worker having a medical checkup before going to work in
      the nuclear plant. Person B is a doctor who works for the nuclear
      power plant company. Ask questions of the worker to see if he is
      healthy enough to work in the plant.

Exercise 9   Integration

A.   The following is an imaginary press conference with the president of
      the United States about the energy crisis. The reporters are asking
      questions. The president is answering them. Fill in the blanks to make
      questions in the simple present tense. Fill in the blanks to answer in the
      simple present tense.

PRESIDENT: Yes.

REPORTER A: Mr. President, according to a recent CBS Survey, 69 percent

of the American public __*doesn't believe*__ in the energy crisis.
                                    (negative, believe)

_____ you _____ the oil companies
                                      (believe)
create shortages to get higher prices? _____

the oil companies ever _____ the supply of oil and
                                (hold back)
_____ the shortages themselves?
        (create)

PRESIDENT: The answer is simple. We _____ a real crisis.
                                                (have)

People who _____ cars know that we
                    (drive)
_____ a real energy crisis because they
        (have)
_____ that there just isn't enough gasoline.
        (see)

REPORTER B: Mr. President, what _____ the average American
                                                                (need)
_____ to do in this crisis?

PRESIDENT: The average American _____ to do many things
(need)
to save energy. First of all, each American _____
(need)
to help at this time of crisis. And I think each American

_____ to help if he possibly can.
(want)

REPORTER C: Mr. President, where _____ most of our oil
(come)
_____ from at this time?

PRESIDENT: Well, a lot of our oil _____ from other countries,
(come)
from the OPEC countries. Of course, our own oil companies

_____ a lot of oil, too. We _____ to
(produce)   (need)
produce a lot more. We _____ to depend on
(negative, want)
foreign oil.

REPORTER C: Mr. President, one more quick question. Why _____
(negative, have)
we _____ enough gasoline these days? People

_____ to know.
(want)

PRESIDENT: And the American people _____ a right to know.
(have)
OPEC _____ the supply of most of the oil in the
(control)
world as well as world oil prices.

REPORTER D: Mr. President, what _____ to the prices of
(happen)
domestic oil when OPEC _____ its prices?
(raise)
_____ the price of domestic oil
(increase)
automatically?

PRESIDENT: Well, U.S. companies _____ a choice. They
(negative, have)
_____ their prices too.
(raise)

66   Chapter 4

REPORTER E: Mr. President, financial reports for big oil companies

_____ huge increases in profits. _____
     (show)

these companies _____ every time we have an
     (profit)

oil crisis?

PRESIDENT: As I said before, we _____ a serious problem
     (have)

here. The really bad shortages, according to the Secretary of

Energy, will come in the mid-1980s. And I _____
     (promise)

you, I _____ to investigate this matter thoroughly.
     (intend)

We all _____ to cut back, every one of us.
     (need)

REPORTER F: One last question. How _____ you _____
     (conserve)

energy at the White House?

PRESIDENT: We _____ the thermostat down to 65° in the
     (turn)

winter and we _____ it up in the summer.
     (turn)

B. Imagine you are one of the reporters. Continue asking the president
questions. Then write answers to the questions.

REPORTER G: _____

PRESIDENT: _____

_____

_____

C. Review the vocabulary of the exercise. Now role play this conversation. Do not read from these lines. Improvise.

Exercise 10   *Integration of Simple Present and Present Continuous*

Directions
Fill in the blanks with either the present continuous or the simple present
tense. (A reporter is interviewing a supervisor at a nuclear power plant.)

REPORTER: We are inside the control room of the Apple Core Nuclear

Power Plant. I _am interviewing_ Mr. Wilkins and
(interview)

_____ questions about nuclear power in general
(ask)

and the Apple Core Plant in particular. What kind of material

_____ _do_ _____ power plants _____ _use_ _____ for
(do)   (use)

nuclear fuel?

MR. WILKINS: Well, for the most part we _____ uranium.
(use)

REPORTER: I'm going to follow Mr. Wilkins and ask him questions. Mr.

Wilkins, what _____ you _____
(do)

right now?

MR. WILKINS: I _____ the safety valves for the plant's cooling
(check)

system.

REPORTER: How often _____ you _____ them?
(check)

MR. WILKINS: We _____ them several times a day.
(check)

REPORTER: How many men usually _____ in this room?
(work)

MR. WILKINS: Half a dozen or so.

REPORTER: What _____ those men _____ over there
(do)

in the corner?

MR. WILKINS: They _____ on protective clothing. When we
(put)

_____ into many areas of the plant, we
(go)

_____ this protective clothing.
(wear)

REPORTER: _____ supervisors _____ the men
(monitor)

and the plant for radioactivity every day?

MR. WILKINS: Oh, yes. Whenever a worker _____ the plant, he
(leave)

_____ himself for radioactivity at the door. The
(check)

man over there _____ radiation levels in this
(record)

room right now. We _____ radiation all the time.
(monitor)

In fact, the equipment shows that nothing _____
(leak)

into the environment right now.

REPORTER: _____ your plant ever _____ leaks?
(negative, have)

MR. WILKINS: Well, occasionally a small amount _____ into
(escape)

the environment. But this _____ very often.
(negative, happen)

REPORTER: Thank you very much, Mr. Wilkins. This has been most

interesting.

Expressing Your Ideas: Speaking and Writing

1. Does your country produce oil? Does it import or export oil? Are there energy problems in your country? What are they?
2. Is there a conflict between big oil companies and people who want to protect the environment in your country? Describe it.
3. Why are there so many oil spills from tankers? How can we prevent them?
4. Are oil prices very high in your country? Are they controlled by the government? Do the prices increase every year? What problems or benefits does this create for the average person?
5. How is electricity produced in your country? Is there a shortage of energy to produce electricity? If so, does your country have a plan to deal with this problem?
6. What are some other sources of energy in addition to oil?
7. Does your country operate or plan to operate nuclear power plants? What are the advantages and disadvantages of nuclear power?
8. Does your country use or plan to use solar energy? What are some of the advantages and disadvantages of solar power?
9. Does your country waste energy? If you think it does, describe how. Many people say Americans waste a great deal of energy. Do you agree? Do you know any examples of this? Describe what you have noticed.

There + Be; Count and Non-count Nouns

Chief Little Elk of Mount Pleasant, Michigan. (*Wide World Photos*)

Theme: *Native Americans and Immigrants*

Grammar: *There + Be; Count and Non-count Nouns*

Dialogue

(ARNOLD, YOLANDA, JACK, and MOLLY are sitting in a coffee shop. YOLANDA is planning to visit her parents in New Jersey this afternoon.)

ARNOLD: How about another cup of coffee, Yolanda? **How much time** do you have before your train leaves?

YOLANDA: **Not much.** There's a train in about thirty minutes.

ARNOLD: It only takes you about ten minutes to get to the train station from here. **There's time** for another cup of coffee.

JACK: Yolanda, were your parents born in this country?

YOLANDA: No, they came here in the fifties.[1] **A great many Puerto Ricans** immigrated to New York around that time.

MOLLY: **How many Puerto Ricans** are there in New York now?

YOLANDA: I don't know exactly, but **there are** more **Puerto Ricans** here than in San Juan.

JACK: It's really amazing to think about the number of different ethnic groups in this country. Just in New York alone **there are thousands** of Greeks, Italians, Chinese. . . .

MOLLY: Jack, how about you? Where are your parents from?

JACK: My parents were born here, but my grandparents came over here from Poland around 1915.

ARNOLD: Immigrants really had **a lot of problems** in those days, didn't they? Did your grandparents know **much English** when they came here?

JACK: No, they knew **very little.** They just knew **a few words** like "hello," "good-bye," "thank you," and "how much."

MOLLY: How did they manage?[2] Did your grandfather have **much trouble** finding a job?

JACK: **There weren't many good jobs** in those days if you couldn't speak English. Luckily my grandparents already had **a few relatives** in this country, and they helped my grandfather find a job.

YOLANDA: What kind of job did he get?

JACK: He worked in a shoe factory for **many years**. He saved every penny and finally bought his own business. They're living a very comfortable life today.

MOLLY: That's a typical American success story, isn't it?

---

1. *in the fifties:* from 1950 to 1960.
2. *How did they manage?:* This question means, "What did they do to overcome all the problems they had?"

JACK: It sure is. My grandparents are Americans now, but they take **a great deal of pride** in where they come from.

ARNOLD: **A lot of people** today are interested in tracing their roots.[3] Most people in this country have an immigrant background. **Very few Americans** can say that their ancestors came over here on the Mayflower.[4]

Part 1   There + Be

A. There + Be

There + be is an extremely common structure in English. We can use it with all tenses. Here we show only the present and past tenses.

STATEMENTS:

there $\left.\begin{array}{c}is\\was\end{array}\right\}$ (not) + a singular noun

there $\left.\begin{array}{c}are\\were\end{array}\right\}$ (not) + a plural noun

There are many different ethnic groups in this country.

Contraction: there is = there's

QUESTIONS:

$\left.\begin{array}{c}is\\are\\was\\were\end{array}\right\}$ there + subject . . . ?

Are there many different ethnic groups in your country?

Examples

The United States is a nation of immigrants. However, the American Indians lived in this country long before the first European immigrants arrived in the fifteenth century. At this time **there were many Indian tribes** in all parts of the country. Each tribe had its own language, its own religion, and its own customs. When the white settlers pushed west, **there were many con-**

---

3. *roots:* family background; where your ancestors came from.
4. *the* Mayflower: the ship that brought the first European settlers to Massachusetts in 1620.

flicts between them and the various Indian tribes. Partly because **there was never a united Indian nation** of all the different Indian tribes, the Indians gradually lost their lands to the settlers.

QUESTIONS

Why **was there a conflict** between the Indians and the settlers during the settlement of the west?

Because the settlers wanted the Indian land to raise cattle and crops, but the Indians wanted to keep the land for hunting.

Were there any peace treaties between the U.S. government and the Indian tribes?

Yes, there were.

Is there land in the United States today which belongs to the American Indians?

Yes, **there is.**

Are there still **many disputes** between the U.S. government and the Indians over land?

Yes, **there are.**

Today **there are** still **many Indian tribes** that live all over the United States. For the most part, they live on reservations. This is land that the federal government gave the Indians to live on after the Indians lost the war with the white settlers. Many Indians are dissatisfied with these reservations. **There is a movement** among American Indians today to reclaim some of their lost land.

B. Contrast of <u>There Is/Are</u> with <u>It Is (It's)/They Are</u>

Explanation

Don't confuse *there is* with *it is* (*it's*) or *there are* with *they are* (*they're*).

Examples

Every year **there is** an Indian festival in Anadark, Oklahoma. **It is** very popular with tourists. **There are** several performances about Cherokee Indian history. **They are** always very emotional performances because the Indians dramatize a tragic period in their history, when the United States government forced them to move away from their land in Tennessee to a reservation in Oklahoma.

Exercise 1   There Is/Are/Was/Were

Directions

Fill in the blanks with *there is, there are, there was,* or *there were.*

Before 1840 *there weren't* many white people in the western part of
(negative)
the United States. In the 1840s white people began to move out West.

_____ many fights between the settlers and the Indians over the land. _____ also fights between white hunters and the Indians. The white hunters killed millions of buffalo. In 1865 _____ 15 million of these animals. By 1885 _____ only a thousand. The Indians needed the buffalo to survive. Without the buffalo and the land, _____ any way for the Indians to keep their old way of life.
(negative)

Many terrible battles took place between the Indians and the settlers. Many lives were lost on both sides. During the last part of the nineteenth century, fighting was especially intense. The Indians made a great effort to try to maintain their way of life. However, they did not have very modern weapons.

In 1880 _____ a tragic confrontation between the United States Army and a group of Sioux Indians in Wounded Knee, South Dakota. The U.S. Army ordered all the Indian men to give them their guns. Two or three of the Indians refused, and the soldiers started shooting.

The fight was very bloody. After it was over, _____ many
(negative)
Indian survivors. An Indian chief, Red Cloud, said, "_____ no hope on earth." Another chief, Black Elk, said, "_____ no center any longer and the sacred tree is dead."

_____ 1,500,000 Indians in the United States today.

_____ still many different tribes, each with its own language and traditions. _____ 300 different Indian languages and dialects which are spoken today. _____ many tribes today who still
(negative)

make their living in the same ways they used to before the white settlers

came, but a few have preserved their old ways. For example,

_____ a tribe in Arizona called the Navajo who still make

beautiful silver and turquoise jewelry. The Navajo use the traditional

designs that have been in their tribe for hundreds of years.

_____ also a revival of interest in Indian art forms, such as

pottery, rugs, and baskets. _____ some Navajo baskets which

sell for over $100.

The Navajo are also an example of a tribe that wants to become part of

industrialized society. _____ valuable deposits of oil, coal, and

uranium on Navajo land. The Navajo want control of the development of

these resources.

Exercise 2

A. Choose a place that had special meaning for you at some point in your
    past. Describe this place and what you used to do there. Use *there is,
    there are, there was, there were.*

B. Choose a place that has changed over the years. Describe what it was
    like in the past. Use *there was/there were.* Then write about what it is
    like today. Use *there is/there are.*

Exercise 3   Contrast of <u>There + Be</u> with <u>It/They + Be</u>

A. Use the past tense. Fill in the blanks with *there was, there were, it was,
    they were.*

Thanksgiving is a national holiday that Americans celebrate in

November. In the early seventeenth century _____ a small

community of people in Massachusetts. _____ people who

had left England to find religious freedom in the New World.

_____ called Pilgrims. In 1621, at the end of their first

year in the new country, _____ a big feast and celebration

to give thanks to God. _____ the first Thanksgiving. At this

feast _____ also many Indians. _____ guests

of the Pilgrims at this feast because they had helped the Pilgrims during

the long and difficult first year in the New World.

B. Use the present tense to describe the picture. Fill in the blanks with
    there is, there are, it is, or *they are.*

In this picture a group of Indians and Pilgrims are celebrating the

first Thanksgiving together. On the table _____ a large

turkey. _____ also a large basket on the table.

_____ a gift from the Indians. _____ full of

vegetables. These vegetables are native to the New World. The Indians taught the Pilgrims how to grow them.

Part 2   Count and Non-count Nouns

A count noun is a noun that has a plural form (usually s or es). It is always possible to put a number in front of a count noun. For example, *one* table, *two* tables. Non-count nouns (mass nouns) do not have a plural form. They are almost always singular, but we never use the indefinite article *a, an* before a non-count noun. Here are some common examples:

water	oil	pollution
coffee	gold	advice
rice	money	

A. Statements about a Large Quantity

Look at the following lists:

For Count Nouns	For Non-count Nouns
a lot of	a lot of
many	a great deal of
a great many	quite a bit of
quite a few	

NOTE: We use the expression *a lot of* when we talk about a large quantity of both count and non-count nouns. *A lot of* is conversational. It is not the preferred written form.

Examples: Count Nouns

The only native Americans are Indians. The United States is really a country of immigrants. Europeans began to arrive in the United States in the seventeenth century. Immigrants are still coming to the U.S.

One of the major periods of immigration was during the nineteenth century. **A lot of people** came to the U.S. to escape the economic or political problems in Europe at that time. In those days the sea journey from Europe to America was very difficult. **Many passengers** became sick. **A lot** died before they reached America. **Quite a few** arrived with nothing but the clothes on their backs. **Many of these new Americans** found a better life in the United States. Some of them later became rich. **A great many famous Americans** are immigrants or the descendants of immigrants.

Examples: Non-count Nouns

Immigrants came for a number of reasons. America was a land of promise. There was **a great deal of available land** ready for farming. The Midwest attracted many settlers because it has **a lot of rich, fertile soil.** The Midwest is known as the breadbasket of the country. Despite the abundance of good farmland, the newcomers who settled here suffered **quite a bit of hardship.** For example, there were prairie fires, droughts, and harsh winters.

NOTES:

1. It is not always necessary to repeat the noun. When you don't repeat the noun, don't use *of* after *a lot.*
2. In general, we don't use *much* before a non-count noun in affirmative sentences, because it will usually sound too formal or incorrect.

B. Statements about a Small Quantity

Use the following expressions to talk about small quantities of count and non-count nouns:

For Count Nouns	For Non-count Nouns
not many	not much
(very) few	(very) little
just ⎫	just ⎫
only ⎬ a few	only ⎬ a little
a few	a little

Examples: Non-count Nouns

Immigrants came to this country because they had **very little hope** of making a better life for themselves in their native land. The difficult conditions in Europe forced them to emigrate. In the 1840s in Ireland, for example, there was a great potato famine. Potatoes were the staple of the Irish diet. Without potatoes, there **wasn't much food,** and many people starved. The journey to America did**n't cost much money** in those days: only about $20.

Example: Count Nouns

Sometimes there weren**'t many opportunities** for the immigrants in America. For example, when the Irish first arrived in Boston, **very few jobs** were open to them, and **only a few** were high paying. **Not many American workers** liked these "new Americans," because they worked for low pay. Because of this, wages for all workers went down. There were many disagreements and problems between the "old" Americans and the "new" ones.

NOTE: Sometimes you see *a lot* in negative statements. However, the most common pattern is *not much, not many* when the sentence is negative.

C. Contrast of *Few/Little* with *A Few/A Little*

Few ⎫
Little ⎬ have a different meaning from ⎰ a few
         ⎱ a little.

Few ⎫
Little ⎬ have a meaning similar to ⎰ not many.
         ⎱ not much.

A few ⎫ have a positive meaning similar to *some* when we are talking
A little ⎭ about a small quantity.

Notice the difference in meaning:

1. *Very few good jobs were open to the immigrants.*
   (In this sentence, we mean that this was a real problem for the immigrants, because the number of jobs was very limited.)
2. *Most of the immigrants had very little education.*
   (In this sentence, we mean that this was a real problem which made it difficult for them to find jobs.)
3. *A few good jobs were open to the immigrants.*
   (In this sentence, we mean there were some good jobs for immigrants, and that at least some immigrants had good job opportunities.)
4. *Some of the immigrants had a little education.*
   (In this sentence, we mean that these immigrants had some education.)

D. Questions

1. Use *how many* + count noun
   how much + non-count noun

How many immigrants came to the United States during the nineteenth century?
   A great many did. Millions came then.
How much English did they know when they arrived?
   In general, they didn't know much.
   They knew just a little.
   They knew only a few words.

2. In yes/no questions, follow these patterns:

   many
   a lot of
   a large number of $\Big\}$ + count noun
   quite a few

   much
   a great deal of $\Big\}$ + non-count noun
   a lot of

Did they have **a great deal of knowledge** about the geography of the land they had to cross?
   No, they had **only a few crude maps.**
Did settlers have **much trouble** crossing the country in covered wagons?
   Yes, they had **a great deal of trouble.**
Did **many immigrants** settle in big cities?
   Many did, but many went west to farm also.
Did **a large number of immigrants** become rich?
   No, they didn't, but a few did.

E. Ways to Count Non-count Nouns

Explanation
It is almost always possible to describe specific quantities of mass nouns; in other words, to count non-count nouns. Here is a list of vocabulary to do this:

a cup of tea	a glass of water	a bottle of wine
coffee	milk	milk
chocolate	wine	medicine

a slice of cake	a piece of cake	furniture	an article of clothing
pie	pie	advice	
bread	fruit	jewelry	
meat	chalk	equipment	
	music	machinery	
	news	luggage	

a course in English
       mathematics
       history
       chemistry

Explanation
To talk about a specific quantity of some non-count nouns, we can also use other vocabulary:

Non-count	Count
trouble	a problem
luggage	a suitcase
homework	homework assignment, homework exercise
information	a fact
mail	a letter
jewelry	a ring, a necklace, a bracelet

Examples
How much English do you know?
  I know quite a bit.
How many courses in English have you taken?
  I've taken several.
How much information do you have on how California was settled?
  I think I know a great deal.
How many facts do you know about how California was settled?
  I can only give you a few specific facts.

Exercise 4   Large Quantities with Count and Non-count Nouns

Directions
Write sentences (use your own paper) beginning with *there is/there are*. Use the expressions *many, quite a few, a great many* for count nouns and the expressions *a great deal of, quite a bit of* with non-count nouns.

Examples

1. (mountains in Switzerland)

There are a great many mountains in Switzerland.

2. (pollution in the oceans of the world)

There is a great deal of pollution in the oceans of the world.

3. (people in the People's Republic of China)
4. (diamond mines in South Africa)
5. (nightlife in New York City)
6. (nice weather in California)
7. (oil wells in Iran)
8. (gambling in Monaco)
9. (cowboys in Texas)
10. (banking in Switzerland)
11. (traffic in Tokyo)
12. (earthquakes in California)

(Remember *a lot of* is correct in all these sentences.)

Exercise 5   A Small Quantity with Count and Non-count Nouns

Directions

Write sentences beginning with *there is/there are.* Use *not many, very few, only a few* with count nouns. Use *not much, very little, only a little* with non-count nouns.

1. (rain in the Sahara Desert)
2. (illegal drugs in the U.S.S.R.)
3. (daylight in Scandinavian countries in the winter)
4. (women political leaders in the world)
5. (agriculture in Saudi Arabia)
6. (tourism in Antarctica)
7. (things you can buy for 5¢ in the U.S.)
8. (peace in the world today)

Exercise 6   Questions

Directions

Complete the questions by filling in the blanks with *much, many, how much, how many.* Then answer the questions using *a lot, a great many, a great deal, quite a few, quite a bit, very few, very little, only a few, only a little,* *a few, a little, not many, not much.* Add *of* when it is necessary. When you see an asterisk (*) next to a question, try to add specific information to tell exactly how much. Use a number.

Example

1. *Do you drink ___*much*___ coffee?

   Yes, I drink a lot. I drink about five cups a day.

2. Did you have _____ problems when you got your visa to come to the United States?

   _____

3. Did your parents or relatives give you _____ advice when you left home?

   _____

4. *Did you bring _____ luggage with you when you came to the United States?

   _____

5. *Do you receive _____ news from home?

   _____

6. _____ letters do you send home each week?

   _____

7. *_____ cash do you usually carry?

   _____

8. Do you have _____ American friends?

   _____

9. _____ times a week do you go to class?

   _____

10. Are there _____ students in your class?

_____

11. Do you have _____ interest in politics?

_____

Exercise 7   A Few/Very Few, A Little/Very Little

Directions
Fill in the blanks with *a few, very few, a little, very little*. Read the sentence completely before you make your choice.

Many Scandinavians immigrated to this country in the last half of the

nineteenth century and the first part of the twentieth century. For example,

over one million Norwegians came during this time. Most of these immigrants

settled in the north-central part of the United States. These settlers left

their native land with _very few_ resources because they were not

allowed much room for storage on the voyage over. Of course, they needed

_____ help when they arrived, and fellow countrymen were

often there to give advice and aid. As newcomers, they quickly learned

_____ words of English, so they could buy what they needed.

From the East Coast where they landed, they traveled west to some of the

best farmland in the country.

In 1862 President Lincoln signed the Homestead Act, which provided that

a man could buy 160 acres of land. The government charged _____

money because it wanted this area to be settled quickly. By this time,

there were _____ settlements in the Midwest, so settlers could

meet, exchange news, and buy goods. When the Scandinavians arrived, there were _____ hostile Indians remaining in this territory. As a result, the settlers didn't have to worry about war; they only had to worry about their survival. They had _____ trouble adjusting to the climate, for example, because of the very hot summers in that part of the country. Another problem was medical care. There were _____ doctors, so people had to rely on home remedies. Most of these settlers became farmers. At that time there were _____ people in this area, so the nearest neighbor probably lived miles away. _____ farm help was available, so families did most of the work themselves. They usually began farming with _____ livestock and equipment. As soon as the farmers earned _____ dollars, they bought farm equipment with the money and invested their profit in the farm. Many eventually became some of the most prosperous citizens in the area.

Exercise 8   Using Countable Expressions with Non-count Nouns

Directions

Fill in the blanks with *much* or *many* and/or use one of the following for the answer: bottle, bag, package, box, pound, loaf (loaves). Use *of* when necessary.

(YOLANDA is planning to invite her co-workers to her apartment for a party tonight. MOLLY is at YOLANDA's apartment now. They are making a shopping list.)

MOLLY: How _*many*_ people are going to come tonight, Yolanda?

YOLANDA: About twenty, I think.

MOLLY: How _____ wine do you want me to get?

YOLANDA: Get three half gallons of white and two _____

_____ red and some whisky.

MOLLY: Okay. How _____?

YOLANDA: Only two _____.

MOLLY: How _____ _____ _____

ice do you want?

YOLANDA: Get me three.

MOLLY: How _____ cheese did you say? I forgot.

YOLANDA: One _____ _____ Swiss cheese and

two _____ _____ Brie.

MOLLY: And how _____ bread?

YOLANDA: Two _____ _____ rye bread and four

_____ _____ French bread.

MOLLY: And how _____ Alka Seltzer?

YOLANDA: You're funny! Actually, I need some. Get me a _____.

Exercise 9   Integration

A. Fill in the blanks with *much, many, (very) few, (very) little, (only) a few, (only) a little, a lot (of), quite a bit (of), quite a few.* Try to use all of these expressions one or more times.

California

California is the most populous state in the United States, and it is the

third largest in area. Americans have always considered California a

kind of "Promised Land." Some have gone there hoping to find gold,

some to find fame and fortune in Hollywood, others to find the easy life of California's golden sunshine and white beaches. Some have found their dreams, but most Californians work hard to make a living from their state's abundance of natural resources.

California has a diverse geography and economy. There *is a* (is/are) *great deal of* commercial fishing, and there _____ (is/are) _____ canning factories. In fact, California leads the nation in the area of fishing. California has _____ _____ excellent vineyards and produces _____ wine. In the past, wine from California was considered inferior to European wine, but today _____ California wine is exported to Europe.

Agriculture is a major part of California's economy, particularly in the interior valleys. However, California has a serious problem with its water supply. The southern part of the state does not get _____ rain and has _____ major rivers. The coastal region has to bring in _____ water from the Colorado River 200 miles away. California agriculture depends heavily on irrigation. Without its complex irrigation system, the state would have _____ agriculture. It could not produce the wonderful fruit and vegetables for which it is famous. There _____ (is/are) citrus groves in California. The California navel orange is famous all over the country.

And what about the gold that the gold miners of 1849 rushed to the
state to find? How _____ gold _____ there
                                         (is/are)
in California today? There _____ _____ gold
                                (is/are)
left, but it is not a significant part of the economy. Today California has
"black gold." Petroleum is now the state's most valuable mineral. Oil
companies are drilling _____ new oil wells, especially off
the coast of Santa Barbara.

California is also famous because it has _____ natural
disasters. There _____ _____ earthquakes in
                      (is/are)
California. Not _____ of the earthquakes do serious
damage, but _____ people predict that one day California
will fall into the ocean. In addition to the earthquakes there
_____ _____ floods and mudslides. Despite
        (is/are)
these problems, very _____ California residents choose to
leave their beautiful state.

B. Now prepare a talk for your classmates on an interesting region of
your country. Use part A as a model for your talk.

Exercise 10   Integration

A. Interview a classmate about life in his or her country. Use the different
question forms for count and non-count nouns in part 2. Give answers
using the following expressions: *a lot, many, a great many, a great deal,
quite a few, quite a bit, not many, not much, (very) few, (very) little,
(only) a few, (only) a little.* Use *of* when necessary. After you ask a
question with one of the count or non-count expressions, you may want
to ask for additional information on the subject. For example, if you
ask, "Is there much pollution in the big cities of your country?" you can
also ask, "What causes this pollution? Is the government trying to
control pollution?"

Here is a list of count and non-count nouns that the interviewer can ask about:

1. Life in the big cities:
    Non-count: traffic   Count: foreigners
             pollution   skyscrapers
             dirt   museums
             noise   restaurants
             crime   nightclubs
             modern architecture   theaters
                                              public universities
                                              private universities

2. Politics and social problems:
    Non-count: unemployment   Count: political parties
             poverty   economic problems
             interest in politics   student demonstra-
             terrorism   tions
             power (the leader of   strikes
                your country)   unions
             religious discrimination   programs to help poor
             racial discrimination   people
             illiteracy

3. The economy:
    Non-count: manufacturing   Count: factories
             fishing   resorts
             mining   tourists
             industry   highways
             import/export trade   railways
             tourism   airports
             oil   mines (gold, silver,
             steel   coal, copper)
             coffee   steel plants
             wheat
             rice

B. Now write a summary of what you have learned from your classmate about his country.

Expressing Your Ideas: Speaking and Writing

1. Does your country have many different ethnic groups? What are they? Are there many immigrants in your country? From which countries? When did they come? What attracts immigrants to your country? Do many people emigrate from your country? Why? To what countries do they usually emigrate? How many immigrants does your country accept each year?

2. Is it easy to become a citizen in your country? What does a person have to do to become a citizen?

3. Are there many jobs and other opportunities for newcomers to your country?

4. Is there much unemployment among immigrants or certain minority groups? Do immigrants generally hold certain kinds of jobs? If so, what are they?

5. Is there much discrimination against immigrants or minority groups? If so, why? Which groups? Are there laws that attempt to limit discrimination? How successful are these laws?

6. Are there many famous people in your country who are immigrants or the descendants of immigrants? Name some.

7. If you decide to remain in the United States as an immigrant, how might this affect your life?

Verb + Infinitive, Verb + Object + Infinitive, Verb + Gerund

The Beatles at Shea Stadium, New York. (*Bill Jerome*)

Theme: Rock Music

Grammar: Verb + Infinitive, Verb + Object + Infinitive, Verb + Gerund

---

Dialogue

(ARNOLD and his father, MR. CALHOUN, are talking on the telephone.)

ARNOLD: Hello?

MR. CALHOUN: Hello, Arnold. This is Dad. How are you?

ARNOLD: Fine, and you?

MR. CALHOUN: Okay. I **invited you to come** to dinner Saturday night, remember? I **expect to see** you this weekend.

ARNOLD: Well, I'm not sure I can make it.[1] I **forgot to tell** you I got a job at a disco Friday and Saturday nights.

MR. CALHOUN: You **don't need to do** that, Arnold. I'll give you the money to go back to school. I'**d like you to go** back and **finish** your degree.

ARNOLD: I'm sick of[2] going to school, Dad. I **want to be** on my own.[3] I **don't want you to give** me money all the time, and besides, I **enjoy playing** my guitar.

MR. CALHOUN: The guitar, the guitar, the guitar! I **don't want to hear** about that guitar!

ARNOLD: Look, Dad, I'm tired of fighting about this. I **decided to drop out** of school[4] and **try** my luck with music, and that's that![5]

MR. CALHOUN: All right. Let's **stop talking** about it. What about next Monday or Tuesday? **Would** you **like to come** for dinner then?

ARNOLD: I'm sorry, Dad. I'**d like to,** but I **need to practice.**

MR. CALHOUN: You can never **hope to make** any money as a musician. **Don't expect me to help** you every time that you need money.

ARNOLD: Dad, I appreciate your advice, but please **stop treating** me like a child.

MR. CALHOUN: All right, I'll try to mind my own business,[6] but I **urge** you **to think** very carefully about your decision.

---

1. *to make it:* to be able to accept an invitation to a party, dinner, or appointment.
2. *to be sick of something:* to be very tired of something or very bored with something.
3. *to be on (your) own:* to be independent and responsible for yourself.
4. *to drop out of school:* to leave school before you get a degree or diploma.
5. *that's that!:* That's final! Let's not discuss it anymore.
6. *to mind (your) own business:* to worry about your own problems; not to interfere in another person's problems or decisions.

Some verbs in English are often followed by a second verb. The second verb can be in two different forms: the infinitive (*to + be*) or the gerund (*be + ing*). The first verb can be in any tense.

Part 1   Verb + Infinitive

A. Affirmative Statements

Explanation

When certain verbs, such as *want*, *need*, and *hope*, are followed by another verb, the second verb must be in the infinitive form. Here is a list of verbs that require the infinitive form for the second verb. This list is not complete. Only the most common verbs have been selected.

afford	dare	hesitate	mean	refuse
agree	decide	hope	need	seem
appear	deserve	intend	offer	threaten
ask	expect	learn	plan	try
attempt	fail	long	prepare	want
choose	forget	manage	promise	would like

Examples

Rock music is an important part of American culture. Rock music first became popular during the 1950s, and it is still popular today, mainly among teenagers and young adults. Teenagers often **want to establish** their own identity and **need to express** their own feelings. Rock music does this for them. Some teenagers even **hope to become** rock stars.

B. Reduced Infinitives

Explanation

Look at the examples below. Notice that in the answers to the questions, you use *to* after the first verb, but it is not necessary to include the second verb or verb phrase. All of the verbs in the above list are used in this way.

Examples

Do many women become rock stars?
   Some **manage to,** but there are many more men than women in rock music.
   NOTE: It is not necessary to say **some manage to become rock stars.**
Do parents like the rock music that their kids like?
   Some **try to.**

C. Negative Statements

Explanation

It is possible to make either the first verb or the second verb negative depending on your meaning.

1. When you want to make the meaning of the first verb negative, follow the general rules for forming negatives.

Example

Many parents and teenagers disagree about rock music. Many parents **don't want to listen** to loud rock music in their homes all the time.

2. When you want to make the meaning of the second verb negative, put *not* after the first verb and before the infinitive (before *to*).

Examples

Many parents **prefer not to listen** when their teenagers turn on rock music.

NOTE: Don't confuse these two different negative forms. The meaning is different.

Some parents **try not to let** loud rock music bother them, because they know it's important to their kids.

Other parents **don't try to understand** and don't permit loud rock music in their house.

Arnold **promised not to smoke** more than a pack of cigarettes a day.

He **didn't promise to give up** cigarettes completely.

Part 2   Verb + Object + Infinitive

A. Verb + (Optional Object) + Infinitive

Explanation

Some verbs followed by the infinitive work in two different ways. They can be followed by an infinitive (for example, *want to do*), or they can be followed by an object and then the infinitive (for example, *want someone to do something*). The following verbs operate in this way:

ask	dare	prepare
beg	expect	want
choose	need	would like

Examples

The Beatles were probably the most popular group in the history of rock. Even Queen Elizabeth of England **wanted to meet** them and **wanted them to visit** Buckingham Palace. She **asked them to accept** a special medal of honor.

From about 1964 to 1970 every Beatles record album sold over a million copies. Every album was new and innovative and had a strong influence on other musicians and young people everywhere. When the Beatles broke up in 1970, people were shocked. They **expected the Beatles to stay** together forever.

B. Verb + Object + Infinitive

Explanation

One group of verbs *always* takes an object before the infinitive when the sentence is in the active voice. Here is a list of these verbs:

advise	forbid	order	teach
allow	force	pay	tell
challenge	hire	permit	urge
command	instruct	persuade	warn
convince	invite	remind	
encourage	motivate	require	

Examples

One of the Beatles, George Harrison, became especially interested in Indian music and philosophy. Ravi Shankar, a famous Indian musician, **taught Harrison to play** the sitar. The sitar is an Indian instrument.

In 1970 there was a war in Bangladesh, East Pakistan. Harrison wanted to help the war victims, so Ravi Shankar **encouraged him to give** a concert. Harrison **invited several other rock stars to play** at the concert. He **convinced everyone to give** the money from the concert to the people of Bangladesh.

Exercise 1   Verb + Infinitive

Directions

Choose the correct tense for the first verb under the blank. Then put the second verb in the infinitive form.

Stevie Wonder is one of the best known "pop" musicians in the United

States. His record albums have won many awards, and many of his songs,

such as "You Are the Sunshine of My Life," are popular all over the world.

Stevie was born in a poor section of Detroit. He was born blind. Even as

a child, he *refused to allow* his blindness to interfere with his life. As a
(refuse/allow)

young child, he _____ the bongos, drums, piano, and harmonica,
(learn/play)

and he _____ songs. When he was twelve, a record company
(learn/write)

_____ him a recording contract. His record became a hit!
(offer/give)

Today Stevie experiments with many different kinds of music, and he

_____ different rhythms in his songs, such as Brazilian, bossa
(try/include)

nova, samba, rock, jazz, and soul. He _____ perfect sound on
                                        (expect/have)

his records and works long hours for this. Sometimes he _____
                                                        (decide/get up)

in the middle of the night to rush down to a recording studio.

Stevie has an active life. He _____ a cane or Seeing Eye dog
                              (negative, need/use)

to get around.

Stevie Wonder can't see with his eyes, but he says, "My mind

_____ to infinity."
(want/see)

Exercise 2   Verb + Infinitive/Verb + Object + Infinitive

Directions
Fill in the blanks with the correct tense of the first verb. Use the infinitive
for the second verb. In some of the sentences an object separates the two
verbs.

Last month Arnold _*invited*_ his father _*to come*_ to
                   (invite/come)

the discotheque where Arnold works. He _____ his father
                                        (want/hear)

_____ him play the guitar. Arnold's father _____
                                                      (refuse/go)

to the discotheque. He said he _____ to noise. Two weeks later,
                               (negative, like/listen)

Arnold and his father had an argument about Arnold's decision to make

music his career. Arnold _____ his father that weekend and
                          (decide/negative, visit)

_____ money from him either because he _____
(negative, take)   (want/be)

independent.

Arnold's father _____ Arnold _____ a living
                 (negative, want/earn)

from music. He _____ Arnold _____ a doctor or a
                (would like/be)

banker, but Arnold _____ to his father and _____
                    (choose/negative, listen)   (follow)

his interest in music.

Exercise 3   Verb + Object + Infinitive

Directions

Read the information about these famous rock stars. Then fill in the blanks with the verbs under the line. You must add an object pronoun between the first verb and the infinitive.

Example

1. Rod Stewart wears crazy clothes. He says he does it because young

    people like crazy clothes. He wears wild clothes because his fans

    <u>*Want him to wear*</u> them.
        (want/wear)

2. Mick Jagger studied at the London School of Economics. He also sang in

    a rock group at that time. His parents _____ his studies.
                                              (encourage/continue)

    They _____ a rock star.
          (negative, want/be)

3. Mick Jagger's fans love him and always scream when he sings. Mick

    Jagger _____ when he is on stage.
            (expect/scream)

4. Peter Frampton is very popular with young teenage girls. After concerts

    they run after him to touch him. Peter has many bodyguards to

    protect him. They _____ Peter.
                       (negative, allow/touch)

5. Stevie Wonder met the woman he loves on the telephone. He fell in love

    with her voice on the phone, so he _____ dinner with
                                         (invite/have)

    him.

Exercise 4   Verb + Object + Infinitive

Directions

Use the grammar pattern verb + object + infinitive and write sentences (on a separate sheet of paper) with the verbs given below:

1. *Remind.* Arnold is very absent-minded. He forgets everything. What things did his mother always have to remind him to do when he lived at home?

2. *Warn.* Molly's mother worries about her a lot because she thinks New York City is very dangerous. What things does her mother always warn Molly to do or not to do?

3. *Want.* What things do language teachers want their students to do? What don't they want their students to do?

4. *Order, encourage, advise, urge, tell.* Arnold's father went to the doctor for a checkup last week. He smokes a lot; he is overweight; he doesn't get much exercise; he never relaxes or takes a vacation. What did the doctor say to him? Use the above verbs.

Exercise 5

Directions

Look at the examples. Notice that in the first answer it isn't necessary to use a long sentence. Use a reduced infinitive (for example, *want to*). Answer the questions *when* or *where* or *what kind by* using a full sentence. Use these verbs in both short and long sentences:

want   need   expect   plan   intend   hope   would like

Examples

Is Arnold going to buy a new guitar?
    Yes, he plans to.
When?
    He plans to buy one next month.

You may also use a negative answer. In this case do not answer in a complete sentence:

Does Arnold want to find a part-time job for extra money?
    He needs to, but he doesn't want to.

Now ask a classmate about his or her plans:

1. Are you going to find a part-time job for extra money?

_____

    What kind of job?

_____

2. Are you going to take another course in English?

_____

When?

_____

3. Are you going to travel abroad this summer?

_____

Where?

_____

4. Are you going to get a job after this course or after you return to your

country?

_____

What kind of job?

_____

5. Are you going to get married?

_____

When?

_____

Part 3   Verb + Gerund

A. Verb + Gerund

Explanation

When some verbs, such as *enjoy*, *avoid*, and *dislike*, are followed by another verb, this second verb is in the gerund form (base form + *ing*). Here is a list of verbs that require the gerund form for the second verb. This list is not complete. We have selected only the most common verbs:

appreciate	dislike	have	postpone	resume
avoid	enjoy	trouble	practice	spend
consider	escape	problems	quit	time
delay	finish	difficulty	regret[7]	two hours
deny		miss	report	several months
			resent	waste time

Examples

The music of the Beatles and other famous groups of the 1960s is based on the music of black rhythm and blues singers of the 1950s like Fats Domino, Little Richard, and Chuck Berry. Little Richard's music was very shocking for the middle class of the 1950s. He **enjoyed singing** about sex and fast cars. Some radio stations **avoided playing** his music, but teenagers loved him. In later life, Little Richard became a Christian preacher. Today he **dislikes listening** to the sexy songs he recorded in his youth.

B. Preposition + Gerund

Explanation

1. Some verbs in English have two parts: a verb and a preposition (*on*, *up*, *off*, for example). When you follow these two-word verbs with a second verb, you must use the gerund form. This is true for any verb that follows a preposition.

Examples

Little Richard **gave up singing** rock music when he became very religious. He didn't **feel like singing** this kind of song anymore. However, Chuck Berry **kept on singing and writing** songs through all the changes in rock.

Here is a list of some common verbs that are followed by a preposition. If the preposition is followed by a second verb, use the gerund form. This list is not complete.

succeed in
keep on (= continue)
put off (= postpone)
give up (= stop)
concentrate on
think about   } + base form + *ing*
prevent someone from
stop someone from
believe in
feel like
discourage someone from

---

7. *regret:* There is one exception to this rule. In formal letters we often use the expression "We regret to inform you that...."

The next verbs are especially confusing because they have the preposition *to* in front of the gerund:

look forward to = anticipate with pleasure
get used to
be used to = get/be accustomed to
confess to
admit to

+ base form + ing

Examples

Many young people **look forward to going** to their first rock concert. Most parents want their children to save money. However, many teenagers **admit to spending** their entire allowance on records.

2.   Some adjectives are followed by prepositions. When you want to use a verb after these adjective phrases, you must use the gerund form.

Examples

"Oldies but goodies" is a common rock expression. It means records that are old but still popular. People are still **interested in hearing** Chuck Berry's songs today. They never get **tired of listening** to his rock classics like "Johnny B. Goode," "Sweet Little Sixteen," and "Roll Over Beethoven."

Here is a list of some common adjectives that are followed by prepositions:

afraid of	tired of	sick of
interested in	worried about	responsible for
		bored with

C. Negative Statements

Explanation

If you want to make the meaning of the first verb negative, follow the general rules for forming negatives.

Example

Little Richard **doesn't enjoy listening** to his old records anymore.

If you want to make the meaning of the second verb negative, put *not* immediately in front of the gerund.

Example

Many radio stations **considered not playing** the first rock records of the 1950s because the records shocked many people.

Look at the following sentences. Notice the use of the same verb, *dislike*:

Yolanda often eats in restaurants. She **doesn't dislike cooking** for herself; it's just that she often does not have the time, and her kitchen is very small. She **dislikes not having** enough space to cook in.

Part 4 Verb Followed by Either the Gerund or the Infinitive

A. Verb + Infinitive or Gerund (Little Change in Meaning)

Explanation

After the following verbs, you may use either the infinitive or the gerund form. In most situations there is not much difference in meaning.

begin	hate	love	start
continue	like	prefer	

Example

People all over the world $\begin{cases} \text{like to listen} \\ \text{like listening} \end{cases}$ to rock music.

B. Verb + Infinitive or Gerund (Change in Meaning)

Explanation

Certain verbs have one meaning when they are followed by an infinitive and a different meaning when they are followed by a gerund. The most common of these verbs are *stop* and *remember*.

1. *Remember to do.* If we say we *remembered to do* something, we mean that we had something to do and we did it.

Example

When Elvis Presley first appeared on TV, the cameramen were told not to show Elvis moving his hips. During the show, they **remembered to focus** on Elvis's face.

2. *Remember doing.* When you use the gerund form after *remember,* you mean that you recall an event or an action.

Example

Today a lot of people **remember watching** Elvis's first television appearance.

3. *Stop doing.* When you use *stop* with a gerund, you mean you are stopping an action.

Example

The Beatles **stopped performing** together in 1970.

4. *Stop to do.* When you use *stop* with an infinitive, you mean you are stopping in order to do something.

Example

I was on my way to the bank, and I **stopped to talk** with a friend. Unfortunately, the bank was closed when I got there.

Exercise 6   Verb + Gerund

Directions

Using the words in parentheses, make some general statements about the life of rock stars. Use the gerund form for the second verb.

Example

1. (appreciate/hear/applause)

   Most rock stars *appreciate hearing applause*.

2. (avoid/use/the main entrance of a theatre)

   Rock stars _____

   because their fans surround them and ask for autographs.

3. (deny/take/drugs)

   Most people think that all rock stars use drugs, but rock stars _____

   _____.

4. (dislike/sing/the same hit songs)   (enjoy/hear/their favorite songs)

   Rock stars _____

   over and over again in concerts, but the fans always

   _____.

5. (negative, finish/play/until 2:00 or 3:00 A.M.)

   When rock stars perform, they usually give two concerts a night, so they

   _____.

6. (miss/see/their families)

   Rock stars have to travel a lot. When they are married and have

   children, they

   _____.

(regret/have/so little time) They _____

to spend at home and they (get tired of/travel)

_____.

Exercise 7   Contrast of Verb + Infinitive and Verb + Gerund

Directions

Choose the correct tense of the first verb. Choose the infinitive or the gerund form for the second verb. There are some verbs in this exercise for which both infinitive and gerund are correct.

During the summer of 1969 one of the most important events in the history of rock music took place in Woodstock, New York. Around half a million people traveled to this small town for a weekend rock music festival. Many more people _wanted to come_ but couldn't get near the area because
                (want/come)
of all the traffic. People _____ traffic backed up for ten miles.
                         (report/see)

The weather was bad on the weekend. It rained every day except for the last one. When the promoters of the concert heard the weather forecast,

they _____ the festival, but finally they _____
    (consider/negative, have)   (decide/go)
ahead with their plans. Some people _____, but most
                         (choose/leave)
_____ and _____ the rain to spoil their weekend.
  (prefer/stay)   (refuse/allow)
They _____ to the music even in the rain.
    (enjoy/listen)

Many of the young people who came to Woodstock believed in a world of music, drugs, and free love. They _____ an example for a new
                       (hope/set)
world, and they _____ society. They called themselves the
       (expect/change)
Woodstock Nation.

Many of the local townspeople _____ so many hippies
      (negative, appreciate/have)

in their town and _____ nudity and drugs so near their homes.
(resent/see)

Some people _____ a lot of trouble with so many people living
(expect/see)

together in a small area for three days, but the visitors _____
(enjoy/share)

everything with each other and _____ or _____
(avoid/argue)   (fight)

with each other or the residents of Woodstock. The local townspeople

_____ the extra business, but _____ up
(appreciate/have)   (negative, look forward to/clean)

after the weekend.

   In the years after Woodstock, many rock promoters _____
(attempt/copy)

this rock festival, but they all _____ the same spirit of happi-
(fail/achieve)

ness, peace, and good music that the Woodstock festival symbolized.

Exercise 8   Integration: Verb + Infinitive,
Verb + Object + Infinitive, Verb + Gerund

Directions
Fill in the correct form of the verb under the line. Choose between infinitive
or gerund for the second verb. Sometimes you will need to add an object.

   Elvis Presley, the great rock guitarist and singer, was born on January 8,

1935, in Tupelo, Mississippi. His parents *liked to take* him to church.
(like/take)

He _____ to the church music and _____.
(enjoy/listen)   (sing)

   Elvis was very close to his mother, Gladys. She _____ out of
(negative, want/be)

her sight, so she walked him to school every day until he was a senior in

high school.

   Elvis _____ a bicycle, but his parents _____
(want/have)   (refuse/give)

him one. Instead they bought him a guitar. Elvis _____ the
(practice/play)

guitar every free moment that he had. He _____ music from
(try/imitate)

the radio.

Elvis's mother _____ the guitar and sing. Elvis also
                      (encourage/play)

_____ football, but she _____ football because
       (like/play)   (urge/negative, play)

she was afraid he would get hurt. She _____ the game. Elvis
                                              (ask/give up)

_____ his mother, so he quit playing football. She also
(negative, want/worry)

_____ a job because she thought it interfered with his school
      (force/quit)

work.

In 1953 Elvis _____ his first album. Soon after, disc jockeys
                    (decide/record)

_____ Elvis's records on their radio stations. Elvis also sang on
    (start/play)

television on the *Ed Sullivan Show,* but the TV network _____
                                                                (refuse/show)

Elvis from the waist down because he wiggled his hips so erotically.

Elvis earned millions of dollars from his records and movies and

_____ people call him the "King" of rock 'n roll.
    (like/hear)

In 1976 Elvis's doctors _____ performing because he was
                               (order/stop)

quite sick. In 1977 Elvis died of a heart attack at the age of forty-two. His

mother had died at the same age.

Exercise 9   *Final Integration*

Directions
Ask a classmate these questions:

1. What did your parents advise you to be?
2. What did you hope to be?
3. What did your teachers encourage you to do?
4. How did you decide? Did you have trouble making up your mind?
5. Did anyone ever discourage you from doing what you wanted to do? How? Why?
6. Do you expect to be successful? Make a lot of money?
7. Do you expect your family to help you? Why or why not?
8. Do you plan to have a family?

9. Do you plan to have a career? Will you postpone having children until you establish a career?
10. At what age do you expect to retire?
11. What do you look forward to doing after you retire?

Expressing Your Ideas: Speaking and Writing

1. Arnold and his father have trouble understanding each other. They are from two different generations. We call this lack of understanding or lack of communication between generations the "generation gap."
   a. Do you have trouble talking with your parents? Do they seem to understand your problems? Do you usually agree or disagree with them? If you are a parent, do you have trouble talking with your children?
   b. Is there a generation gap in your country? Is this problem greater in the United States? Why or why not?
   c. What are some of the differences between people your own age and people your parents' age? Are there many similarities?
   d. Do your parents approve of the way you dress, talk, and behave? If you are a parent, how do you feel about how your children and their friends dress, talk, and behave?
   e. Do parents often expect their children to spend more time at home than the children want to spend there?
   f. Do parents usually give financial help to their children who are over the age of eighteen? At what age do they stop helping them? Do you think parents sometimes use money to control their children when they are trying to become independent? Give examples.
2. What are popular professions among young people in your country? In the United States? What professions do parents usually want their children to choose? Do parents often try to force their children to become something that they don't want to be? Did your parents encourage you to be something you didn't want to be?
3. What kind of music do you like? What kind of music did you enjoy listening to when you were a teenager? Do you and your parents have different tastes in music?
4. Is rock music popular in your country? What other kinds of music are popular? Which rock stars or groups are famous in your country? Who are your favorites?

Time Clauses and the
Real Conditional

Pele: one of the world's greatest soccer players. (*Bill Jerome*)

Theme: *Physical Fitness and Sports*
Grammar: 1. *Time Clauses: Past, Present, and Future*
                 2. *Real Conditional*

Dialogue

(YOLANDA and MOLLY are jogging in the park. MOLLY started jogging about two months ago, but today is YOLANDA's first day.)

YOLANDA: Molly, I'm exhausted. It's only seven in the morning! Let's stop for a few minutes.

MOLLY: Don't quit yet. Push yourself a little. Just a few minutes more. **When I started jogging, it was really difficult for me, too.**

YOLANDA: Have pity on me then. This is my first time.

MOLLY: Come on, Yolanda. **After you jog another month or two, you'll be ready for the marathon.**

YOLANDA: The marathon!!! How many miles is the marathon?

MOLLY: It's about twenty-six miles. **If I jog every day, I'll enter it next fall.**

YOLANDA: Count me out.[1] I'm tired now after only half a mile. I'm going to stop.

MOLLY: Okay, but don't sit down. Keep on[2] walking for a while. That's important. **When you stop exercising suddenly, sometimes you get muscle cramps.**

YOLANDA: I'm in terrible shape.[3] **I'm going to go back to bed as soon as I get home.** Is jogging really good for me?

MOLLY: Yes, but you won't feel the benefits right away. Doctors say that **the heart gets stronger after you jog regularly for a month or so.**

YOLANDA: I know. Everybody's talking about how wonderful jogging is. It's the latest fad.[4]

MOLLY: That's true. Look. The park is full of joggers. Everybody jogs nowadays.

YOLANDA: Well, **unless you come by my apartment every morning and drag me out of bed, I won't do it.**

MOLLY: Okay, I'll come and get you. It's nice to have company. I really want to lose some weight and get in shape.[5] I'm tired of being out of condition.

---

1. *Count me out:* I don't want to be part of this. Don't include me.
2. *Keep on:* Continue.
3. *I'm in terrible shape:* I am not in good physical condition. We say someone is in bad or terrible shape when his or her physical condition is poor, usually because of not exercising.
4. *fad:* something that becomes very popular for a short period of time.
5. *get in shape:* get your body in good physical condition by exercising.

YOLANDA: The new Molly!

MOLLY: **I'm going to do this until I look and feel the way I want to.**

Part 1 Time Clauses

Explanation

A time clause is a part of a sentence which has its own subject and verb and begins with a time expression such as *before, after, when, as soon as,* or *until.* It is not a complete sentence.

time clause	main clause
When I started jogging,	it was difficult for me.

We can place the time clause at the beginning or end of the sentence.

A. Time Clauses about the Past

Examples

Jesse Owens is a famous name in the history of American sports. **When he was a student at Ohio State University,** he broke several world records in track. Later, at the 1936 Olympics, he broke the world record for the 200 meter race and the broad jump. The 1936 Olympics took place in Munich **when Hitler was in power.** Hitler was angry **when Jesse Owens, a black man, won several gold medals.** Hitler wanted Germans to win in order to prove his theories of racial superiority. **Before Owens received his medals,** Hitler left the stadium. Owens didn't receive full recognition for his victory **until he returned to the United States. As soon as he arrived in New York,** crowds of reporters and people greeted him.

B. Time Clauses about the Present

Examples

Americans love to watch spectator sports. They are also becoming more and more interested in participatory sports and physical fitness for reasons of health. Some studies show that **when people exercise properly,** they have 50 percent fewer heart attacks. **After a person jogs regularly for a period of time,** his pulse rate and blood pressure go down.

C. Time Clauses about the Future

Explanation

Notice that in the examples for the past and present time clauses, the tense of the verb in the time clause is the same as the tense of the verb in the main clause.

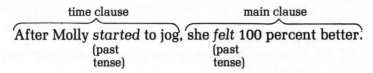

After Molly *started* to jog, she *felt* 100 percent better.
(past tense)   (past tense)

When we use time clauses to talk about a time in the future, the tenses in the two clauses are different. The verb in the time clause is in the simple present tense, and the verb in the main clause is in the future tense (*will* or *going to*).

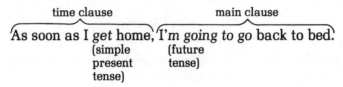

As soon as I *get* home, I'm *going to go* back to bed.
(simple present tense)   (future tense)

D. Questions

Explanation

When you ask a question that contains a time clause, the question form is used only for the verb in the main clause. The time clause can come at the beginning or end of the question. Don't use the question form in the time clause.

Examples

main clause   time clause

MOLLY: How old **were you** *when you started smoking*, Arnold?
ARNOLD: Around thirteen or fourteen.
MOLLY: *When you're nervous,* **do you smoke** a lot?
ARNOLD: Yeah, and especially before I play.
MOLLY: **Do you reach** for a cigarette *as soon as you get up in the morning?*
ARNOLD: Yes, I have one or two cigarettes before I eat breakfast, but I won't tomorrow.

Part 2   Clauses with *If* and *Unless* in the Future: The Real Conditional

A. *If* Clauses

Explanation

When we talk about a future time and use an *if* clause, we call this sentence a *real conditional* sentence. The actions in both the clauses will occur in the future. We use the simple present tense in the *if* clause and the future tense (*going to* or *will*) in the main clause.

if clause   main clause

If I *jog* every day, I'll *enter* the marathon next fall.
(simple present tense)   (future tense)

Examples

ARNOLD: You know, it's going to be hard for me to quit smoking when I'm at the disco. Everyone smokes there. What'll I **do** *if someone* **offers** *me a cigarette?*

MOLLY: *If I'm there,* I'**ll take** it away from you.

ARNOLD: Yeah, but when I play, I'm always very nervous. *If I* **don't have** *a cigarette in my mouth tonight,* I'**ll go** crazy.

MOLLY: *If you really* **need** *something,* we'**ll give** you chewing gum.

B. Unless Clauses

Explanation

Unless means *if not* when the verb in the *unless* clause is affirmative. Sentence (1) means the same as sentence (2):

1. **Unless** Molly comes to get Yolanda every morning, Yolanda won't jog.
2. **If** Molly doesn't come to get Yolanda every morning, Yolanda won't jog.

You can't use *unless* with a negative verb when the verb in the main clause is negative.

Incorrect: I won't stop smoking unless you don't help me.

Correct: I won't stop smoking unless you help me.

Examples

YOLANDA: Listen, Arnold stopped smoking two weeks ago. Let's take him out to dinner to celebrate.

MOLLY: Okay. *Unless* we *find* a restaurant with a no-smoking section, Arnold **won't enjoy** his dinner at all. He still wants to light up when he smells cigarette smoke. When are we going to go?

YOLANDA: We'**ll go** Saturday night *unless* Jack and Arnold **have** other plans.

MOLLY: And let's treat him to a really nice dinner.

YOLANDA: We'**ll do** that *unless* we'**re** broke.[6] Let's check our pocketbooks first.

A SPECIAL NOTE ABOUT COMMAS

When the time clause or *if/unless* clause is at the beginning of the sentence, it is followed by a comma.

After you jog regularly for a month or so, your heart gets stronger.

If Molly jogs every day, she'll enter the marathon next fall.

When the time clause or *if/unless* clause is at the end of the sentence, there is no comma:

Your heart gets stronger after you jog regularly for a month or so.

Molly will enter the marathon next fall if she jogs every day.

---

6. *to be broke:* to have no money.

Exercise 1   Time Clauses: Past, Present, and Future

A. Fill in the correct tense of the verb: simple present, simple past, or future.

Physical fitness programs sponsored by corporations are a fast-growing trend in the American business world. More than four hundred large corporations now offer exercise programs to their employees. The business world is fast becoming convinced that employees

__*work*__ more productively when they __*are*__
  (work)   (be)

physically fit. When an employee _____ out because of
                                      (stay)

illness, it _____ a company a lot of money. Employee health
              (cost)

problems cost business more than $3 billion a year.

Many corporations build their own exercise centers. Xerox Corpora-

tion _____ $3.5 million when it _____ its
       (spend)   (build)

exercise center in Leesburg, Virginia, a few years ago. A large

corporation in California is building a facility for 2,000 workers. When

it _____ complete, the center _____ two
    (be)   (have)

racquet ball courts, a sauna, an exercise room, two pools, a volleyball

court, two tennis courts, a basketball court, and a track.

When a company _____ that it cannot afford to build its
                    (decide)

own center, it often _____ for its workers to enroll in
                         (pay)

independent exercise centers. Cardio-Fitness is an example of such a

center. Cardio-Fitness charges its members $550 a year. Most of the

members are sponsored by their corporations. The center always

_____ the applicants' medical histories very carefully
       (review)
before they _____ the exercise program. After the clients
                  (begin)
_____ a series of tests, the center _____ them
       (take)   (give)
an individual program to follow.

Medical evidence that exercise makes for a healthy heart is growing.

When Dr. Ralph Paffenbarger, Jr. of Stanford University _____
                                                              (conclude)
a fifteen-year study in 1979, he _____ that people who
                                        (find)
exercise regularly have fewer heart attacks. Companies have found

that workers _____ with stress better when they
                    (cope)
_____ regularly. In Chicago a printing company called
       (exercise)
Excello Press _____ to build an exercise room after an
                     (decide)
angry employee _____ his lunchbox into a printing press
                      (throw)
and caused $100,000 in damage. When the president of the company

_____ about the incident, he _____ that his
       (hear)   (realize)
employees needed an outlet for their tensions and frustrations. One

employee of the federal government is delighted with her new exercise

program, which she participates in during work hours. Before she

_____ the program, she _____ tense all the
       (start)   (be)
time and suffered from severe headaches. Now she feels much more

relaxed.

The business world believes that company exercise centers are

becoming an important fringe benefit. Business experts predict that in

the future, before an executive _____ accepting a job with
                                      (consider)

a corporation, he or she _____ about exercise facilities
                                    (ask)
the same way that people now ask about other benefits, such as medical

coverage or vacation time. Some people predict that the employer's

interest in the physical well-being of employees will grow. In the future,

employers _____ at several other factors when they
                        (look)
_____ health programs. They will consider such things as
     (consider)
nutrition, weight control, and coping with stress in addition to exercise

programs.

   Others are not so optimistic. These pessimists say that the economy

is entering a very difficult period. They predict that when company

profits _____ , the exercise programs_____
              (drop)   (be)
the first benefit to be eliminated.

B.   Read the exercise again. With your classmates try to retell as much of
     the information as possible without looking at it. Try to use time clauses.

Exercise 2   Future Time Clauses

Molly is going to run in a women's minimarathon in Central Park in two
months. Here are some of the things she is going to do *before* or *after* she
runs the race:

1.   buy a new running suit
2.   practice extra hard
3.   run an extra mile every day for practice
4.   feel proud of herself
5.   celebrate with her friends
6.   take a long hot shower
7.   probably get new blisters on her feet
8.   feel very, very tired
9.   fill out an entry form
10.   pay an entrance fee

Directions

Use the information above to make sentences with time clauses. Use these time expressions: *when, before, after, as soon as, until.* Use these verbs in your time clauses: *enter, run, finish, complete.*

Example

Before Molly runs the marathon, she's going to pay the entrance fee.

Exercise 3

A. You are planning to enter a sports event (for example, a race or a game) or you are planning to start a new exercise program to get in shape (for example, jogging or swimming). Write sentences and tell what you're going to do before, after, and when you start. Use time clauses with *when, before, after, until, as soon as.*

Before I start my new exercise program, I'm going to have a medical checkup.

B. Your government is sending you to the moon. You are going to be one of the first settlers in a moon colony. Describe this adventure before takeoff, after takeoff, and after your arrival on the moon. Use time clauses.

Before I do anything else, I'm going to see a lawyer and make a will.

C. You and your wife or husband just visited the doctor. You're going to have your first child. How are you going to prepare for the birth of your child? What are you going to do after the child arrives? Make sentences using time clauses.

Exercise 4   Real Conditionals

Directions

Fill in the blanks with the correct tense of the verb under the line.

1. Professional athletes earn very high salaries. Tickets to games are

   already very expensive. If athletes' salaries **Continue** to

   (continue)

   increase, the price of tickets **will increase** too. If the price of

   (increase)

   tickets _____, many people _____ to games.

   (increase)   (negative, go)

If people _____ tickets, the owners of the teams
(negative, buy)
_____ money.
(lose)

2. Scientists are studying cigarette smoking. According to a 1979 report,

unless people _____ smoking, 320,000 people per year
(stop)

_____ prematurely. The tobacco industry is trying to show
(die)

that smoking is not really dangerous. Unless people _____
(continue)

to buy cigarettes, the tobacco industry _____ a great deal
(lose)

of money. Many people want the government to stop all cigarette adver-

tising. The tobacco industry wants to continue advertising because it

_____ profits unless it _____ .
(negative, make)   (advertise)

Exercise 5   *If/Unless*

A. Look at the picture of a hockey game and then write sentences in the
real conditional. Use *if* and *unless*.

Example *If hockey player #8 hits player #13, there will be a big fight. Unless the policeman stops the fans, they will climb over the fence.*

B.   Eva is a thirteen-year-old girl. She has studied ballet since she was seven. A national ballet company just asked her to join its ballet school. Eva has a choice to make. If she joins this school, she won't have time for other activities that girls like because she will practice for hours every day. Write sentences in the real conditional. Use *if* and *unless*.

Example *If Eva practices all the time, she won't have time for parties and movies.*

If she doesn't join the ballet school, she won't get good professional training.

C.   Now write about a choice you think you will make soon about your future. Write sentences about what will or won't happen if you decide one thing or another. Use *if* or *unless* in your sentences.

Example *Unless I continue my education, I won't get the job I want.*

D.   Arnold's father is a banker and works all the time. He never exercises, and he smokes and eats too much. Write sentences about what will or won't happen to Arnold's father if he continues this way. Use *if* and *unless*. Use your imagination.

Example *Unless Arnold's father goes on a diet, he will damage his heart.*

E.   Choose a crisis or problem in the world today (energy, world peace, hunger, the Mideast conflict, poverty, pollution, nuclear weapons, etc.) and write about it, using the real conditional.

Exercise 6 Problem Solving

Directions
Discuss these problems in small groups in your class. Report back to the other groups the pros and cons of each possible solution to the problem.

A. The person you love is from a different country. She or he has a completely different cultural and religious background. You are faced with many choices:

> whether or not to marry
> whether or not to convert to this person's religion
> what kind of marriage ceremony to have
> where to live (in whose country)
> how to raise your children (in what religion and with the values and customs of which country)

Discuss each choice that you have to make, and tell what all the consequences will be for each possible decision. For example, tell what will happen if you marry the person and what will happen if you don't.

B. Susan is a mother in her thirties. She has two children, aged two and six. Susan is well educated and had a good job before she stopped work to have children six years ago. Now she is beginning to feel frustrated and bored with staying at home. She is trying to make a decision whether or not to start work again. She will feel more fulfilled if she goes back to work, but she is concerned about her children, especially the two-year-old. Discuss her choices in this situation and all the consequences each decision will bring. Here are the choices:

> whether to go back to work or continue to stay at home as a mother and housewife
> whether or not to leave the children in a day-care center or with a baby-sitter
> whether to work part time or full time
> whether to make a decision for herself or follow her husband's wishes (her husband prefers for her to stay home)

Exercise 7 Integration of Future Time Clauses and the Real Conditional

Directions
Imagine you are a very famous and clever robber. You have carefully planned a robbery with your gang. Tell each one of them what he is going to do when certain signals are given. The members of your gang are very nervous and ask a lot of questions about what will happen if something goes wrong. Invent a dialogue between the gang leader and the members of the gang.

LEADER: This is a perfect crime. It can't fail if you follow my instructions. We'll all be rich tomorrow if you do exactly as I say. Now, John, when Robert comes into the jewelry store, you're going to walk up to the salesman and ask him about a diamond necklace for your wife.

JOHN: But what will happen if. . . .

(Now you continue this dialogue.)

Expressing Your Ideas: Speaking and Writing

1. Are people in your country interested in physical fitness? What do people do to keep in shape? What do you do?
2. Is jogging very popular in your country? Why do you think jogging is so popular in the United States? What are some of the benefits of jogging? Which sports are most beneficial in helping a person maintain good physical condition?
3. Which sports do people in your country play? What is the most popular sport? Tennis? Golf? Track?
4. In the United States, women are becoming more and more involved in sports. Is this true in your country? Which sports do women play?
5. Does your country participate in the Olympics? What did you think when the United States and other countries decided not to go to the Moscow Summer Olympics in 1980? Is it possible to separate sports from politics?
6. Who are some of the famous athletes in your country? Is it possible to make a lot of money from sports?
7. Is sports a big business in your country? In the United States, sports-wear and sports equipment are big business. Are they in your country?

Can, Could, Be Able To

Bucky Dent of the Yankees forcing out Singleton at 2nd base. (*William Hotz/Sunpapers*)

Theme: *More Sports*

Grammar: *Can, Could, Be Able To: Permission, Ability, Possibility*

Dialogue

(JACK and ARNOLD are at a baseball game in Yankee Stadium. ARNOLD is a real baseball fan. JACK isn't.)

JACK: Look at No. 39. He **can't hit** anything.

ARNOLD: Yeah, the Yankees[1] are playing badly again this year.

JACK: What do you mean, again? I thought they won the World Series [2] last year.

ARNOLD: Yeah, they did, but they started the season[3] badly. They **couldn't win** anything in the first part of the season.

JACK: So how did they win the Series?

ARNOLD: Well, finally they **were able to break** their losing streak.[4] They **were able to win** most of their games in the second half of the season.

JACK: Here comes Reggie Jackson.

ARNOLD: He **can hit** almost anything.

JACK: **Can** he **play** outfield[5] well?

ARNOLD: I think he **can.**

JACK: Didn't the Yankees lose one of their best players at the beginning of this season?

ARNOLD: Yes, he broke his finger, but they think he**'ll be able to play** in a few more weeks.

JACK: **Can** you **get** us tickets for next week's game?

ARNOLD: Sure, I **can. Can** you **give** me the money in advance? I'm broke[6] as usual.

---

1. *the Yankees:* a New York baseball team.
2. *the World Series:* a group of games for the championship.
3. *season:* The baseball season is from April through October.
4. *to break a losing streak:* to stop losing one game after another.
5. *play outfield:* There are three players who take positions far out in the baseball field. They play outfield.
6. *to be broke:* to have no money.

The following are modal auxiliary verbs: *can, could, should, ought to, have to, must, might, may, had better,* and *would rather.* A modal auxiliary is used before another verb. We often use modals when we want to give advice, prohibit, give permission, or talk about ability. In this chapter we are going to look at the modal *can.*

Part 1   Present Tense: Can, Could, Be Able To

Explanation
Can and *could* have many different meanings. In this chapter we are only going to talk about a few of these meanings. We use the base form of the verb after *can, could,* or *be able to.*

STATEMENTS

can (not) + base form

Reggie Jackson can hit almost any ball.

be (not) able to + base form

Reggie Jackson is able to hit almost any ball.

QUESTIONS

Can + subject + base form?

Can Reggie play outfield?

Could + subject + base form?

Could you lend me your book on baseball?

Be + subject + able to + base form?

Is Molly able to play baseball?

A. Ability

Explanation
When we have the capacity to do something, we usually use *can. Be able to* and *can* are frequently interchangeable in the present tense.

Examples
The Tarahumara Indians live in the Copper Canyon in the Sierra Madre Mountains of Mexico. They are excellent runners. They **can run** for forty-eight hours without getting out of breath. They play an unusual form of football. The game continues through the night. The players **are able to see** the

ball at night because friends run next to them with torches. These people live in a canyon with very steep walls. Even donkeys **can't climb** up and down the canyon safely, but the Tarahumara Indians **can.**

B. Possibility

Explanation
We also use *can* when we mean it is possible to do something. We usually don't use *be able to* for this meaning.

Example
Doctors think we **can learn** a lot about health and exercise from the Tarahumara Indians.

C. Permission and Prohibition

Explanation
There are two ways to ask for or give permission: with *may* or with *can.* *Can* has the same meaning as *may,* but *may* is more formal. In the negative, *can't* means it is not permitted. For these meanings we almost never use *be able to.*

Examples

MOLLY: I just read an article about the Tarahumara Indians in Mexico. Read it! Maybe they will inspire you to jog.

YOLANDA: Okay. **Can** I **borrow** it?   (or)   **May** I **borrow** it?

MOLLY: Sure, you **can take** it, but you **can't keep** it for more than a few days. It's due at the library next week.

NOTE: We often use *could* when we ask for permission. Some people think it is more polite than *can.*

Could I **borrow** that book?

Part 2   Past Tense: <u>Could</u>, <u>Was/Were Able To</u>

Explanation
We use *could* or *was/were able to* to express ability, possibility, and prohibition when we talk about the past. In negative statements *couldn't* and *wasn't/weren't able to* are very similar in meaning. In affirmative statements they are usually similar in meaning, but there are some cases where we don't use *could.* When we want to talk about a specific event or a specific achievement, we don't use *could.* We use *was/were able to.*

Examples
Baseball is a favorite American sport. Jackie Robinson is one of the most famous players in the history of baseball. In high school he was an all-round

sportsman.[7] He **could play** baseball, basketball, football, and track. Of course, he **wasn't able to play** all of these professionally. So he chose baseball because he **could play** it the best. In 1945 he became the first black to join major-league baseball. He didn't start off the first season well, but by the end of the year, he **was able to finish**[8] with the highest batting average in the league.

Before 1945 only white baseball players **were able to join** organized baseball. When Jackie joined his first all-white team, the team **couldn't play** in several towns in the South because these towns didn't allow interracial teams to play. Because of Jackie's courage, more and more blacks **were able to join** organized baseball.

Part 3   Future Tense: <u>Can, Will/Won't Be Able To</u>

Explanation
We use either *can/can't* or *will/won't be able to* to talk about possibility or ability in the future.

Examples
YOLANDA: Molly, some friends of mine organized a baseball game in the park for next Saturday. **Can** you **go?**

MOLLY: I **can go**, but I don't know how to play. I **won't be able to hit** the ball.

YOLANDA: I'll teach you. Practice with me for a few evenings. You'**ll be able to play** by next Saturday.

Part 4   Questions

Examples

1. **Can** women **play** for organized baseball today?
   No, they can't, but some women are fighting to change those rules.
2. **Are** women **able to earn** the same money as men in sports?
   No, they aren't. For example, women golfers earn much less than men.

---

7. *all-round sportsman:* someone who can play many sports well.
8. We cannot use *could* in this sentence because we are talking about a specific one-time achievement in a difficult situation. In all the other sentences in the example, it is possible to use *could* or *was/were able to*. Here are two more examples where you cannot use *could:*
1. I was sick yesterday, but I **was able to take** my math test in the afternoon because the doctor gave me some medicine.
2. Molly had a cramp in her leg, but she **was able to finish** the mini-marathon before it got really bad.

3. When **will** women **be able to compete** against men in the Olympics?
    Who knows?
4. **Could** women **compete** in the Olympics in ancient Greece?
    No, they couldn't. They finally organized their own Olympics.

Exercise 1   Question Practice

Directions
Read the following information and then ask a question using *can/can't, be able to* in the past, present, or future.

Example
1. Molly can't beat Yolanda at tennis now.

    When _____ *will she be able to beat* _____ her?
                            (beat)

    After she practices a lot.

2. Molly runs a lot more than Yolanda, and she runs more often.

    Who _____in the next mini-marathon?
                    (participate)
        Molly _____.

3. Who _____faster, Molly or Yolanda?
                    (run)
        Molly _____.

4. Bob Hayes, a famous athlete, was sick when he was a child. He won an

    Olympic medal for running.

    Why _____ sports as a child?
                    (negative, play)
        Because he had polio.

5. Girls didn't play on the same baseball teams as boys until 1978.

    Why _____ on boys' teams?
                    (negative, play)
    Because the rules didn't allow them to.

6. Mickey Mantle was a great baseball hitter.

What _____ that was unusual?
                (do)
He hit left-handed and right-handed.

7. Mark Spitz was a champion swimmer.

What _____ in the 1972 Olympics?
             (achieve)
He won five gold medals.

8. Jim Thorpe won a gold medal in track and field. The Olympic Committee

took it away from him.

Why _____ the medal?
           (negative, keep)
Because he had once played professional football and earned money.

Only amateur athletes can participate in the Olympics.

Exercise 2 Present and Past Tense: <u>Can</u> and <u>Be Able To</u>

A. Choose one of the superheroes from the following list:

Superman	The Incredible Hulk
Batman	Spiderman
The Bionic Man/the Bionic Woman	Bruce Lee
Wonder Woman	

Write five sentences about one of these superheroes. Tell what he or she can do. Is there anything that he or she cannot do? Tell what.

Example
Superman can bend steel with his bare hands.

B. Now you are one of these superheroes and there are many things in the world that you want to change. What can or will you be able to do to bring about these changes?

Example
I am Wonder Woman. I work to eliminate crime and corruption. There is an international plot to steal all the gold at Fort Knox.[9] I will be able to stop

---

9. Fort Knox: Where the gold is kept for the United States Treasury.

this crime. I will be able to hear the conversation of the robbers with my superhearing. I'll be able to find their secret meeting place because I have x-ray vision. . . .

1. Now finish this story.
2. Now choose another superhero you want to be and write your own story.
C. King Kong had enormous strength. He could do many things. For example, he could uproot a tree with one hand. What were some of the other things he could do? What were some of the things he couldn't do? Why?

Exercise 3   _Could, Was/Were Able To_

Directions
Fill in the blanks with *could, was/were able to*. Remember that in some affirmative sentences, you can only use *was/were able to*.

The American colonies decided to become independent from Great

Britain in 1776. There were many reasons for this. According to the

colonies, they _couldn't pay_ the high taxes that the British demanded.
          (negative, pay)

They were also unhappy because they _____ their own
              (negative, elect)

governors. In 1776 there were thirteen colonies. Each colony was very

different from the others, and often the colonies didn't get along.

However, on July 4, 1776, the thirteen colonies _____ their
            (forget)

differences, and they united to declare their independence from the British.

The Revolutionary War lasted from 1776 to 1781. George Washington and

his army had many problems. At first, Washington didn't win many battles

because his army wasn't well trained. Also, Washington _____
            (negative, buy)

equipment and guns because the government didn't have much money. The

problem was that the Continental Congress _____ taxes.
            (negative, collect)

Congress _____ tax laws, but it _____ the colonies
   (pass)   (negative, force)

to pay. Eventually, after a lot of debate and disagreement, Congress

_____ enough money to equip the army. Finally, in 1781,

(collect)

Washington _____ the war, and the American colonies became

(win)

the United States of America.

Exercise 4   *Could, Be Able To*

Directions

Some of the sentences in the following reading are numbered. Change the numbered sentences, using the affirmative or negative form of *could* or *was/were able to* and the base form of the verb. (Use a separate sheet of paper).

Example

(1) *At first, only runners could compete.*

The Olympic Games

The Olympics began in ancient Greece in the year 776 B.C. The Greeks held these contests during the summer months once every four years. (1)At first only runners competed. Later there were competitions in boxing, chariot racing, and long-distance running. (2)In the Greek Olympics, only free men competed. (3)Women, foreigners, and slaves didn't participate. (4)Women didn't even watch the Olympics. (5)Later, however, women established their own games, which were called the Heraea. The Olympics and the Heraea disappeared when the Romans conquered Greece.

In the nineteenth century Pierre de Courbertin, a Frenchman, worked hard to revive these games. (6)Finally, he organized the first modern Olympics in Athens in 1896. Other Olympics followed. (7)Again, at first only men entered the competitions. (8)Finally, women participated in the Olympic games in 1912. (9)Nowadays amateur athletes from many nations of the world compete in a variety of sports events, including track and field, water sports, gymnastics, skiing, and figure skating.

Expressing Your Ideas: Speaking and Writing

1. Tell about a famous athlete or someone you know who had to overcome a difficulty. What could or couldn't the person do when he or she had this difficulty or handicap? How was the person finally able to overcome the difficulty? What can or can't this person do today?

2. In this chapter you read about the special abilities of the Tarahumara Indians. Tell about a group of people who have a special or unusual ability.

3. In this chapter you read about the American struggle for independence. Tell about a period in your country's history. For example, describe a time when your country was not independent, or describe a time when your country had a different form of government. Tell what the government and the people could and could not do at that time. Then explain the outcome of the situation. How was the new government able to develop or not develop? Were these changes beneficial to the people or not? Why?

4. Tell about a time in your life when you weren't able to do something that you very much wanted to do. What were some of the reasons for this? Were you finally able to solve this problem? How?

The Past Continuous Tense

Theme: UFOs[1] and Other Unexplained Phenomena
Grammar: The Past Continuous Tense

Dialogue

MOLLY: Did you see that program about UFOs on TV last night? It was really incredible!

JACK: You don't believe in UFOs, do you?

MOLLY: I don't know what to think. The program was really convincing. They interviewed a man from New Jersey. He **was driving** through a park at night **when** a bright light **surrounded** his car and ——

JACK: He was probably drunk.

MOLLY: —he got out of his car and saw a flying saucer[2] only fifty feet away from him.

JACK: And I suppose when it landed, some little green men got out.

MOLLY: They weren't green, but when the door of the flying saucer opened, ten little creatures walked out.

JACK: Oh, sure they did. Tell me more, Molly. Then what happened?

MOLLY: Then they dug up some earth and put it into some little plastic bags.

JACK: Plastic! I suppose they have an oil industry on Mars, too. And what **was** the man from New Jersey **doing while** all these little creatures from Mars **were digging**?

MOLLY: He **was** just **standing** there and **watching** them. Then all of a sudden one of the creatures started to walk toward him.

JACK: Did the creature introduce the man to all his little green friends? Did they shake hands . . . or antennae, I mean?

MOLLY: No! The man ran back to his car and drove away as fast as he could.

JACK: Come on, Molly. You don't really believe that story.

MOLLY: This man didn't seem like a kook.[3] He was just an average guy, just like you or me. You know, Jack, it *is* possible.

---

1. *UFOs:* Unidentified flying objects.
2. *flying saucer:* a spaceship from another planet; another word for UFO.
3. *a kook:* a crazy or very peculiar person.

We use the past continuous in several different ways. In this chapter we will talk about several of the different meanings of this tense.

The form of this tense is:

Statement: subject + $\begin{Bmatrix} was \\ were \end{Bmatrix}$ (not) + base form + ing

Molly was watching television at 10:00.

Part 1   Interrupted Actions

A. Statements

1. Explanation

When we want to say that we were in the middle of doing something when something else interrupted us, we use this pattern:

subject + past continuous + *when* + subject + simple past

a man was driving home when a bright light surrounded his car.

Example

In the summer of 1977 two young people **were walking** along a street in New York City *when* they **looked up** and **saw** a UFO above the World Trade Center. It didn't look like an airplane, but it had blinking lights. The same night another man **was jogging** on a beach near New York City *when* an object with flashing lights **appeared** above him.[4]

2. Explanation

Sometimes the past continuous is used in the *when* clause. This does not change the meaning of the sentence. In this case *when* has the same meaning as *while*.

Examples

Two young people **were walking** along a street in New York City **when** they **looked up** and **saw** a UFO.

$\begin{rcases} When \\ While \end{rcases}$ two young people **were walking** along a street in New York City,

they **looked up** and **saw** a UFO.

---

4. Details on some of these and other sightings mentioned in this chapter are in *UFO Exist!* (Putnam, 1976) by Paris Flammonde.

3. Explanation
The *when* clause can come at the beginning or end of the sentence.
Examples
Muhammad Ali was jogging in the park *when he saw a flying saucer.*
(or)
When Muhammad Ali saw a flying saucer, he was jogging in the park.

B. Questions

(Question word) + $\begin{Bmatrix} was \\ were \end{Bmatrix}$ + subject + base form + ing?

What was the man doing when he saw the U.F.O.?

Examples
In 1972 a young man was climbing a mountain in Wyoming when he saw a flying saucer and strange creatures.

Was the flying saucer **coming** toward him when he saw it?
  Yes, it was.
What **was** he **doing** when he saw the flying saucer?
  He was resting from the climb.

C. Contrast of Simple Past and Past Continuous in
Sentences with <u>When</u> Clauses

Notice the difference in meaning between these sentences.

1. In August 1952 a young man **was driving** a boat through a swamp in Florida when he saw a UFO.
2. The young man **drove** away quickly when he saw the UFO.

Explanation
In the first sentence the man was driving the boat through the swamp *first.* THEN he saw the UFO. In the second sentence the man drove away immediately AFTER he saw the UFO. In this sentence *when* means *after.*
  Note the question formation:

1. What **was** the man **doing** when he saw the UFO?
  He **was photographing** wildlife.
2. What **did** he **do** when he saw the UFO?
  He **raced** away because he was afraid.

Here are other examples: Two boys **were skating** on a lake *when a bright object appeared* above the trees near the lake. The UFO remained there for several minutes. The boys **went** over to inspect the trees *when it took off.* The tops of the trees were cut off and parts of the trees were burned.

What **were** the boys **doing** when the UFO appeared?
They **were skating.**
What **did** they **do** when the UFO took off?
They **went** over to inspect the trees.

Exercise 1 *Past Continuous with Interrupted Action*

A. Uri Geller is a famous Israeli psychic. A *psychic* is a person who has special mind powers. A psychic can do unusual things: read other people's minds or move objects without touching them. Some people believe in Uri Geller's special powers; others say Geller is dishonest and tricks people. Donald Singleton, a reporter for the *New York Post,* once spent several days with Geller. The following exercise is based on an article Singleton wrote after that experience. Fill in the blanks with the past continuous or the simple past form of the verb. All of these sentences show interrupted action in the past.

Uri Geller says that when he is in a room, strange things happen.

Frequently, he says, he is not trying to make these things happen. He

gave the reporter an example. One time he went to a friend's house for

dinner. This friend had a rare and beautiful rock on a shelf in the living

room. They __were eating__ dinner in the dining room when this
       (eat)

rock ___flew___ through the dining room door and _____
    (fly)   (fall)

to the floor with a loud noise. Geller says he _____ about
                                 (negative, think)

the rock when this _____.
                 (happen)

    Geller _____ this story to the newspaper reporter when
          (tell)

the reporter _____ a fork on the table next to them. When
          (notice)

he _____ at the fork a second time, it _____
     (look)   (move)

from side to side on the table and _____. Geller was
(bend)
surprised when the reporter told him about the fork.

Later that same night Geller and the reporter _____ in
(wait)
the lounge of a theater when the reporter _____ a strange
(hear)
noise. When he _____ across the room, the soda machine
(look)
_____ ice all over the floor. Geller says that he didn't try
(throw)
to make the machine do that.

After several days with Geller, the reporter didn't know how to

explain all the strange things that he had seen.

B. Ask questions to get more information about the situation.

Example

1. One night in August 1952 a man from Long Island, New York, saw
   a UFO. It landed not far from him, and three small beings got out.
   They walked around for a few minutes and then got back in their
   ship and left.
   What _was the man doing_ when _the UFO landed_?
   He was taking a walk.

2. In May of 1955 a New York photographer and his girl friend were
   in a park when a huge object with a circular shape appeared above
   them. The man photographed the UFO, and the photograph later
   showed something that looked like a large doughnut.

   What _____ when _____?
   He was taking photographs of his girl friend.

3. A woman from Brooklyn saw a UFO from her car window in
   January 1975. The UFO was in the sky above an apartment building.
   The ship had a circle of blinking lights around it.

   Where _____ when _____?
   She was going to visit some relatives.

4. On December 1, 1971, Muhammad Ali was in Central Park in New
   York City when he saw something bright with the shape of a light
   bulb in the sky.

   _____ when _____?
   No, he wasn't taking a walk. He was jogging.

5. A Manhattan man sighted a UFO in 1974. He saw something pink with the shape of a triangle in the clouds. After some time it moved off to the north and disappeared.

What _____ when _____?

He was watching the sunset. It was a beautiful summer evening.

C. Tell about your experience:

1. Think about some time in your life when something happened that frightened you or when something happened that you couldn't explain. Tell what you were doing when this happened. Try to think of more than one incident.

2. Invent a story about a day when everything went wrong from morning to night. Tell what you were doing when each of these things went wrong. Try to use two different patterns:
   I was doing (something) when (something) happened.
   (or)
   While I was doing (something), (something) happened.

Example

Yesterday was a terrible day for me. The day was a disaster beginning with the moment that I got up. I was having a wonderful dream when the alarm clock woke me up. I tried to go back to sleep for a few minutes to finish my dream, but I couldn't. Later, while I was making my morning coffee, I knocked the can of coffee off the counter by accident, and it spilled all over the floor.

Now continue the story of your disastrous day. What minidisasters happened while you were:

shaving (or) putting on makeup	getting on the bus
getting dressed	riding in an elevator
waiting for the bus in the rain	having lunch in a restaurant

If you have a real story about a day in your own life when everything went wrong, tell it.

Exercise 2   Contrast of Past Continuous and Simple Past

UFOs and psychic powers like Uri Geller's are difficult to explain. Here are some other stories about a strange creature. Some people believe that there is a strange creature called a "bigfoot" that lives in the Pacific Northwest of the United States. A bigfoot is a nine-foot-tall hairy creature that is half man and half ape. Some people believe there are two hundred of these creatures. Many residents of this area of the United States say that they have seen these creatures. Here are their stories:

The first story happened on the Nooksak River in the state of Washington.

Early one morning three men *were fishing* (fish) when they *heard* (hear) some strange noises near the shore and _____ (smell) something very unpleasant. When they _____ (point) their flashlight at the shoreline, they _____ (see) a large hairy creature. The men had left a bag of fish on the shore. When they _____ (catch) the bigfoot with their lights, it _____ (try) to steal some fish from the bag. The bigfoot _____ (turn) and _____ (run) away when it _____ (see) the men.

In the spring of 1973, an Oregon high-school teacher _____ (drive) on a quiet country road when he _____ (see) a bigfoot on the far side of a lake. The creature _____ (pick) berries when the man _____ (see) it. The man stopped his car and took his rifle out, but when he _____ (try) to shoot the bigfoot, he _____ (negative, can) because the creature looked so human.

A woman in the same area _____ (sit) in her living room and _____ (watch) television when a large hairy arm _____ (come) through her window. When she _____ (scream), her husband _____ (come) from the next room with a gun. When he _____ (open) the front door, a bigfoot _____ (stand) there. It _____ (turn) and _____ (run) away when it _____ (see) the gun.

Part 2   Past Continuous with a Specific Time

Explanation

When we want to say that we were in the middle of doing something at a specific time in the past, we use the past continuous.

Examples

Jack called Molly at 10:00 P.M. Molly **was watching** the news on TV then.

We use the past continuous (*was watching*) because we want to say that the action began before the specific time (10:00 P.M.) and perhaps continued after it. We can't use the simple past (*watched*) to express this meaning in this case. Notice the difference in this situation:

Molly had a lot of things to do yesterday. She went shopping in the afternoon. She studied until about 8:00 P.M. At 9:00 P.M. she sat down and **watched** TV.

In this situation, we can't use the past continuous (*was watching*). Here we mean that Molly began watching TV at 9:00 P.M.

Exercise 3   Past Continuous with a Specific Time

In the summer of 1977 there was a total blackout[5] in New York City and surrounding areas. The electricity went out at 9:25 P.M. New Yorkers were doing a variety of things that night at that time. Use your imagination and complete the following sentences about what people were doing at 9:25 on the night of the blackout.

Example

1. _Some people were watching TV_ at 9:25 that evening. They couldn't see the end of their favorite TV programs.

2. A number of people _____ at 9:25. They didn't know if they should pay for their half-eaten dinners or not. The waiters didn't know what to do either.

3. Some New Yorkers _____. If they had an electric stove, they had to throw their half-cooked dinners in the garbage.

---

5. *blackout:* a total failure of electricity in an area.

4. One man _____.

   He had to wait until the next morning to finish the last page of his

   murder mystery.

5. Quite a few people _____.

   They had to wait for hours until security men got them out of the

   elevators and helped them down blackened stairwells.

6. Some children _____.

   Their parents stopped reading the bedtime stories and let the children

   come into their bedrooms to sleep.

7. One journalist _____

   for *People* magazine. He had to finish writing the story by candlelight

   so that the story would be ready for publication the next morning.

8. Some people _____.

   They had to come back another time to see the end of the movie.

9. Many New Yorkers _____.

   They had to sit in the hot subway cars for hours before help came.

10. A teenage boy _____.

    He couldn't find his dog in the darkness and ran home. Fortunately,

    the next day the dog returned.

11. A lot of children _____.

    They didn't know about the blackout until the next day.

Part 3   Simultaneous Actions in the Past

Explanation
We often use the past continuous in both clauses to show that two actions were happening at the same time in the past. We can use both *when* and *while*, but we use *while* more often for this meaning.

Example
Jack didn't watch the program on UFOs last night because he was at the observatory. *While* Molly **was watching** the program, Jack **was looking** at the stars through a telescope.

Exercise 4

1. Think of a party that you went to where you did not have a good time. What were you doing while all the other people were enjoying themselves?

    While _____, I _____.

2. Arnold worked in a discotheque last night. He was annoyed because people didn't listen to his music very carefully. What were they doing while Arnold was playing?

    _____ while Arnold _____.

3. The president of the United States gave a very long and boring speech to Congress yesterday. What were many of the congressmen doing while he was giving his speech?

    _____ while _____.

4. Yolanda's friend Lisa gave birth to her first baby a week ago. Lisa's husband was very nervous. What was he doing while Lisa was giving birth?

    While _____, her husband _____

    _____.

5. Yolanda decided to go on a diet for about a week. Last night she and Molly went out to a restaurant for dinner. Molly had a chocolate sundae for dessert; Yolanda had nothing. What was Yolanda doing while Molly was eating her chocolate sundae?

    _____ while _____.

Exercise 5   Integration

Directions

Imagine that you saw a UFO. A reporter is asking you to describe what you saw. Do this exercise with a classmate. One of you is the person who saw the UFO. The other person is the reporter. Invent a dialogue. The reporter wants to know:

1. what the person saw
2. what the person was doing when he or she saw it
3. where it was
4. what it looked like
5. what time he or she saw it
6. what it was doing while he or she was watching it

Expressing Your Ideas: Speaking and Writing

1. What do you know about UFOs? How do you explain them? Do you or anyone you know believe in UFOs or life on other planets?
2. Do you believe in some things that you can't explain rationally—for example, psychic phenomena? Tell why you do or do not believe in these things. Talk about any examples that you have from your own life or that you have heard about from a friend.
3. Do you or people that you know believe in ghosts or other supernatural beings? Are there stories about supernatural creatures that most people in your country know about? Who are these creatures and what do they do?

10 Comparison of Adjectives, Adverbs, and Nouns

Boy leaning against building.

Theme: *Cities*

Grammar: *Comparison of Adjectives, Adverbs, and Nouns*

Dialogue

ARNOLD: I'm sick and tired of living in New York. It's dirty. It's noisy. It's crowded. I need **more space.**

JACK: That's true, but what city is really **better?** Where would you like to live instead?

ARNOLD: Maybe San Francisco. It's **much cleaner** and **much more beautiful than** New York.

YOLANDA: It's **less crowded,** and it's **safer,** too.

JACK: I don't know if it's really **safer.** Maybe there's **less crime** in San Francisco, but if you think about it, San Francisco is **just as dangerous.**

ARNOLD: Oh, do you mean the earthquakes?

JACK: Yeah. California has **more natural disasters than** any other area of the country: earthquakes, mud slides, forest fires—

ARNOLD: Okay. Forget San Francisco. What about Chicago?

MOLLY: Chicago? I lived there when I was a child. It was all right, but I'd rather live in a small town than a big city like Chicago.

YOLANDA: I wouldn't. A small town **isn't nearly as exciting as** a big city. There aren't **as many things** to do.

ARNOLD: Yeah. If I move, I want to go to a big city like Chicago.

MOLLY: Arnold, I don't think you'd like Chicago. You hate the winter in New York. The winters in Chicago are **worse than** they are here. It's **much windier** there.

ARNOLD: All right. Forget Chicago. What about New Orleans? It's **warmer than** New York. And it's a great city for musicians.

JACK: Yeah, it's great for jazz, but does it have **as many opportunities** for rock musicians **as** New York does?

ARNOLD: Probably not. I guess I'm stuck here in New York.

MOLLY: The grass always looks greener on the other side of the fence.[1]

---

1. *The grass always looks greener:* This expression is about envy. It means that what you don't have always looks better than what you do have.

Part 1   Comparison of Adjectives

A. Comparisons to Express the Idea of More

Explanation

When we want to compare and contrast things, we often use these patterns:

> short adjective (one syllable) + er + than
>
> *San Francisco is cleaner than New York.*
>
> more + long adjective (two or more syllables) + than
>
> *San Francisco is more dangerous than New York.*

Example

San Francisco is built high on a hill overlooking the Pacific Ocean. The streets high up on the hill are **steeper than** the streets downtown. On some of these steep streets, people even have difficulty parking their cars. Almost every morning the fog rolls in from the Pacific. It is **foggier** in the morning **than** it is in the afternoon when the sun burns off the fog. Most people who visit both New York City and San Francisco think San Francisco is **more beautiful than** New York, especially when they see the sunlight on the Golden Gate Bridge.

SPECIAL CASES

1. Spelling:
    a. You must double the consonant when you add -er to some adjectives:

    fat → fatter
    big → bigger
    slim → slimmer

    Please turn to the chapter on the present continuous to review the rules for doubling consonants. Use the same rules here.

    b. With one- and two-syllable adjectives ending in y, change y to i and add -er.

    foggy → foggier
    happy → happier
    windy → windier

2. Some people use -er with some two-syllable adjectives (*narrow, handsome*). In general, you are correct if you use *more* with two-syllable adjectives (except for those that end in y).

    The streets high up on the hill are *narrower than* the streets downtown.

    The streets high up on the hill are *more narrow than* the streets downtown.

3. Do not add -er to adjectives with an *ed* ending.
   tired → more tired
   bored → more bored
4. Look at this pattern:
   $\frac{a}{an}$ + comparative adjective + singular noun

   San Francisco is very cosmopolitan. It's famous for its ethnic diversity and different life-styles. San Francisco is **a more cosmopolitan city than** the other cities in California.
5. Irregular forms:
   good → better than
   bad → worse than
   far → farther than

   In the middle of San Francisco Bay is a famous island called Alcatraz. It used to be a federal prison. Many prisoners tried to escape by swimming to shore. The currents were **worse than** the prisoners thought they were. The shore was **farther away than** they expected.
6. When you want to express the idea of "very" with a comparison, use *much* or *a lot*:

   There are no prisoners on the island of Alcatraz today. When Alcatraz was a prison, the island looked **a lot drearier than** now. Alcatraz is going to become a public park. The island will be **much more attractive** when the park is finished.

B. Comparisons to Express the Idea of Less

1. Explanation
A common pattern for expressing a comparison that means less is:

> *not as* + adjective + *as*
>
> *Yolanda thinks a small town isn't as exciting as a big city.*

Examples
Pittsburgh, the home of the steel industry, is an important industrial city in Pennsylvania. In the late 1940s, Pittsburgh had a very serious problem with air pollution. Pittsburgh burned a lot of cheap coal to make steel. Civic leaders decided that cheap coal was **not as important as** clean air. Industry had to put air filters on smokestacks. The clean-up was **not as difficult as** industry expected and **not as expensive.**

Today the air in Pittsburgh is actually **not as smoky or polluted as** the air was twenty years ago.

NOTE: In British English the pattern is:
not + *so* + adjective + *as*

2. Explanation

Another way to express a similar meaning to *not as* + adjective + *as* is this form:

---

less + long adjective (two or more syllables) + *than*

A small town is less exciting than a big city.

C. Comparisons that Express the Idea of Equality or Near Equality

Explanation

When we are comparing two things, and we want to say that the two things are the same in some way or close to the same in some way, we can use these patterns:

$$
\left.
\begin{array}{r}
\text{as } + \text{ (adjective) } + \text{ (as)} \\
\text{just as } + \text{ (adjective) } + \text{ (as)}
\end{array}
\right\} = \text{ equal}
$$

$$
\left.
\begin{array}{r}
\text{nearly as } + \text{ (adjective) } + \text{ (as)} \\
\text{almost as } + \text{ (adjective) } + \text{ (as)} \\
\text{isn't quite as } + \text{ (adjective) } + \text{ (as)}
\end{array}
\right\} = \text{ almost equal}
$$

Examples

Denver, Colorado, is another city with an air pollution problem. Citizens in Denver are **just as concerned** about their air **as** the citizens of Pittsburgh were. The air in Denver doesn't look **nearly as dirty as** the air in Pittsburgh did, but in fact it's more dangerous because it contains many poisonous substances.

D. Questions

Explanation

We often use three different types of questions to make comparisons:

1. *Are large cities more interesting than small towns?*
    Arnold thinks they are. What do you think?

2. *Who is friendlier: people in cities or people in small towns?*
    People in small towns are. (short answer)
        (or)
    People in large cities are.

    Which is more interesting: country life or city life?
    Country life is. (short answer)
        (or)
    City life is.

3. *Are prices as high in small towns as they are in large cities?*
    In some small towns, prices are higher than in large cities.

E. Parallelism

Explanation

Look at these two sentences for an example of parallel structure:

The architecture of New Orleans is more European than **the architecture of Chicago.**

The architecture of ~~New Orleans~~ is more European than **Chicago.**

We cannot say: *The architecture of New Orleans is more European than Chicago.* We are comparing the architecture of two cities, not *architecture* and *cities.* This is an example of an incorrect sentence because parallel structure is not used.

Sometimes we don't want to repeat the noun (*architecture*) a second time. We use a pronoun instead of the second noun if the referent (antecedent) is clear. These patterns are especially useful in written English.

A. Use *that* to replace a mass noun.

Use *those* to replace a plural count noun.

Examples

The European architect Le Corbusier devised a dream city early in the 1920s. He called it the Radiant City. The skyscrapers in Le Corbusier's city were taller and more majestic than **those** of any city of the time. The design of the Radiant City was more formal than **that** of any real city. It had twenty-four skyscrapers and underground streets, which were all within a great park.

B. Use *one* to replace a singular count noun preceded by an indefinite article. (For example: *a building, a city.*)

Use *the one* to replace a singular count noun preceded by a definite article and followed by an adjective clause. (For example: *the building (that) he designed as a young man. . . .*)

Examples

At the same time Le Corbusier was designing the Radiant City, an American architect, Daniel Burnham, was planning an ideal city in Chicago. He called his ideal city the City Beautiful. Burnham wanted to build a whole city around a cultural center. The ideal city of Le Corbusier was more influential in the United States than **the one** that Burnham designed. Le Corbusier's city, with its skyscrapers and underground streets, was actually more practical and modern than **the one** that was designed for beauty alone.

Exercise 1   Comparison of Adjectives: Affirmative Statements

Directions
Fill in the blanks with the correct form of the comparative adjective. Use
these forms: -er (than), more . . . (than), less . . . (than)

The story of the North End of Boston is a story of great change. In the

early 1940s the North End was a terrible slum. It was _**older than**_

 (old)

the rest of Boston and ___**closer**___ to the area of heavy industry.

 (close)

Rents were _____ they were in other areas of Boston, so the

 (expensive)

North End attracted floods of new immigrants every year. But this meant

that the North End was _____ any other part of Boston. Because

 (overcrowded)

of this overcrowding and because there weren't adeqate sanitary conditions

the North End of Boston was _____ any other area of Boston, and

 (dirty)

the residents of the North End were _____.

 (healthy)

Between 1940 and 1960 the North End changed radically. The people who

lived there rehabilitated the neighborhood. They did many things to make

the neighborhood _____. They planted trees and painted their

 (attractive)

houses. They cleaned the streets and alleyways. They became

_____ about garbage and in general took pride in making the

 (careful)

neighborhood look _____. People did not want to leave the North

 (good)

End because the rents were generally _____and because the North

 (low)

End was _____ many other sections of Boston.

 (appealing)

City planners were amazed and puzzled by this change. Bankers were still

hesitant to give out loans to the people from the North End. It was a

_____ risk _____ the bankers wanted to take be-

 (big)

cause this section of Boston was still considered a slum. Nevertheless, the

North End was _____ and the people were _____
(clean)   (friendly)
in many other neighborhoods of Boston. The North End became an example

of how neighborhoods can change when people really care about them.

B. Describe a neighborhood or place you know that has changed. Compare
    what it was like in the past with what it is like now.

Exercise 2   Comparison of Adjectives: (Not) As . . . As

Complete the blanks with the correct comparative form of the adjective. Use
as . . . as, not as . . . as.

   Los Angeles is one of the largest and richest cities in the United States.

Yet it is not *as safe as* many other American cities. In fact, the
                    (safe)
crime rate in New York and in Chicago is not _____ that in Los
                                               (high)
Angeles. Sociologists and urban planners have studied these cities to try to

understand their problems. Jane Jacobs, the author of *The Life and Death of*

Great American Cities, believes that a crowded area sometimes is not

_____ a suburban area. She believes that city streets often
(dangerous)
aren't _____ or _____ dark surburban streets.
          (empty)   (isolated)
Certain residential areas can be just _____ inner city streets.
                                         (dangerous)
People in expensive neighborhoods are sometimes just _____
                                                          (afraid)
to come home alone at night _____ people in more crowded

neighborhoods. According to Jacobs, the North End of Boston is

_____ anyplace else because it isn't _____ and
(safe)   (isolated)
the people on the streets know each other. Even late at night people can

come home and not be in empty streets. Perhaps this is why the crime rate

in the North End of Boston is not _____ the crime rate in all the
(high)

other areas of Boston.

Exercise 3   Paired Questions

Directions
Some people think their hometown is better or worse than other places in
the world. Ask a friend about his or her hometown and its people. Study the
examples and use the same patterns in your conversation.

Examples

(noisy)   FRIEND: Is your hometown as noisy as this city?
          YOU: Actually, my hometown is noisier during the day, but
                 at night it's quieter.
(crowded)   FRIEND: Are the streets of your hometown as crowded as they
                 are here?
          YOU: No, the streets aren't as crowded because they're
                 wider and there aren't as many cars.
          FRIEND: Which is more industrialized, this city or your
                 hometown?
          YOU: This city is.

You may want to use these adjectives:

expensive	decadent	ambitious	interesting
dangerous	big	outgoing	reserved
attractive	exciting	polite	overcrowded
polluted	lively	aggressive	unpleasant

Exercise 4   Parallelism

Directions
Look at the following sentences. Some of them have a problem of comparing
two things that are very different and therefore not really comparable.
Correct each of the sentences that contains a faulty comparison. Some
sentences are correct.

Example

1. The parks of Boston are not as dangerous as Chicago.

You should write this sentence this way:

The parks of Boston are not as dangerous as the parks of Chicago.
    (or)
The parks of Boston are not as dangerous as *those* of Chicago.

2. The air of Denver is as dangerous to breathe as Los Angeles.

    _____

3. The public transportation system of San Francisco is more efficient

    than Los Angeles.

    _____

4. The population of New York is greater than Chicago.

    _____

5. The suburban area of Los Angeles is larger than that of New York.

    _____

6. The parking problem in New York is much more severe than New

    Orleans.

    _____

7. The museums and cultural centers in large cities are more numerous

    than small towns.

    _____

8. The people in small towns are friendlier than most big cities.

    _____

9. The jazz of New Orleans is more exciting than that of New York City.

    _____

10. The bridges of San Francisco are more beautiful than New York.

_____

11. Earthquake tremors in San Francisco are more frequent than north-
eastern cities.

_____

Exercise 5   Integration of Comparative Adjectives

A. Choose the correct form of the comparative adjective. Choose from one of these patterns: -er than, more ... than, as ... as, less ... than, not as ... as. You must use each of these forms at least once.

Example

1. New York/ large/ Montreal.

   New York is larger than Montreal.

2. Paris/ old/ Cairo.

   _____

3. In 1940 Shanghai/ industrialized/ Marseilles.

   _____

4. Dublin/ far from London/ Naples.

   _____

5. Cairo's climate/ dry/ London's.

   _____

6. Tokyo/ crowded/ Hong Kong.

   _____

7. London/ famous for its Renaissance art/ Florence.

   _____

8. For swimming, the Mediterranean/ good/ the North Sea.

---

9. A first-class hotel room in Paris/ expensive/ a first-class

hotel room in Geneva.

B. Now write a paragraph about apartments in New York City and in your hometown. Use these expressions and add some of your own:

expensive   difficult to find
spacious   convenient to shopping areas

Part 2   Adverbs and Comparison of Adverbs

A. Adverbs

Explanation
A word that describes or gives more information about a verb is called an *adverb*. We don't use adverbs after the verbs *be, seem, feel*. We use adjectives after these verbs because an adjective gives information about the subject of the sentence, not the verb. When you add *-ly* to many adjectives, they form adverbs:

$$strong \; + \; ly \rightarrow strongly$$
$$quick \; + \; ly \rightarrow quickly$$

There are a few common adverbs that don't end in *-ly*. The adjective and adverb forms of the following words are the same:

hard   long   straight
fast   high
late   wrong

Examples
In the 1960s many people worked *hard* to clean up Pittsburgh. (*Hard* tells you how they worked.) They believed *strongly* in a clean environment.
GOOD AND BAD
The adverb form of *good* is *well.*
The adverb form of *bad* is *badly.*

Examples

In some cities of the United States, the highways are built very *well*, but they are maintained very *badly*.

NOTE: Some adjectives end in -*ly*. Do not confuse these with adverbs:

friendly
lively

These adjectives do not become adverbs. We form adverbial expressions with these adjectives in this way:

The people in Boston greeted me *in a friendly manner*.
The people in the streets of New Orleans danced *in a lively fashion*.

B. Comparison of Adverbs

Explanation

Many adverbs end in -*ly*. To make a comparison, use this form:

$$\left.\begin{array}{l} \text{more} \\ \text{less} \end{array}\right\} + \quad \text{adverb} \ + \ \text{than}$$
$$\text{(not)} \quad as \quad + \ \text{adverb} \ + \ as$$

Examples

The London Underground System is older than the New York Subway System. The London subways run **more smoothly than** the New York subways and **more efficiently,** too. However, the London subways don't stop **as frequently as** the New York subways, and they don't run all night.

There are some very common adverbs that do not end in -*ly*: *hard, fast, late*. To make a comparison use this form:

adverb + er + than

harder than
faster than
later than

Example

The Japanese National Railways run **faster than** American and British trains.

Exercise 6 Forming Adverbs

Directions

Here is a list of adjectives that you are going to match with the descriptions below:

slow	happy	fast	creative
careless	graceful	hard	obsessive

Read each of the following descriptions. Then finish the sentences by forming adverbs from the adjectives above. Do not use any adverb more than once.

Example

1. In some cities people drive their cars and pay no attention to the rules

   of the road. These people drive _carelessly_.

2. At rush hour traffic moves very _____.

3. The Concorde is a new airplane that travels across the Atlantic Ocean

   in record time. The Concorde travels very _____.

4. A person who studies with a dictionary all the time and has to translate

   every single word from his first language studies _____.

5. Some students spend a lot of time studying before an examination. The

   night before their examination, they study very _____.

6. Yolanda is a wonderful dancer. People watch her on the dance floor

   because she moves _____.

7. Arnold likes to invent new rhythms and songs for his music. He is

   always coming up with new ideas. He writes _____.

8. Fairy tales often end with the princess finding the prince. They live

   _____ ever after.

Exercise 7   Comparison of Adverbs

A. Fill in the blank with the adjective or the adverb form. Decide if you
   need -ly or not.

   People who travel to large cities often have a hard time, especially if

   they do not speak the language ___ _well_ ___. The people in a big
                                       (good)

   city often seem _____ and _____. The
                      (unpleasant)   (cold)

foreigner often feels _____ and _____ during
                                (confused)   (unhappy)
his first days. Some visitors have a _____ time asking for
                                              (hard)
directions. People often look at them _____, answer
                                              (contemptuous)
_____, or walk away _____. When they call
     (abrupt)   (quick)
a phone operator for information, the operators often speak

_____ and in a _____ voice. Often it is
     (fast)   (strange)
_____ to understand the operator's accent. If they ask the
   (difficult)
operator to repeat something, the operator sometimes answers

_____ and hangs up _____.
     (angry)   (sudden)
    Many foreigners respond _____ to these experiences
                                   (emotional)
because they are not accustomed to such behavior. They speak

_____ about how they are treated. They say people should
   (passionate)
try to treat foreigners _____ and _____.
                              (polite)   (friendly)

B. Have you ever traveled abroad? Tell about the experiences you had.

Exercise 8   More Comparison of Adverbs

A. Many people think that men and women are very different from one
    another. What do you think? Write sentences comparing men and
    women. Use the expressions in parentheses.

(speak politely)   1. Women _____

(drive recklessly)   2. Women _____

(work hard)   3. Women _____

(spend money   4. Men _____
  carelessly)
(express feelings   5. Women _____
  honestly)

(dance well)   6. Men _____

(cook well)   7. _____

(dress stylishly)   8. _____

_____   9. _____

B.   Discuss your ideas with classmates. Do you think your opinions are stereotypes? Where do stereotypes come from?

C.   Write about a stereotype that was discussed in class. Tell what the stereotype is, whether you think there is any truth to it, why you think people believe it, and what effects it has on the way people treat each other.

Part 3   Comparison of Nouns

Explanation
Sometimes we want to compare the number or amount of two nouns. Remember that count nouns can be plural and mass nouns are always singular. (See Chapter 5.)

A. Comparisons to Express the Idea of More
When the number or amount of one thing is greater than the number or amount of some other thing, we use this pattern:

more + plural count noun + than
          mass noun

Examples
New York City has **more skyscrapers than** San Francisco.
There is **more smog** in Los Angeles **than** in San Francisco.

B. Comparisons to Express the Idea of Less
When the number or amount of one thing is smaller, we use these patterns:

1. not + as   many   + plural count noun   + as
                  much   mass noun

Examples
There aren't **as many museums** in Los Angeles **as** in New York.
Washington, D.C., doesn't have **as much nightlife as** San Francisco (does).

2. $\begin{matrix} fewer \\ less \end{matrix}$ + $\begin{matrix} \text{plural count noun} \\ \text{mass noun} \end{matrix}$ + *than*

Examples

Columbus, Ohio, attracts **fewer tourists than** Denver does.

There is **less tourism** in the Midwest **than** there is on the West Coast.

Exercise 9   *Comparison of Nouns: Two Cities*

Directions

Choose two cities you know well. Compare them, using these nouns. Try to use all of the patterns for comparison of nouns

Example

1. (big office buildings) _There are more big office buildings in New York than in Athens._

2. (expensive restaurants) _____

   _____

3. (pollution) _____

   _____

4. (traffic) _____

   _____

5. (crime) _____

   _____

6. (noise) _____

   _____

7. (interest in art) _____

   _____

8. (boutiques) _____

   _____

9. (hospitals) _____

_____

10. (crazy people) _____

_____

11. (nightclubs) _____

_____

12. (cockroaches) _____

_____

13. (cultural life) _____

_____

14. (manufacturing) _____

_____

Exercise 10   Integration

A. Fill in the blanks with the correct form of the adverb or the comparative form of the adverb, adjective, or noun.

Chicago is one of the most important cities in the United States.

Located on Lake Michigan, Chicago is _____ in area
                                          (big)
_____ any other city in the United States except New York

City. Before 1871 most of the buildings in Chicago were made of wood.

Then, in the Great Fire of 1871, flames swept through Chicago

_____ firefighters could put them out. This fire killed
    (quick)
several hundred people and left almost 90,000 homeless. Afterward,

the city was rebuilt _____. The new buildings, made of
                         (rapid)

stone and steel, were _____ the ones built before the fire.
(safe)

They were also architecturally _____. The architecture of
(innovative)

Chicago became famous in the early 1920s. The first skyscrapers were

built then. There were _____ there _____ in
(skyscrapers)

in any other city of the time.

Between World War I and World War II, Chicago became famous

because of its underworld[2] activities. Chicago was the home ground for

Al Capone, one of the world's most famous gangsters. There was

_____ in Chicago at this time _____ at any
(crime)

time in the city's history. Many gangster movies of the time were set in

Chicago. Some of them glorified the life of a gangster. In fact, the

gangsters were _____ in real life _____ they
(ruthless)

were in the movies that were made about them. They controlled the

bars and illegal gambling houses. At that time Chicago had

_____ any other city in the United States, and the Mafia
(speakeasys)[3]
controlled them.

After World War II, things quieted down in Chicago. Today there are

_____ and _____ there was in Al Capone's
(gang wars)   (street violence)
time. Most people think there isn't _____ there was
(organized crime)
before. Certainly, gangland violence was _____ in Al
(visible)
Capone's time.

---

2. underworld: the world of gangsters and organized crime.
3. speakeasys: nightclubs in the 1920s that served liquor when it was against the
law to buy and sell liquor.

Why else is Chicago famous? There is _____ at O'Hare
                                      (air traffic)
International Airport _____ in any other airport in the

country, and Chicago is _____ for its shipping industry
                          (important)
_____ any other United States city because it is on Lake

Michigan. The meat-packing industry is _____ it is in
                                           (large)
many other cities in the United States. Although Chicago doesn't have

_____ New York City, it does have the tallest skyscraper
   (skyscraper)
in the world, the Sears Building.

Exercise 11   Integration Exercises

1. Compare yourself now with how you were at some time in the past. For
    example, are you happier now? Why or why not? Are you more com-
    fortable with people? More confident? Thinner? Heavier? Kinder?
    Wiser? Explain.

2. Compare yourself to someone in your family. For example, are you more
    intelligent? More practical? More concerned about politics or social
    issues? Choose someone in your family and write about him or her,
    comparing yourself to this person. You might want to use some of these
    adjectives:

conservative	rich	good in school	absent-minded
creative	practical	neat	timid
serious	imaginative	friendly	shy
ambitious	good in business	considerate	attractive

3. Describe a city 100 years from now in comparison to what the city is
    like now. Compare the people, the buildings, the stores, the hospitals,
    the taxes. For example, are the people happier? Busier? More relaxed?
    Are jobs easier to find? Are schools more or less plentiful? Are there as
    many public services? Talk about the technological changes, the trans-
    portation system, the communications systems, the food, the living
    arrangements, and the types of family structures.

4. Two people are talking about a problem in American cities. One person
    is you. The other person is a banker. He believes the city is in danger of
    going bankrupt. He is suggesting ways to solve the city's problems. He
    wants higher taxes, fewer public services, and less government inter-
    ference in business. You are agreeing or disagreeing with him. Write a
    dialogue.

5. Make up a questionnaire for a singles dating service. You need to get a lot of information about the person and about what he or she likes so you can match people up. Make up a list of questions. For example:

    Is strength as important to you as beauty?

    Is an intelligent person more exciting to you than an attractive person?

    Is a good conversation as interesting to you as a good movie?

    Now get several people to fill out your questionnaire. Then write a report explaining which two people match up the best. Explain in your report why these two people are good for each other.

Expressing Your Ideas: Speaking and Writing

1. What are some of the problems in the city you are living in now? For example, is traffic a problem? Air pollution? Health care? Noise? Housing? Are these problems more serious than they are in your hometown? Are there solutions? If so, what do you think they are?

2. If you moved to another city, where would you prefer to live? In what ways would that city be better than where you're living now? What other differences would there be?

3. Do you remember your first impression of the city you're now living in? Did you expect things to be different? Explain how.

4. Do you like to travel? Do you think most big cities resemble each other or are there major differences?

5. What are some of the advantages and disadvantages of living in the city?

6. How do people in your country feel about Americans and the way they live? What do you think Americans feel about people from your country and the way they live? Where do you think these ideas come from? Are they stereotypes?

7. Did your family ever move from one city or town to another when you were growing up? What was the new city like? Did you like it better than where you lived before? How did the move affect you? Was it difficult to leave your friends and make new friends?

The Superlative of Adjectives and Nouns

Gunther Goebel-Williams, the world's most famous animal trainer. (*Bill Jerome*)

Theme: The Best and the Worst

Grammar: Superlative of Adjectives and Nouns

Dialogue

MOLLY: Hi, Yolanda. Hi, Arnold. What did you do today?

YOLANDA: We took my niece Susie to the circus.

ARNOLD: It's called **the "Greatest** Show on Earth."

YOLANDA: I had **the most fun** I've had in ages.[1]

MOLLY: Where's the circus?

ARNOLD: It's at Madison Square Garden.[2] It has **the most seats** of any place in the city.

YOLANDA: We sat in **the least expensive seats** in the Garden, but we could see everything.

MOLLY: Did Susie like it?

ARNOLD: She loved it, especially the trapeze acts.[3] They had **the most** incredible trapeze artists in the world.

YOLANDA: And **the funniest clowns.**

ARNOLD: **One of the best trapeze artists** was dressed as a clown. He did wonderful stunts[4] without a net under him.

YOLANDA: He wore a ridiculous outfit,[5] really—**the baggiest pants** in the world. I don't know how he balanced on the tightrope.[6]

ARNOLD: He was actually **one of the most talented athletes** in the whole show.

YOLANDA: And **the silliest.** Susie couldn't stop laughing.

ARNOLD: There was a fat lady. They claimed she was **the fattest woman** in the world. She weighed more than four hundred pounds!

YOLANDA: They had **the skinniest man** too. He looked like a string bean.

MOLLY: It sounds like fun. I bet Susie ate a lot of junk.

ARNOLD: Yeah. She ate cotton candy and hotdogs and popcorn.

YOLANDA: I ate a lot too. I ate **the most hotdogs** of the three of us. I ate four, and I feel a little sick now.

MOLLY: No wonder, four hotdogs!

---

1. *in ages:* for a very long time.
2. *Madison Square Garden:* an indoor stadium in New York City. Large rock concerts, the circus, and a wide variety of sports events take place here.
3. *trapeze acts:* acts performed on ropes and swings high up in a circus tent.
4. *stunts:* very difficult, highly unusual acts that require a lot of skill.
5. *outfit:* everything that someone is wearing. Usually an outfit is coordinated in color and style.
6. *tightrope:* the rope high at the top of a circus arena or tent. This is also referred to as the *tightwire* or *high wire.* It is the rope that people walk across to show skill in balance.

Explanation

We use the superlative when we want to show that one person or thing out of a group of three or more is unique in some way. To form the superlative, use these patterns:

Part 1 Superlative of Adjectives

the + short adjective + est + noun

The clown wore the baggiest pants of anyone in the circus.

the + most + long adjective + noun

The clown was the most talented athlete in the circus.

the + least + long adjective + noun

They sat in the least expensive seats in Madison Square Garden.

Examples

The Ringling Brothers' Barnum and Bailey Circus is **the biggest circus** in the United States. It has **the most spectacular acts** of any circus in the country. One of the star performers, Gunther Gebel Williams, is probably **the most famous animal trainer** in the world. His methods are unusual in that he uses kindness rather than punishment to train his lions, tigers, panthers, and elephants. **The most popular clown** in the United States, Emmett Kelly, worked for the Ringling Brothers' circus for many years. He was never **the funniest** or **liveliest clown** in the circus, but there was something in his sad face that touched people's hearts.

It is possible to give the same information in the superlative and comparative forms:

Gunther is probably **the most famous animal trainer** in the world.
Gunther is probably **more famous than** any other animal trainer in the world.

The meaning of these two sentences is the same, but the grammatical structure is different.

Part 2   Superlative of Nouns

The + { most / fewest } + count noun

The + { most / least } + non-count noun

Examples

Ringling Brothers' gives **the most performances**, sells **the most tickets**, and makes **the most money** of any circus in the United States. Some of the attractions of the Ringling Brothers' circus include freak shows, clown shows, animal acts, trapeze acts, juggling acts, and parades. Which of these acts has **the most appeal** for adults? For children? Which of these acts holds **the least appeal** for adults? For children? Why?

Part 3 One of the, Two of the, Three of the + Plural Count Noun

Look at this pattern:

One (*of the* + superlative adjective + plural count noun) + singular verb

Note that the noun is PLURAL. The verb is singular because the subject of the verb is *one.*

Examples

One of the trickiest stunts of all time was performed on a high wire in New York City. In 1974 Philippe Petit walked across a wire between the towers of the World Trade Center. Then he walked back and forth several times. Finally he was arrested for trespassing.

Some people felt he was **one of the most foolish people** of all time since this is **one of the windiest places** in New York. Others said he was **one of the bravest people** in the world because he accomplished such a difficult stunt. What do you think?

Part 4 More Information about Superlative Forms

A. Prepositional Phrases

Explanation

We frequently use prepositional phrases with *in* or *of* when we use the superlative. Here are some common expressions:

in the family	of the men in my family
in the class	of the women in my class
in the United States	of the major cities in the United States
in the world	of the industrialized countries of the world
	of these three things
	of all time
	of all

B. Present Perfect and the Superlative

Explanation

We often use the superlative with the present perfect. This structure is discussed fully in chapter 16.

Example
Michu is *one of the shortest men who* **has ever lived**. He is less than 40 inches (100 cm) tall. He is with the Ringling Brothers' circus.

C. Special Cases

1. Irregular forms:

adjective	comparative	superlative
good	better than	the best
bad	worse than	the worst

Examples
Many children dream of running away from home to join the circus. The life of a circus performer seems very glamorous. Some of **the best things** about circus life are the excitement, the applause, and the romance. However, there are also drawbacks to this life. One of **the worst aspects** of circus life is the lack of stability caused by the constant moving from town to town.

2. There are some adjectives that form the superlative with either *-est* or *most:*

Example

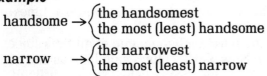

handsome → the handsomest / the most (least) handsome

narrow → the narrowest / the most (least) narrow

Exercise 1   *The Superlative of Adjectives*

Directions
Here are some facts about the United States. Supply the superlative form of the adjective under the line: the _____-est, the most _____, or the least _____.

1. _____ mountain in the United States is Mount McKinley
   (high)
   in Alaska. It is 20,320 feet (6,194 meters) high.

2. _____ lake in the country is Lake Superior. It is 31,820
   (large)
   square miles.

3. Several years ago Lake Erie, another of the Great Lakes, was

   _____ lake in the United States. It was so polluted that
   (polluted)

nothing could live in it, and it was pronounced a dead lake. However, government and business have been working to clean it up, and life has begun to return to Lake Erie.

4. _____ city in the country is St. Augustine. It was founded
   (old)
   in 1565 by a Spanish explorer.

5. _____ state in the United States is Nevada. It has approx-
   (populous)
   imately 500,000 inhabitants for 110,540 square miles (286,299

   square km).

6. _____ state in the United States is Rhode Island. It is
   (small)
   44 miles (70 km) long and 35 miles (56 km) wide.

7. Some of _____ farmland in the world is in Bucks County,
   (rich)
   Pennsylvania.

8. Although the cost of living in New York City is very high, it is not

   _____ city in the United States. For example, the average
   (expensive)
   price of a house in San Francisco is higher than it is in New York.

9. Some of _____ caves in the eastern part of the United
   (spectacular)
   States are the Mammoth Caves in Virginia. There are fantastic

   natural sculptures of stalactites and stalagmites in the caves. One of

   _____ is a stalactite that drips magical water. The guides
   (interesting)
   say that if a bald man puts his head under this stalactite, his hair will

   grow back.

10. One of _____ sights in the United States is the Grand
    (spectacular)
    Canyon. The Colorado River rushes through a deep, colorful gorge.

    The gorge is one mile (1.6 km) deep and four to eighteen miles (6.4 to

    29 km) wide.

11. _____ city in the United States is New York. It has
    (big)
    approximately eight million people.

12. _____ university in the United States is Harvard
    (old)
    University in Cambridge. It was founded in 1636 in order to train

    Puritan ministers.

13. Salt Lake in Utah is _____ lake in the United States.
    (salty)
    When people jump in, their bodies immediately float to the surface.

14. Macy's Department Store in New York City is called _____
    (big)
    department store in the world. It covers one city block.

Exercise 2

Write sentences with the correct superlative form of the adjective.
Complete the sentences. You can work in a group and share your knowledge
or look up the information in a dictionary.

Example

1. The Nile *is the longest river in the world* _____ .

2. Mount Everest _____ .

3. Rolls-Royces _____ .

4. China_____ .

5. The cheetah _____ .

6. The lion_____ .

7. The giraffe _____.

8. The blue whale _____.

9. The great white shark _____.

10. The Great Wall of China _____.

11. The Sears Building in Chicago _____.

12. The Alaska pipeline _____.

13. The Caspian Sea _____.

14. The Verrazano Narrows Bridge _____.

15. Greenland _____.

Exercise 3   Superlative of Nouns

Directions
Complete the blanks with *the most/the fewest* + count noun or *the most/the least* + the noncount noun.

1. Alaska produces _____ oil of any state in the United States.

2. New York, California, Ohio, and Massachusetts have an unusually large number of colleges. Ohio is the leader. Ohio has _____ colleges of these four states.

3. Death Valley, California, is one of the driest places in the United States. Some years it has _____ rain of any area—less than 2 inches (5 cm) of rain per year.

4. California has _____ inhabitants of any state. In 1970 the population was approximately 20,000,000.

5. Nevada has _____ representatives in Congress of any state in the country. Because of its small population, it has only one representative.

6. California grows _____ lettuce of any state in the country. Lettuce, along with celery and radishes, has _____ calories of any food.

7. Florida gets _____ snow of any state in the United States.

Exercise 4   Superlative of Adjectives

Directions
Complete the following questions by filling in the blanks with the superlative form of the adjective. Then answer the question.

1. Who is _the best_ cook in your family?

   _____

2. What is one _____ things that happened in your life today?

   _____

3. What is _____ problem in your country today?

   _____

4. In your opinion, why is the oil crisis one _____ crises in the world today?

   _____

5. Where are some of _____ mountains in the world?

   _____

6. Who is _____ leader in the world today?

   _____

7. Is the United States _____ country in the world?

_____

8. What do you think is one of _____ political issues in the

United States today?

_____

9. Is pollution one of _____ problems?

_____

Exercise 5 Superlatives of Adjectives: Describing Famous People

Directions

Here are some adjectives:

beautiful	good	bad	convincing
sexy	funny	famous	interesting

Here are some entertainers and famous people in movies:

Charlie Chaplin	Alain Delon	Ingmar Bergman
Marilyn Monroe	Woody Allen	Kurasawa
Elizabeth Taylor	Robert Redford	Sergei Eisenstein
Jean-Paul Belmondo	Paul Newman	Toshiro Mifune
Marlon Brando	Jane Fonda	Jean Renoir

Write sentences about these people or others you know. Tell about what you think is the most striking quality of the actor, actress, or director. You may use other adjectives and write about other people.

Example

Marilyn Monroe had the sexiest figure of any actress in the world, but she wasn't the most beautiful. Elizabeth Taylor was more beautiful.

Exercise 6 Integration of Comparative and Superlative

Directions

Fill in the blanks with the correct comparative or superlative form of the adjective, adverb, or noun. Read the entire question before you fill in the blank.

1. Although the Mississippi River is *longer than* any river in the
   United States, it isn't *the longest* river in the world. The Nile is.
   (long)

2. Texas used to be _____ state in the United States, but
   (large)

   today it isn't _____ state. Alaska is.
   (large)

3. The Empire State Building in New York City used to be _____
   (tall)

   in the world, but today it isn't _____ in the world. The
   (tall)

   Sears Building in Chicago is.

4. The United States used to produce _____ oil of any

   country in the world, but now it doesn't produce _____

   Kuwait or Saudi Arabia.

5. Although the Caspian Sea is _____ freshwater lake in the
   (large)

   world, it isn't _____ of all lakes in the world.
   (deep)

6. Mount McKinley is _____ point in North America, but it
   (high)

   isn't _____ Mount Everest is. Mount Everest is
   (high)

   _____ mountain in the world.
   (high)

7. The Arctic Ocean is one _____ of all the oceans in the
   (cold)

   world, but it isn't _____ it used to be. It has been warming
   (cold)

   up each year.

8. Greenland is _____ island in the world, but it isn't
   (large)

   _____ . Japan is.
   (populous)

9. The King Ranch in southern Texas is _____ ranch in the
   (large)

   United States. It is 1,000,000 acres (404,700 hectares). It is larger than

   the state of Rhode Island.

10. The North Pole is completely dark on December 22. It has

_____ sunshine of any area in the world on December 22.

On June 22 the opposite is true. The North Pole has _____

sunshine of any place on earth on June 22. The "midnight sun" is

famous.

11. Death Valley, California, has recorded some of the _____
                                                          (high)
temperatures in the world. Sometimes the air temperature reaches

134° F (57°C). The air temperature isn't _____ the
                                              (hot)
ground temperature, which sometimes reaches 165°F (74°C). Some

rocks are _____ a frying pan. You can fry an egg on them.
              (hot)
_____ point in the United States is also located in Death
    (low)
Valley. It's 282 feet (86 meters) below sea level.

12. Mount St. Helens is a volcano in the state of Washington. There was a

small eruption in 1857. In 1980 the volcano erupted again. This was

_____ eruption in the continental United States. It was one
    (destructive)
of _____ natural disasters in United States history, caus-
        (bad)
ing over a billion dollars in damage. The destructive force was

_____ than that of the first atomic bombs. In fact, it was
    (great)
almost as great as the force of the largest atomic bombs. It rained down

almost _____ mud and ash _____ Vesuvius

did in A.D. 79. People in nearby Yakima, Washington, reported that it

was almost _____ night at noontime on the days of the
                (dark)
eruption. The streetlights automatically turned on. Fortunately, it did

not cause _____ deaths _____ other volcanic

eruptions, such as Vesuvius, Mount Aetna (1669), or Krakatoa (1883).

Krakatoa was _____ eruption in history, taking 36,000
                         (bad)
lives.

Expressing Your Ideas: Speaking and Writing

1. Tell about the hardest choice you have ever had to make. Tell why it was so difficult to make this choice and how it was important in your life.
2. Describe the most unusual person you've ever met (or the richest, smartest, most naive, most sophisticated, nastiest person).
3. Talk about the best or the worst day of your entire life. What happened?
4. Describe one of the most embarrassing moments of your life. Tell what made it so embarrassing and what happened as a result.
5. Talk about a famous person in the world today or in history. Who in your opinion is or was the most interesting person in politics? The most or least intelligent ruler of a country? The most impressive actor or actress? The most creative person you've ever met?
6. Describe the most frightening (or most fascinating or most beautiful) place you have ever seen.
7. Talk about the most expensive present you have ever bought for someone. Tell about what this person meant to you and why you bought this present. Tell how the person reacted to the gift.
8. Describe the most unpleasant experience or the most pleasant experience you have had since you came to the United States.

Have To and Must

Arnold in the army.

Theme: *The Military*

Grammar: *Have To* and *Must*

Dialogue

(MOLLY, YOLANDA, ARNOLD, and JACK are walking down a street in a very poor neighborhood.)

YOLANDA: Look at those buildings over there. They're falling apart.[1] Isn't it awful that people **have to live** in them?

JACK: What do you mean? They **don't have to live** there. There are other places to live.

YOLANDA: Oh, come on, Jack! Open your eyes. These people are really poor. Where are they going to get the money to live in decent buildings?

ARNOLD: That's right. The government doesn't help them.

JACK: What are you talking about? What about all the money the government spends on welfare?[2]

YOLANDA: That's a drop in the bucket.[3] Really, there **must be** a better way to help the poor.

ARNOLD: I agree with you. The government spends millions on the military, but it doesn't spend much on social programs.

JACK: That's because the military is vital to our defense. Social programs aren't.

ARNOLD: You sound like my father. Why **do you have to be** so conservative all the time?

MOLLY: Wait a minute, Arnold. Jack's right. The Soviets are increasing their military strength every day.

JACK: Yeah, we **mustn't forget** that.

ARNOLD: You don't know what you're talking about!

JACK: Come on, Arnold. You don't have to be so insulting. Our opinions are valid too. We just have a different point of view.[4]

YOLANDA: Why don't we all go have a drink? We **don't have to fight** about our ideas.

---

1. *falling apart:* disintegrating; becoming old and worn out.
2. *welfare:* money the government gives to elderly, handicapped, or poor people who don't have enough money to live on.
3. *a drop in the bucket:* a very small amount.
4. *point of view:* opinion, way of looking at something.

Part 1   *Have To*

A. *Affirmative Statements*

Explanation

We use *have to* and *has to* to talk about something that is necessary to do. Use *had to* to talk about something in the past that was necessary to do.

Examples

Today the United States has a volunteer army. There are many things that a volunteer **has to do**. He **has to go** through basic training for seven weeks. During basic training the volunteers **have to get up** between 4:30 and 5:00 A.M. They **have to learn** the discipline and routine of army life.

Before 1973 the army was not voluntary. Most men eighteen years and older **had to serve** in the army for two years.

FUTURE TIME: Sometimes we form the future of *have to* with *will*; sometimes we just use *have to*.

Examples

1. The army **will have to do** more studies to decide if the new volunteer army is better than the old army.
2. The army **has to do** more studies in the future to decide if the new volunteer army is better than the old army.

B. *Negative Statements*

Explanation

We use *don't have to* and *doesn't have to* to talk about something that is not necessary to do. Use *didn't have to* to talk about something in the past that was not necessary to do.

Examples

Today's army gives the men more freedom. Today a man with a moustache **doesn't have to shave** it off. Volunteers today **don't have to get** short haircuts. Before 1973, they had to.

NOTE: When you say that someone *doesn't have to do* something, you mean that there are other possibilities or choices:

Volunteers **don't have to get** short haircuts. They can wear their hair a medium length.

C. *Questions*

Examples

1. **Do** men **have to have** a high-school diploma for the army?
      No, they **don't**.
      (or)
      No, they **don't have to**.

2. **Do** women **have to?**   (or)   **Do** women **have to have** one?
Yes, they **do.**
(or)
Yes, they **have to.**
3. *How old* **does** a volunteer **have to be?**
He or she has to be eighteen or older.
4. Do volunteers like to get up at 4:30 A.M.?
No, they don't, but they **have to.**
5. *Why* **did** men **have to join** the army before 1973?
Because it was the law.

AFFIRMATIVE AND NEGATIVE STATEMENTS

Subject	Helping Verb	Has to Have to	Base Form	
A volunteer		has to	go	through basic training for seven weeks.
A volunteer	doesn't	have to	shave	his moustache.

QUESTIONS

Question Word	Helping Verb	Not	Subject	Have to	Base Form	
Why	did		men	have to	join	the army before 1973?
How old	do		volunteers	have to	be ?	
Why	do	n't	volunteers	have to	shave	their moustaches nowadays?

Exercise 1   *Have To/Had To*

Arnold was in the old army from 1971 to 1973. He hated it. He had to do many things that he didn't want to do.

A.   Look at the five pictures and make sentences for each about what Arnold had to do when he was in the army.

1. *Arnold had to salute his officers.*
He had to wear a uniform.

2. _____

_____

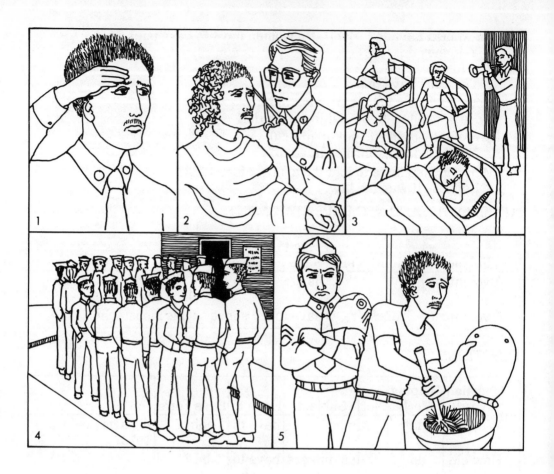

3. _____

_____

4. _____

_____

5. _____

_____

B. Ask questions using *have to* or *has to*. Write an answer for each question. Use your imagination for the answers.

1. (Look at picture 1.) (always)

   Did Arnold always have to salute his officers? Yes, he did.

2. (Look at picture 2.)

   How often _____

   _____

3. (Look at picture 3.)

   What time _____

   _____

4. (Look at picture 4.)

   How long _____

   _____

5. (Look at picture 5.)

   Why _____

   _____

C. Arnold has a friend whose younger brother, John, is in the volunteer army today. Some things about army life are the same. Some things are different. Write a sentence about John. Then tell what Arnold had to do.

   These things are the same:

   1. (salute his officers)

      John has to salute his officers. Arnold did too.

   2. (get up early)

      _____

3. (go to rifle training)

_____

4. (peel potatoes)

_____

5. (obey orders)

_____

These things are different today:

1. (get a short haircut)

John doesn't have to get a short haircut, but Arnold had to.

2. (shave his moustache)

_____

3. (get a pass to leave the base)

_____

4. (eat army food all the time)

_____

Exercise 2   Role Playing

Directions
Do this exercise with a partner. One of you is an angry sergeant. One of you is a rebellious soldier who has realized he or she doesn't like army life. The sergeant has many unpleasant duties for the soldier to do. The soldier insists that he doesn't have to do all of these duties. Act out an argument.

Exercise 3   Integration

A. Tell or write about a time when your life changed and you took on increased responsibilities. What additional things did you have to do? For example: you had a child and you had to get up during the night to feed her or him.

B. Tell or write about a time when a change took place and you didn't
    have to do things you had to do before. For example: you left home and
    you didn't have to tell your parents what time you came home at night.

Part 2 Must

A. Affirmative Statements

Explanation
Must also means that it is necessary to do something. Its meaning is similar
to *have to* and *has to*. We often use *must* to talk about rules or to give a
strong order. Americans use *have to* and *has to* in more situations than
must for this meaning. Use the base form of the verb after *must*.

Examples
It is the first day of basic training. The sergeant is telling the new volunteers the rules for the army.

SERGEANT: All right, men. You're in the army now, and don't forget it. You
           must obey all orders. You **must answer** with, "Yes, sir" or "No,
           sir." You **must salute** every officer.

We can also use *must* + the base form to talk about the future:

SERGEANT: Tomorrow, you **must get up** at 4:30 A.M.

To express this meaning of *must* in the past, we use *had to*.

When Arnold was in the army, his sergeant told him that he **had to get up**
at 4:30 A.M.

B. Negative Statements

Explanation
We use *must not* (*mustn't*) to say that something is not permitted. In the
negative *must* and *have to/has to* are very different in meaning. Remember
that *don't have to/doesn't have to* means it is not necessary. Look at these
sentences for a contrast of *must not* and *doesn't have to/don't have to*:

1. In the United States all drivers must have a driver's license. A person
    mustn't drive unless he or she has a valid license with him. (It is
    prohibited by law.)
2. A foreigner can drive with an international driver's license for a year.
    He **doesn't have to get** an American license right away. (It isn't
    necessary for him or her to get a license for one year.)

Examples

SERGEANT: Men, here are some things you **must not do**. They are against the rules. You **must not drink** when you are on guard duty. You **must not leave** your rifle anywhere. You **must not be** late for anything. One rule is different now. You **don't have to get** a pass when you leave the army base anymore, but you **must not stay** out all night.

C. Questions

Explanation

We do not use *must* in questions very often. We usually use *do/does* + subject + *have to* for questions.

Examples

1. **Must** volunteers **wear** uniforms in today's army?
      Yes, they must.
2. **Do** volunteers **have to wear** uniforms in today's army?
      Yes, they do.

Sentence (1) is grammatically correct, but we do not use this form very often. The form in sentence (2) is much more common.

Exercise 4   Must

An experienced soldier who fought in World War II is speaking to a group of young, inexperienced soldiers about war. They're going to fight their first battle tomorrow.

A.   Write sentences using *must* or *must not*.

1. (keep alert) *You must keep alert.*

2. (get your gun wet) _____

3. (try to be brave) _____

4. (panic) _____

5. (walk alone) _____

6. (obey all orders) _____

B. Rewrite the following sentences. Decide which is correct: *must not* or *don't/doesn't have to*.

1. Muslims and Jews are not permitted to eat pork.

   Muslims and Jews mustn't eat pork.

2. Muslims must pray five times a day. It isn't necessary for Christians to pray five times a day.

   Christians *don't have to pray five times a day.*

3. One of the Ten Commandments says that people are not permitted to kill other human beings.

   One of the Ten Commandments says _____

4. A religious Muslim must go to the mosque on Friday. It isn't necessary for Christians to go to church on Fridays.

   _____

5. It is prohibited for a Roman Catholic clergyman to marry.

   _____

6. It isn't necessary for a Protestant, Jewish, or Muslim clergyman to stay single.

   _____

7. A religious Muslim is not permitted to drink alcohol.

   _____

Exercise 5   Must, Has/Have To, Must Not, Don't/Doesn't Have To

A. You are the dictator of an imaginary country. You have just gained power. You are announcing the new laws of the land. Make sentences using *must*, *has/have to*, *mustn't*, and *don't/doesn't have to*.

THESE THINGS ARE PROHIBITED:
Example

1. have pictures of anyone but me in your homes

   You must not have pictures of anyone but me in your homes.

2. go out on the streets after 9:00 P.M.

   _____

3. hold political meetings without written permission

   _____

4. _____

   _____

5. _____

   _____

THESE THINGS ARE ABSOLUTELY NECESSARY TO DO:

1. report any change of address to me

   _____

2. get permission to work

   _____

3. turn over 50 percent of all your income to the state

   _____

4. _____

   _____

5. _____

   _____

THESE THINGS ARE NOT NECESSARY TO DO:

1. worry about anything ever again

_____

2. go to school

_____

3. do military service if you're 65 or older

_____

4. _____

   _____

5. _____

   _____

B. It's one year later. Because of your unpopular laws, there is a strong possibility of revolution in your country. The revolutionary leaders are demanding many changes. You are answering their demands. Write a dialogue between you and one of these revolutionary leaders.

Exercise 6   Integration

A. MOLLY and her MOTHER are arguing because nowadays MOLLY is coming home very late from her dates with JACK. Molly's MOTHER always worries about her daughter and wants her to be home by midnight. Use *have to, don't have to, must* or *mustn't*. Write a dialogue between MOLLY and her MOTHER. It is 3:00 A.M. when MOLLY walks into her house.

MOTHER: *Where were you? It's 3:00A.M! I waited up all night for you. I was very worried.*

MOLLY: *You didn't have to wait up for me.*

_____

(Continue the dialogue.)

B.   Arnold's father, MR. CALHOUN, is at the doctor's office because he doesn't feel very well. The doctor, DR. NORMAL, is telling MR. CALHOUN that he must change certain bad habits. For example, MR. CALHOUN smokes too much, drinks four martinis a day, gets very little sleep, and works very long hours. Write a dialogue between DR. NORMAL and MR. CALHOUN. The doctor wants to help MR. CALHOUN. MR. CALHOUN doesn't want to change. The doctor is telling MR. CALHOUN what he must do to lower his blood pressure and live longer. Use *have to, don't have to, must,* and *mustn't.*

C.   Contrast your life in the United States with your life in your own country. You can use *have to, must, can,* and *could* and the negatives.

Expressing Your Ideas: Speaking and Writing

1.   Is the military budget high in your country? Does your country spend more on defense or on social programs? Do you agree with your country's policy on this? Why or why not?

2.   Is your country in conflict with other countries? If so, which countries? Why do you think this conflict exists?

3.   Describe the military in your country. About how many people are in it? Does it have modern weapons? Does it buy arms from other countries? How long do people have to serve in the military? What do you think about this?

4.   What do you think about women in the military? Do women have to serve in your country?

5.   What are some of the issues involved in voluntary versus compulsory military service? What are the arguments on both sides of the issue?

6.   A conscientious objector is someone who refuses to fight with his or her country's army because he or she is opposed to war and killing for strong religious or moral reasons. Can a person in your country refuse to fight for these reasons? Do you think people have a right to refuse military service?

7.   Do you think every country has to have an army? Why or why not?

8.   Do you think there will ever be world peace? Why or why not?

9.   In your opinion what are some of the things that have to happen before there can be world peace?

10. Were you ever in the army in your country? Tell about your experience. What did you learn from your experience in the army?

13 May, Might, Must, and Could

Jack's fantasy.

Theme: *Leisure Time*

Grammar: *May, Might, Must, and Could*

Dialogue

(MOLLY is in Vermont on a ski vacation. JACK did not go with her. He's talking to YOLANDA now.)

YOLANDA: Lucky Molly! She **must be having** a wonderful time up there in Vermont.

JACK: Yes, she **must be**. But why did she go alone? She didn't say much about that before she left.

YOLANDA: You know, I was a little surprised that she went alone, too.

JACK: Why didn't she ask me to go with her? Something **must be** wrong.

YOLANDA: Why? Did you two have an argument about something?

JACK: No. I thought everything was fine. But now I'm beginning to wonder. **Could** she **be thinking** of breaking up[1] with me?

YOLANDA: Jack, she **couldn't be thinking** of that. Molly tells me almost everything.

JACK: She does?

YOLANDA: Stop worrying. She never said anything to me about breaking up with you.

JACK: I'm afraid she **might fall** in love with one of those handsome ski instructors. She **might forget** me. She **may not come** back. I **may** never **see** her again.

YOLANDA: Wow, Jack. You **must** really **be** in love.[2] Don't worry so much. Of course she'll come back.

JACK: I sure hope you're right.

YOLANDA: Look, Jack. You **could call** Molly. I have the telephone number of her hotel.

JACK: I thought of calling her last night, but then I changed my mind. Why hasn't she called me? She **must not be thinking** of me at all.

YOLANDA: Oh, come on. Why don't you give her a call? Who knows? She **might be missing** you very much.

JACK: Do you think so? Hey, I have an idea. I **could take** the bus up to Vermont tomorrow. I **could** really **surprise** her.

YOLANDA: But she'll be home in two days.

JACK: Oh, yeah. That's right. I guess I can wait.

---

1. *to break up with someone:* to end a relationship; to stop going out with someone.
2. *to be in love:* To be in love has a different meaning from *to love*. We can say, "I love my parents," but we can't say, "I am in love with my parents." For a relationship between a man and a woman, we can say both "Jack loves Molly" and "Jack is in love with Molly." *To be in love* has a romantic meaning.

In this chapter we show you these modal auxiliaries in the present continuous, the simple present, and the future. See chapter 19 for the past.

Part 1   *May* and *Might*

A. Statements

Explanation

May and *might* are used to talk about possibility when we are uncertain about something. *May* and *might* have the same meaning when we talk about possibility.

SIMPLE PRESENT AND FUTURE OF MAS AND MIGHT

$$\text{subject} + \begin{Bmatrix} may \\ (\text{or}) \\ might \end{Bmatrix} (not) + \text{base form}$$

Molly may forget me.
She might not come back.

CONTRACTIONS: We don't usually use contractions with *may*/*might* + *not*.

Examples

Americans love to play games. After dinner we often spend an evening playing games with friends. One reason we love games **might be** because many Americans are very competitive. Yolanda has several games that are very popular. They are Scrabble,[3] Monopoly,[4] Simon,[5] and backgammon.[6]

Tonight Yolanda and Arnold invited Jack over for dinner. They **might not go** out after dinner because it's very cold outside tonight. They **may stay** in and **play** games.

B. Questions and Short Answers

Explanation

Look at this question: "Might we play games after dinner?" We rarely form questions with *might* in this way. This question sounds very unnatural. If we use *may* or *might* in a question, we usually say,

---

3. *Scrabble:* a word game.
4. *Monopoly:* a game in which people try to buy imaginary property and try to accumulate paper money.
5. *Simon:* a "computer" memory game.
6. *backgammon:* a board game of chance and skill played with dice and markers.

"Do you think + subject + $\begin{matrix} may \\ might \end{matrix}$ + base form. . . .?"

For example, "Do you think we might play games after dinner?" Another way to ask this question is to use the future tense: "Are we going to play games after dinner?"

We often respond to questions about possibility with a short answer using *may* or *might*.

Examples

JACK: What are we going to do after dinner tonight? Are we going to play Monopoly?

YOLANDA: We **might**. Would you like to?

We don't repeat the main verb in a short answer unless the main verb in the question is *be*.

Example

JACK: Yolanda, I know you have to work until 6:00. Is dinner going to be late?

YOLANDA: It **might be**. We might not eat until 8:00. But why don't you come over around 7:30?

Exercise 1 <u>May</u>, <u>Might</u>

A. Talk about possible reasons for the following situations in class. Use *may* or *might* + base form.

1. Arnold never dances at parties. Why not?

   a. *He might not like to dance.*

   b. _____

   c. _____

2. Jack is planning to spend the whole day in bed. Why?

   a. _____

   b. _____

   c. _____

3. Jack is upset because Molly is away in Vermont. What do you think he's going to do to welcome her back home?

a. _____

b. _____

c. _____

4. The rivers and oceans of the world are becoming polluted. Make predictions about what might happen to marine life and to people who depend on fish for food.

a. _____

b. _____

c. _____

d. _____

5. Some scientists feel pessimistic that we will be able to produce enough food for the world's growing population. What do these scientists think may happen?

a. _____

b. _____

c. _____

d. _____

6. Other experts have a more optimistic view that technological advances may solve many of our present problems. What do they think may happen?

a. _____

b. _____

c. _____

d. _____

B. Read the following paragraph. Notice that we don't use *may* or *might* in every sentence. We vary the style with *maybe* or *perhaps* and *will*.

Jack is planning to take a long trip this summer. He isn't sure where to go. He might take a trip around the United States. If he does, perhaps he will visit some of the beautiful national parks in the country. He might choose to travel by bicycle through the countryside of France. Maybe he will stay in youth hostels if he goes to France. Jack might choose to visit the Mayan ruins in the Yucatan Peninsula in Mexico. If he goes to Mexico, he will probably want to read some books about the Mayan Indians before he goes. He may also want to study some Spanish.

Choose one of the following topics and write a paragraph similar in form to the one that you have just read.

1. Write about some ideas you have about your own future.
2. Write about some world conflict and tell what you think might happen in the future.
3. Write about some problems in the United States or in your country and state how these problems might affect the future.

Part 2 Must

Explanation

We use *must* to express what we think is a logical assumption or a deduction which is based on evidence that we have. It means that we have only one possibility in mind. We use *must* when we mean, "I'm almost sure." We use *may* or *might* when we mean, "I'm not sure, but it's possible." When we use *must* to make a deduction, we are usually talking about the present. Deductions with *must* about the future are not very common. To make a deduction about the future, we usually use *probably* and the future tense. Remember that *must* also has the meaning of obligation or necessity. (See chapter 12.)

---

subject + must (not) + base form

Jack must be in love. He can't think of anyone but Molly.

Examples

(JACK is at YOLANDA's apartment now with ARNOLD.)

JACK: Look at all those games. You **must** really **enjoy** games, Yolanda.
ARNOLD: She does. And she enjoys winning, too.

JACK: You **must be** a really good player then.

YOLANDA: I am.

NOTE: We don't often use *must* to form a question. When we use *must* in short answers, the rules are the same as for *may* and *might*.

Exercise 2   Must

A. Read the following short dialogues and make logical deductions based on the information. Use *must*.

1. ARNOLD: I stayed up playing at the disco until 3:00 A.M. last night,

    and I had to get up at 7:00 this morning.

    YOLANDA: You ___*must be very tired*_____.

2. YOLANDA: I just tried to phone Jack. There was no answer.

    ARNOLD: He _____ at home.
              (negative)

3.   JACK: Who was the actress who played the role of Scarlett

    O'Hara in *Gone with the Wind*? I can't remember her

    name.

    YOLANDA: I can't remember, either. Let's ask Arnold. He's an

    expert on old movies. He _____ the

    answer.

4. (ARNOLD is looking out the window. It is winter.)

    YOLANDA: I wonder what the temperature is outside.

    ARNOLD: It _____ really cold. The wind is

    really blowing and everybody is wearing a heavy coat.

B. Here is some information about strange beings from an imaginary planet. Make deductions with *must* based on the information.

1. These strange beings have no ears, but they have long antennae that twitch when there is a noise.

_____

2. They have eyes in the front, side, and back of their heads.

_____

3. They never wear clothes. Their climate is very warm.

_____

4. They can speak hundreds of different languages, they have a highly developed technology, and their doctors have found a cure for every disease.

_____

5. There are no cemeteries on this planet.

_____

6. These beings never carry a weapon, and no one ever fights.

_____

Exercise 3   Contrast of *May/Might* with *Must*

Directions

Fill in the blanks with *may/might* or *must* and the base form of any verb that you think is logical to complete the sentence. Use *must* if you have good reason to be almost sure of your deduction. Use *may/might* if you are thinking of only one of several possibilities.

Examples

1.   JACK: Do you remember that friend of Arnold's that we met a few

               weeks ago at the disco?

    MOLLY: Do you mean Juan?

JACK: Yes. What country does he come from? Do you remember?

MOLLY: I know he speaks Spanish. He *might come* from Spain, or he *might come* from a country in South America.

JACK: Oh, wait a minute! I remember that he told me that his parents live in Madrid.

MOLLY: Oh, he *must come* from Spain then.

2. ARNOLD: Molly, do you know where Yolanda is? I called her apartment, and there was no answer.

MOLLY: I don't know. She _____ at the office.

ARNOLD: Oh, yeah, now I remember. She has to work late tonight. She _____ at the office.

3. ARNOLD: I don't feel well.

YOLANDA: What's wrong?

ARNOLD: I'm not sure. I _____ a simple cold, or I _____ the flu.

YOLANDA: Let me feel your forehead. Hey, you're burning up.

ARNOLD: I _____ a fever.

4. ARNOLD: Look at that beautiful Rolls-Royce over there. I'd like to have a car like that, but I'll never be able to afford one.

JACK: The owner of that car _____ a lot of money.

5. (YOLANDA and ARNOLD are sitting in the park. They are watching a mother with four young children.)

YOLANDA: Look at that poor woman. I don't envy her. She looks so tired.

ARNOLD: It _____ easy to take care of all those children.
                (negative)
You _____ a lot of patience to raise four
           (need)
children.

6.   ARNOLD: What are your plans for the weekend?

JACK: I'm not sure yet. I _____ some museums on

Saturday, or I _____ home and study. What

about you?

ARNOLD: I don't know either. Yolanda and I _____ a

movie tomorrow.

Part 3   Present Continuous of <u>May, Might,</u> and <u>Must</u>

$$\text{subject} + \left\{\begin{array}{l} may \\ might \\ must \end{array}\right\} (not) + be + \text{base form} + ing$$

Molly must be having a wonderful time.

Examples
(JACK, ARNOLD, and YOLANDA are playing Monopoly.)

ARNOLD: What's the matter with you, Jack? You're losing very badly. You **must not be concentrating**.

JACK: No, I can't keep my mind on the game.

YOLANDA: You **must be thinking** of Molly.

JACK: I am. I keep wondering what she's doing now. Just think! She **may be sitting** in front of a beautiful fire with a glass of cognac. Or she **might be dancing** in the arms of one of those ski instructors.

YOLANDA: Oh, come on, Jack. Stop worrying. She's probably asleep now. It's late.

See the rules for questions with *may/might* or *must*. They are the same for the continuous form of these modal auxiliary verbs. When we answer a question that is in the present continuous tense with a short answer using *may/might* or *must*, we use:

$$\text{subject} + \begin{Bmatrix} may \\ might \\ must \end{Bmatrix} + be$$

Examples

(ARNOLD is looking out the window.)

JACK: Hey, Arnold. Is it raining outside?

ARNOLD: It **must be**. People are carrying umbrellas. But it must be raining very lightly. I can't see the rain very well.

JACK: Where did Yolanda go?

ARNOLD: She's in the kitchen.

JACK: Is she serving the dessert now?

ARNOLD: I think she **might be**.

Exercise 4   Present Continuous of <u>May, Might,</u> and <u>Must</u>

Directions

Read each situation. Then make sentences using the present continuous of *may/might* or *must*.

1. Yolanda's grandmother is sitting at a window and she's thinking about some of the happy moments in her life. What are some things that she might be thinking about?

   a. *She might be thinking about the birth of her first child.*

   b. _____

   _____

   c. _____

   _____

   d. _____

   _____

2. Jack and Molly are having a small argument. What do you think they are arguing about?

a. _____

b. _____

c. _____

d. _____

3. An old man is driving an old car up a very steep hill. There are a lot of cars behind him.

a. He _____very fast.
(negative, drive)

b. The other drivers _____ angry.
(get)

4. A man is standing in front of the teller's window in a bank. He's holding a gun and wearing a mask. What do you think he's doing?

_____

Part 4 Could: Alternative Solutions, Possibility, and Impossibility

A. Alternative Solutions: Future

Explanation

When someone has a problem, we can suggest alternative solutions with *could*. This is a polite way to make a suggestion. We can also suggest solutions to ourselves; for example, in the dialogue, Jack says, "I *could take* the bus to Vermont tomorrow."

---

subject + *could* + base form

You could call Molly.

Examples

JACK: Arnold, I want to do something really special for Molly when she gets back from skiing. I want to show her that I really missed her.

ARNOLD: You **could write** a poem for her.

JACK: Be serious!

YOLANDA: You **could get** tickets for that new show on Broadway. She really wants to see it.

ARNOLD: You **could meet** her at the airport with a dozen red roses.

JACK: Yeah. I **could do** that. That's a good idea.

B. Possibility: Present

Explanation 1

Could has the same meaning as *may/might* when we use it in the present continuous.

> subject + *could* + *be* + base form + *ing*
>
> *Jack is afraid that Molly {could/may/might} be thinking of breaking up with him.*

Examples

JACK: I keep wondering what Molly's doing now. Just think! She {could/may/might}

be sitting in front of a beautiful fire with a glass of cognac. She {could/may/might} **be dancing** in the arms of one of those handsome ski instructors.

Explanation 2

Could also has the same meaning as *may/might* with the verbs *be* and *have*, even when they are not in the continuous form.

Examples

(YOLANDA's telephone is ringing.)

YOLANDA: Who could that be? It's so late.

JACK: It {could/may/might} be Molly.

(YOLANDA answers the phone.)

YOLANDA: Hi, Molly. How are you? Oh, no! Really? Your leg?

ARNOLD: Uh oh. It sounds like Molly hurt herself.

JACK: She $\left\{\begin{array}{l}\textbf{could} \\ \textbf{may} \\ \textbf{might}\end{array}\right\}$ **have** a broken leg.

YOLANDA: Jack, come here and speak to Molly. It's nothing serious; she only sprained her ankle. She's coming home tomorrow.

Explanation 3

We frequently use *could* in questions about possibility. It is not necessary to use "Do you think. . . . ?" The rules for short answers are the same as those for *may/might* and *must.*

Examples

Could Jack **be** jealous?
　Yes, he **could be.** In fact, he probably is.
Could Jack **be losing** Molly?
　He's afraid that he **could be.**
Could Molly **be looking** for another man?
　She **could be,** but Yolanda doesn't think that she is.

C. Impossibility: Present

Explanation

When we are talking about possibility and use *could not (couldn't),* we mean that we think something is impossible. We also use **cannot** (*can't*) for this meaning.

Example

According to Yolanda, Molly $\left\{\begin{array}{l}\textbf{couldn't} \\ \textbf{can't}\end{array}\right\}$ **be thinking** of breaking up with Jack.

This is because Molly tells Yolanda everything, and she has never mentioned anything about that.

In affirmative sentences about the present moment, *may/might* and *could* have the same meaning. In negative sentences, the meaning of *could not* is different from the meaning of *may not* and *might not.*

Example

Molly telephoned and said she sprained her ankle very badly. Look at these two sentences:

a.　Molly ~~might not~~ be skiing now.
b.　Molly *couldn't* be skiing now.

Sentence (b) is logically correct in this situation. We know it is impossible for someone to ski with a badly sprained ankle.

Exercise 5 _Could_: Alternative Solutions

Directions
Read the following situations and offer several possible solutions, using _could_.

1. Arnold is worried because he never has enough money. His only income is from playing in discos three or four nights a week. What could he do about this problem?

   a. _He could get a part-time job as a waiter._

   b. _____

   c. _____

   d. _____

2. Yolanda's colleague at the law office lives in a very expensive apartment. She spends half her salary on her rent. She never has much money left for entertainment. What could she do about this problem?

   a. _____

   b. _____

   c. _____

   d. _____

3. Juan, one of Arnold's friends, is having trouble meeting Americans. What could he do to meet Americans?

   a. _____

   b. _____

   c. _____

   d. _____

4. What is a problem that your hometown or country faces? What are some things that the government could do to improve the situation?

a. _____

b. _____

c. _____

d. _____

Exercise 6 *Could:* Possibility

Directions
Think about members of your family or friends. What do you think they are doing at this moment? Use the present continuous of *could* for your sentences, but remember that *may/might* mean the same thing here.

1. _____

2. _____

3. _____

4. _____

5. _____

Exercise 7 *Couldn't:* Impossibility

Directions
Read the following situations and then write sentences with *couldn't* in the present continuous.

1. YOLANDA: Hi, Molly. Where's Jack? Is he studying in the library?

   MOLLY: No, he *couldn't be studying* there because it closed half

   an hour ago.

2. Yolanda is lying on her bed. The radio is playing. Her windows are

   open. Children are screaming in the street below, and three garbage trucks are collecting trash just underneath her window. Is Yolanda sleeping? _____ because there is so much noise.

3. JACK: This is a great party. Do you think Molly is enjoying herself?

    YOLANDA: She _____ herself. She's been talking to that boring man for more than an hour. She can't get away from him.

4. JACK: Molly's phone has been busy for two hours. Who's she talking to?

    ARNOLD: Maybe she's talking to her mother.

    JACK: No, she _____ to her mother. Her mother went to Europe on vacation.

Exercise 8   Integration of <u>May/Might</u> and <u>Could</u>

Directions
Read the following situations and then decide whether to use *may/might, could,* or their negatives. In each situation remember to choose between the base form or the continuous form of the verb after *may/might, could.*

1. Yolanda is wearing a pretty dress and high heels. She's putting on her best jewelry.

    She may be getting ready to go to a party.

    (You would also be correct here if you chose to say, *She might be getting* or *She could be getting.*)

2. JACK: Is Yolanda at home?

    MOLLY: No, she _____ at home because I just saw her
                        (negative)
    on the street.

3. Molly ate four hotdogs, two bags of popcorn, some peanuts, and drank

   five beers at a baseball game about an hour and a half ago. She

   _____ very hungry right now.
   (negative)

4.   MOLLY: Are you going to the disco to hear Arnold tonight?

   YOLANDA: I'm not sure. I _____. But I _____
                                                        (negative)

   because I have a lot of work.

5.   ARNOLD: Look at those men over there. Why are they digging up the

   street again?

   YOLANDA: I don't know. I suppose they _____ in a new
                                            (put)

   waterpipe.

6.   JACK: What am I going to do? I have to hand in this paper

   tomorrow, and I can't type it myself by then. I type too

   slowly.

   YOLANDA: You _____ it to my friend Susan. She's a good
                    (take)
   typist and she doesn't charge very much.

7.   ARNOLD: Jack, why don't we all take a drive to the country next week-

   end?

   JACK: That sounds like a great idea, but I _____ the
                                                 (negative, have)
   car next weekend. I have to take it into the garage for some

   repairs. They _____ the repairs before
                  (negative, finish)
   Saturday.

Exercise 9 Integration of <u>May</u>, <u>Might</u>, <u>Must</u>, and <u>Could</u>

Directions

Choose a classmate who comes from a city or country that you have never visited. Make speculations about what you think life might be like there. Talk about the climate, the geography, the political situation, the food, transportation, industry, housing conditions, the pace of life, or any other area that interests you. Try to use *may, might, must,* or *could* or their negative forms when you make your speculations. Your classmate will tell you if you are right or wrong.

Chapter 14

Should, Ought To, Had Better, Would Rather, and Supposed To

These people are going to ask Ms. Know-it-all for advice.

Theme: *Personal Problems*

Grammar: *Should, Ought To, Had Better, Would Rather,*
Supposed To

Dialogue

MOLLY: Yolanda, I'd like your advice about something. I think I **should move** out and **get** my own apartment.

YOLANDA: It's about time.[1] What finally made you decide?

MOLLY: I can't stand[2] living with my mother anymore. She wants me to do everything her way. I know I **should move out**, but I'm afraid of hurting her feelings. What **should** I **do?**

YOLANDA: Well, first of all, you **shouldn't feel** guilty about moving out. In my opinion everybody has to leave home and become independent someday. Have you told your mother about your plans?

MOLLY: No, I've tried to tell her several times, but she always says, "I'**d rather not talk** about it now. Let's talk about it later."

YOLANDA: Your mother probably still thinks daughters **are supposed to live** at home until they get married.

MOLLY: She does. This is really going to blow her mind[3] when I tell her that I'm going to move out.

YOLANDA: You **ought to tell** her about it right away. You'**d better not keep** putting it off[4] or it will only get harder to tell her.

MOLLY: Okay, I'll tell her tonight. What do you think about this: **should** I **get** my own place or **should** I **find** a roommate?

YOLANDA: What **would** you **rather do**, live alone or with someone?

MOLLY: I think I'**d rather live** alone, but apartments are so expensive now.

YOLANDA: That's true. You'**d better make** a budget for yourself and see what you can afford. I'll help you with it and with anything else I can.

MOLLY: Thanks, Yolanda. I really appreciate it.

---

1. *It's about time*: In this context, "it's about time" means that Yolanda thinks Molly has already waited too long.
2. *I can't stand*: I really don't like
3. *blow her mind*: shock her (slang)
4. *to put something off*: to postpone

Part 1   Should

Explanation

We use *should* when we want to offer advice or express a moral belief. It means: "In my opinion, it is good or advisable for you to do this."

To talk about the general present or future we use:

> Subject + *should* (*not*) + base form
>   (*shouldn't*)
>
> *Molly thinks she should move into her own apartment.*
>
> (Question word) + *should* + subject + base form   ?
>
>   *Should Molly move out of her*
> Yes, (subject) should.
> No, (subject) shouldn't.   *mother's apartment?*

Examples

In many countries of the world people think that young men and women **should live** with their parents until they get married. They believe that young women especially **should not live** alone.

> **Should** young adults **live** with their parents until they get married?
>> Yes, they **should.**
>>> (or)
>> No, they **shouldn't.**

When **should** young people **leave** home, in your opinion?

NOTE: *Should* can also be used to express a different meaning. Sometimes we use *should* to mean: "I have a good reason to expect, think, or assume that something is true."

Examples

> MOLLY: How long do you think it will take me to find an apartment?
>   (or)
>   How long **should** it **take** me to find an apartment?
> YOLANDA: It **shouldn't take** you more than about a week or two.

Part 2   Ought To

Explanation

Ought to has the same meaning as *should*, but *should* is used more frequently. We use *ought to* in affirmative statements, but it is not very common in negative statements or in questions. In negative statements and questions, we usually change automatically to *should*.

> Subject + *ought to* + base form
>
> *Molly thinks she ought to get her own apartment.*

Examples

Many young Americans place great value on independence. Many believe that young people **ought to leave** home after graduation from high school or college. They believe they **ought to enjoy** a period of freedom and independence before getting married.

Exercise 1   *Should*

In the United States many newspapers have an advice column. The writer for the column (columnist) asks readers to send in letters explaining their problems and asking for advice. The columnist then publishes the letter in the newspaper and follows it with some advice.

In the exercises for this section there are some typical problems that people write about when they ask columnists for advice. Imagine that you are the columnist and use the modal auxiliary verbs in the directions to offer your opinions and advice. You can discuss with your classmates first, and then write a reply in the form of a letter to Molly.

Directions

Use *should* and *shouldn't* to offer advice for this problem. Offer advice only about the future and general present, not about the past.

1. Dear Ms. Know-It-All,

    I am 24 years old. I live with my mother, but I would like to move out and get my own apartment because my mother still treats me like a child. She complains if I stay out late with my friends. She tries to tell me how to spend my money and how to live my life. We argue all the time.

    I love my mother very much, but I need to feel independent. I try to tell her that we will get along much better if we don't live together, but she doesn't want me to leave home. What should I do?

    Molly

Dear Molly,
Your problem is very common nowadays.
I'm sure our readers will be interested in

reading about this. In my opinion, you should move into your own apartment.

(Now continue this letter and offer some specific advice.)

Exercise 2   Should and Ought To

Directions

Use *should*, *ought to*, and *shouldn't* to answer these letters.

2.   Dear Ms. Know-It-All,

My father-in-law died about two years ago. Of course my mother-in-law was very upset and lonely, so my husband invited her to live with us. I don't know what to do—I'm going crazy. My mother-in-law and I don't get along very well. She's a wonderful person and is very helpful to me in many ways, but she thinks she's the boss in our home. If I try to discipline the children and tell them that they can't do something, they go running to their grandmother and she tells them they can do it! My husband and I have no privacy. What's worse is that she constantly criticizes me to my husband behind my back. I'm afraid this is going to break up our marriage. What should I do?

Jane

3.   Dear Ms. Know-It-All,

Our daughter is 21 years old and is in her last year of college. She has been dating her boy friend for about four months. The other day she told us that she moved into his apartment. When we asked her if they plan to get married, she said she doesn't want to get married yet because she is too young.

We are very upset about this because we believe it is wrong for young people to live together without being married. Our daughter tells us that we are old-fashioned and that all of her friends live with their boy friends. Is she right? What should we do?

Mr. and Mrs. Old-fashioned

Exercise 3   Should and Ought To

Directions

Imagine that a friend is coming to you with a problem and asking for your advice. With a classmate, act out and (or) write a dialogue between you and your friend using questions with *should*. Answer with *should* or *ought to*. Include some *yes/no* questions and short answers. Also include some *wh-* questions (*what, when, how, who, why*) with long answers.

1. Your friend comes to you with this story:

   We recently found some marijuana in our son's bedroom. He's fifteen years old. Last year he was an excellent student, but this year he hasn't been studying very much and he's doing poorly.

2. Another friend comes to you with this story:

   Last night I was emptying the pockets of my husband's suit because I wanted to take it to the dry cleaner's, and I found several pieces of paper with the names and telephone numbers of women. A few months ago I found papers like this too, but when I asked my husband about them, he got very angry and said I was acting ridiculous and childish. He told me that he loved me very much and that I had no reason to be jealous. Then he refused to talk about it anymore. I think he's seeing other women.

Part 3   Had Better

Explanation

Had better has a similar meaning to *should*. We use it to offer advice. However, its meaning is usually stronger than *should*. When we use *had better*, we usually mean, "If you don't do this, there will be a bad consequence or result." We often follow advice using *had better* with an *or* clause which explains the bad consequence.

We often use *had better* to give someone a warning. Because *had better* is stronger than *should*, don't use *had better* when you are talking to a person in a position of authority. It can be insulting.

GENERAL PRESENT AND FUTURE

Statements: subject + *had better* + (not) + base form

you had better make a budget.

Contractions: I'd, you'd, he'd, she'd, we'd, they'd
(There is no possible contraction with *not* and *had better*)

Questions: We don't use *had better* in questions very often. One exception is when we make suggestions with *had better*: "Hadn't you better do this?"

Examples

(Yesterday MOLLY found an apartment that she likes. She's going to sign the lease later today. She and YOLANDA are talking about it.)

MOLLY: Here's the lease for my apartment. Would you read it with me?

YOLANDA: Okay. You'**d better not sign** it before we read it very carefully, because it's a legal agreement. You'**d better be** sure that certain

Should, Ought To, Had Better, Would Rather, and Supposed To   **219**

things are in the lease or the landlord will never give them to you. For example, you want the landlord to paint before you move in.

MOLLY: Yes, and the landlord promised to give me a new refrigerator.

YOLANDA: Well, you**'d better ask** him to put it in writing or he might forget his promise.

Exercise 4   _Had Better_

Directions
Use *had better* or *had better not*.

1. MOLLY: How do you feel, Yolanda? Is your cold any better?

   YOLANDA: No, it's worse. I feel terrible.

   MOLLY: You _____ to work tomorrow. You
   (negative, go)
   _____ home and rest.
   (stay)

2. JACK: I need some cash. I have to go to the bank.

   ARNOLD: You _____ or you'll be too late. The bank is
   (hurry)
   going to close in about fifteen minutes.

3. MOLLY: I'm a little worried about Yolanda. She looks tired all the

   time.

   ARNOLD: Yes, she works too hard. She _____ some rest
   (get)
   or she's going to make herself sick.

   MOLLY: Yes, she _____ working late so many nights.
   (stop)

4. MOLLY: Are we going to go out tonight, Jack?

   JACK: I don't know. I have a big exam tomorrow. I think I

   _____ tonight.
   (study)

   MOLLY: Yes, we _____ out or you might be too tired
   (negative, go)
   tomorrow.

Part 4   _Would Rather_

Explanation

Would rather means _prefer_. _Would rather_ is a way to compare two choices, so we use it when we make a choice between two or more alternatives. In the negative, _would rather not_ is often a polite way to say, "I don't want to do that."

GENERAL PRESENT AND FUTURE

Statements: Subject + _would rather_ (not) + base form + (than)...

Molly would rather live alone.

Contractions: _I'd, you'd, he'd, she'd, we'd, they'd_
(There is no possible contraction with _not_ and _would rather_.)

Questions:
(Question word) + _would_ + subject + _rather_ + base form ?

What would you rather do?

Examples

In many countries young married couples live with the husband's or wife's parents. In the United States, most young married couples **would rather move** into a tiny one-room apartment than live with their parents. They **would rather not depend** so much on their parents.

In your country, which **would** most young married couples **rather do**: live with their parents or live in their own home?

Would you **rather live** in your own home or live with your husband's or wife's parents?

NOTE: Sometimes we answer "Do you want to . . . ?" or "Would you like to . . . ?" questions with _would rather not._

Examples

Does Molly want to live with a roommate?
She**'d rather not.** She**'d rather live** alone.

Exercise 5   <u>Would Rather</u>

Directions

Use *would rather* or *would rather not*

Example

1. Read the first letter to Ms. Know-It-All (in Exercise 1) about Molly, who
    lives with her mother.

    Would Molly rather live with her mother or in her own apartment?
          (live)
    She'd rather live in her own apartment.

2. Read letter 2 (in Exercise 2) about Jane and her problems with her
    mother-in-law.

    _____ living with her mother-in-law or ask her
          (continue)
    mother-in-law to move out?

    _____

    Where _____ Jane's mother-in-law _____ :

    with her son's family or in her own home?

    _____

3. Read letter 3 (in Exercise 2) about the daughter who is living with her
    boy friend. Does the daughter want to marry her boy friend now? (Give
    a negative short answer using *would rather*.)

    No, _____

4. Read the problem in Exercise 3 about the son who smokes marijuana.

    What _____: study or get high on marijuana?

    _____

5. Read the problem in Exercise 3 about the wife who thinks her husband
   is seeing other women. Does her husband want to talk to her about the
   problem? (Give a negative short answer using *would rather*).

   No, _____.

Exercise 6   *Would Rather* and *Had Better*

Directions

Sometimes people make choices not because they want to, but because they
know it is better for them. Write a sentence with *would rather*. Then follow
it with a sentence with *had better*.

Example

1. (MOLLY and JACK are going to a movie theater.)

   MOLLY: Which should we take, the subway or the bus?

   JACK: We don't have much time. The movie starts in only twenty

   minutes. *I'd rather take* the bus because it's quieter and

   cleaner than the subway but we *had better take* the subway

   because it's faster and we're a little late.

2. (MOLLY is trying to decide between two apartments that she looked at.
   One of them is big and in a very good location, but the rent is more than
   she can afford to pay. The other one is smaller and the location is not as
   good, but the rent is reasonable. YOLANDA is giving her advice.)

   YOLANDA: I know you _____ the big apartment, but you

   _____ the small apartment or you won't have

   any money left for your other expenses.

3. (MOLLY wants to get a dog when she moves into her apartment. She likes
   big dogs better than small ones, but she knows that her apartment will
   be too small for a big active dog.)

YOLANDA: What kind of dog are you going to get?

MOLLY: I _____ a big dog, but I _____
(negative)

because my apartment is very small.

4. (YOLANDA's younger brother is going out the door now to meet some
friends. He has a basketball in his hands. He hasn't been getting very
good grades in school recently.)

YOLANDA'S MOTHER: I know that you _____ basketball than

study, but I think you _____ or you

will fail your next test.

Part 5 Continuous Forms of Modals

Explanation
When you want to use *should*, *had better*, or *would rather* to talk about the
present moment (now), use this form:

> subject + {
> *should*
> *had better*   (not) + *be* + base form + *ing*
> *would rather*
> }
>
> *Molly would rather be living in her own apartment than at home.*

Examples
Molly and Yolanda are walking from building to building looking at apartments for rent. Molly's feet hurt because she's wearing shoes with very
high heels. She **shouldn't be wearing** high heels today because they aren't
comfortable for walking. She **should be wearing** comfortable shoes with low
heels.

Molly and Yolanda are tired of looking for apartments. They **would
rather be sitting** in a cafe and having a drink right now than walking
around and looking for apartments.

Exercise 7 The Present Continuous of <u>Should</u> and <u>Would Rather</u>

A. Use the present continuous form of *should*. Choose carefully between
affirmative and negative.

Arnold and Yolanda are walking in the park. Yolanda is only wearing a light sweater, so she's a little cold. She _shouldn't be wearing_ such a light sweater. She _____ a jacket.

A teenager is carrying a big radio, which he is playing very loudly. The music is bothering people who came to the park for some peace and quiet. The boy _____ his radio so loudly.

There's some new grass with a big sign that says: "PLEASE DON'T WALK ON THE GRASS." Some children are playing baseball on the grass. They _____ there. They _____ in another place.

A child is picking some flowers next to a sign that says: "PLEASE DON'T PICK THE FLOWERS." His mother isn't watching the child. The child _____ the flowers. His mother _____ him.

B. Write questions and answers. Use the present continuous form of *would rather*.

1. There is a basketball game on television now, but Jack is studying for an examination, so he can't watch it.

   What _would Jack rather be doing_ right now?

   He'd rather be watching the ball game on TV.

2. Yolanda's younger sister, Julia, is fifteen years old. It's Saturday night and she's babysitting to earn money for college. Her friends are out dancing at a disco now.

   What _____?

   _____

3. Arnold's father wants to lose weight, so he's on a diet. He's eating half a grapefruit for dessert now, but he's thinking about a chocolate ice cream sundae.

What _____

_____

Part 6   Be Supposed To

Explanation

When we say that a person *is supposed to* do something, we mean that (1) another person, or (2) the law, or (3) the rules of society or good manners expect or require the person to do this.

GENERAL PRESENT, FUTURE, AND PAST

Statements:
Subject + be { am, is, are, was, were } (not)   supposed to + base form

Molly's mother thinks daughters are supposed to live at home until they get married.

Questions:
(Question word) be + subject + supposed to + base form?

What time is Molly supposed to come home?

Examples

In some countries sons and daughters are expected to treat their parents with great respect. For example, children **are supposed to respect** their parents' opinions. They **aren't supposed to question** their parents' authority in any way. Also, when parents grow old, children **are supposed to take** care of them.

EXPLANATION: We often use *be supposed to* to mean that we expect or want a person to do something, but he or she isn't doing it.

Examples

(MOLLY's landlord promised to paint her apartment yesterday, but the painters didn't come. MOLLY is talking to the landlord.)

MOLLY: Mr. Jones, the painters **were supposed to come and paint** my apartment yesterday. They didn't come. What happened?

LANDLORD: I'm sorry. I thought you **weren't supposed to move** in until next week. We made a mistake. Don't worry. They'll be there tomorrow.

Exercise 8   Be Supposed To

A. Jack's younger brother, Bob, is fourteen years old. Tomorrow night he is going to have his first date with a girl. He is asking Jack for advice about how to act on his date. Using *be supposed to,* complete the questions and the answers.

BOB: Jack, I don't know what to do tomorrow night. I don't know anything about girls or dating.

JACK: Don't worry. You'll be fine.

BOB: I have all these questions.

JACK: What's your first question?

BOB: Well, _____*am*_____ I _*supposed* *to pick*_ her up or can we (pick)

just meet someplace?

JACK: I think on a first date you should pick her up.

BOB: Should I help her with her coat and open doors for her and everything?

JACK: Yes, I think so.

BOB: And who _____? _____ for
         (pay)   (pay)

everything?

JACK: In my opinion the man should pay on the first date.

BOB: _____ her when I take her home?
         (kiss)

JACK: I can't tell you everything. You decide.

B. Imagine that a person who is a foreigner in your country is asking advice about good manners in your culture. What are or aren't you supposed to do at the dinner table? What aren't you supposed to talk about at the table? If someone invites you to his or her house for dinner, are you supposed to come on time or about half an hour late?

Example

In the United States when you are invited for dinner, you're supposed to arrive on time. It's a nice idea to bring a small gift such as a bottle of wine or flowers. At the table you're supposed to put your napkin on your lap before you start eating. You aren't supposed to put your elbows on the table.

(Now talk to your class or write about manners in your country.)

C.   How was life different 100 years ago for women? What did people believe that women were or weren't supposed to do? Write about some of the things women were or weren't supposed to do. For example, women weren't supposed to work outside the home. They were supposed to stay home and manage the household and take care of the children.

And what about men? What did people believe men were and weren't supposed to do 100 years ago?

D.   We often use *was/were (not) supposed to* when we talk about a mistake that we made or about something another person expected us to do, but that we didn't do. Use *was/were (not) supposed to* + base form in the following sentences.

Example

1.   ARNOLD: What happened last night, Yolanda? I didn't see you at

the discotheque. You ___were supposed to come___ and hear my

band play.

YOLANDA: I know, I'm sorry. I was exhausted last night.

2.   MOLLY: Can I borrow $10, Jack? I _____ to the

bank at lunchtime, but I forgot, and I didn't remember

until after 3:00, when the bank had already closed.

JACK: Sure. Is that all you need?

3.   JACK: Here's the red wine that you asked me to buy, Molly.

MOLLY: Oh, no! You _____ red wine. We're
                    (negative)
having fish tonight. You _____ white

wine. But never mind.

4. (MOLLY has just come home.)

   MOLLY'S MOTHER: Molly, it's 2:00 A.M. You _____

   home by midnight. I was really worried about you.

   MOLLY: I'm sorry. But you really shouldn't worry about me.

Exercise 9   Contrast of Have To and Should

Directions
Remember that *have to* (*has to*) means "it is necessary" and that *should* means "It is advisable or good in this situation." Choose which is better: *have to/has to* or *should*.

1. MOLLY: You have a bad cold, Jack. I think you **_should go_** to
   (go)

   bed early tonight.

   JACK: I know I **_shouldn't stay_** up late, but I **_have to take_**
   (negative, stay)   (take)

   an important exam in one of my classes tomorrow.

2. ARNOLD: Look at this photograph of Los Angeles in the newspaper.

   You can see the air pollution over the city.

   YOLANDA: Everybody in Los Angeles drives. They never walk. People

   _____ so much. They _____ public
   (negative, drive)   (use)

   transportation or they _____ .
                                    (walk)

   ARNOLD: Yes, but public transportation isn't very good in L.A. It's

   very difficult to get from one place to another without a car.

   People in L.A. _____ a car to get to many
                          (use)

   places.

3. Here is some information about renting apartments. Both the landlord

and the tenant have obligations:

By law every landlord _____ a tenant a written lease, and
(give)
the tenant _____ it. It's a good idea to know exactly what
(sign)
is in a lease. The tenant _____ the lease very carefully
(read)
before he or she signs it. Almost all tenants _____ the
(give)
landlord a security deposit, which is usually one or two months' rent in

advance. By law, if a tenant decides to leave the apartment when the

lease ends, he _____ the landlord thirty days in advance
(notify)
that he is leaving. If he doesn't notify the landlord, the landlord

_____ the security deposit. Some cities have a law that
(negative, return)
says a landlord _____ an apartment every three years.
(repaint)

Here are a few good rules for apartment hunters to follow:

a. You _____ more than about 33 percent of your
(negative, spend)
monthly paycheck for rent.

b. You _____ to find out about security and safety in
(try)
the building. You _____ to several of the tenants
(talk)
about service, maintenance, and safety in your building.

c. You _____ a walk around the neighborhood to see if
(take)
you like it.

Exercise 10   Integration of Modals

A. Read the following letter:

> Dear Ms. Know-It-All,
>
>   My wife is a businesswoman with a very successful career as a young executive. She frequently comes home from work very late because she has meetings or has to go out with the other executives for drinks at a bar to talk business. Of course, most of the other executives are men, and I am becoming very jealous. We never have any time together and I'm tired of making dinner all the time.
>
> Jealous

Here is Ms. Know-It-All's answer to this man's letter. Fill in the blanks. Try to use all of these modal auxiliaries: *should, ought to, had better, would rather, have to/has to,* and the modal auxiliaries that we use to talk about possibilities or alternatives (*may, might, could*) and logical deductions (*must*). In this exercise use *must* to talk about logical deductions. Use *have to/has to* to talk about necessity.

Dear Jealous,

You _____ very unhappy about this situation. You are
        (feel)
probably afraid that your wife is having an affair with one of her co-

workers. Perhaps you're afraid that your wife _____ with
        (be)
her co-workers than with you. Have you talked with her about this problem

yet? If you haven't told her yet, she _____ how you feel. You
        (negative, know)
_____ about it, but you _____ angry or yell.
  (talk)   (negative, get)
Today men _____ that their wives' careers are important
        (realize)
and that there are many times when a woman _____ late at
        (stay)
the office and can't be home in time for dinner. Who knows? She

_____ these late meetings, but perhaps she has no choice.
(negative, enjoy)
    However, it is important for couples to have time together. If couples

never spend time together, their marriage is in trouble and

_____ in divorce. You _____ to make your wife
   (end)   (try)
understand this. You _____ something about this problem
                          (do)
soon or it will only get worse.

B.   (LISA is a friend of Yolanda's sister, SANDRA. She's only twenty-one years
     old. She has been dating her boss, John, who is forty-five years old, for
     about two months.)

LISA: Sandra, I need to talk to you. I didn't sleep at all last night. I

        was up all night thinking.

SANDRA: You _____ tired. What is it?
                    (be)

LISA: John asked me to marry him last night.

SANDRA: What? John _____ old enough to be your father.
                         (be)
          How old is he?

LISA: Forty-five. But he's a wonderful man. I really love him and I

        know he loves me. Age isn't everything. But I can't decide

        whether or not to say yes. Help me.

SANDRA: His age isn't so important now, but it _____
                                                     (become)
          important later when you want to have children. You

          _____ about this very carefully. You
              (think)
          _____ a decision too quickly. Also, ten years
            (negative, make)
          from now you'll be thirty-one and you _____ a
                                                     (be)
          completely different person. You and he _____
                                                     (negative, share)
          the same interests then.

LISA: That's true of any couple. I don't know. You're probably right, but now I feel that I _____ John than any other
(marry)
man I've ever known. I love him.

SANDRA: Yes, but you've only been going out with him for two months. You _____ him well enough to make this
(negative, know)
important decision.

LISA: Maybe you're right. Thanks for your advice. I need to think about my decision some more.

Exercise 11   More Integration

Directions
Try to use the modals you studied in this chapter and chapter 13: *may, might, could, must, should, ought to, had better, would rather,* and *be supposed to.*

1. Look at Sandra's advice to her friend, Lisa, who is thinking about marrying her **forty-five-year-old boss. Do you agree with Sandra's advice?** Why or why not?
2. Think of a personal problem that you have or invent a humorous imaginary problem. Write a dialogue between you and a friend in which you explain your problem and ask your friend for advice. Try to use all of the above modals and include some questions using them.

Expressing Your Ideas: Speaking and Writing

1. In your country, when do young people move out of their parents' home and start living in their own place? Is it different for sons and daughters? How and why?
2. What are the advantages of living with parents? What are the disadvantages? What kind of problems do young adults have when they live with their parents?
3. Should young adults live with their parents until they get married? Why or why not? When should they move out, in your opinion?
4. Are you living with your parents or relatives now? Would you rather be living in your own apartment? Why or why not?

5. In many countries young married couples live with their in-laws after marriage. Is this good? Why or why not?

6. In the United States many young people believe that a couple should live together for some time before they get married. What do you think about this? Why is it a good idea or a bad idea?

7. In many cities in the United States the number of people who live alone is growing. Do many people in your country live alone? How do you feel about this? Would you rather live alone or with roommates?

8. What problems occur when a person lives with a roommate? When a person lives alone?

9. Is it difficult to find an apartment in the city where you live now? Are apartments very expensive? Is it easier or more difficult to find a good apartment in your country than in the United States?

10. How do people find apartments? Name some of the ways. What should you be sure of before you sign a lease for an apartment?

11. How did you find the place where you are living now? Was it difficult to find it? What did you have to do?

12. If you are a parent, do you want your children to continue living with you until they get married? When do you think your children should leave home?

Too, Enough, So, and Such

Mountain climbing.

Theme: *Exploration and Achievement*
Grammar: <u>Too</u>, <u>Enough</u>, <u>So</u>, <u>Such</u>.

Dialogue

(JACK, MOLLY, ARNOLD, and YOLANDA are going on a weekend camping trip to Mount Marcy, the highest mountain in New York State. Right now they are packing for the trip.)

JACK: You're going to love this trip. Mount Marcy is **so high that you can see for miles.**

YOLANDA: I'm really looking forward to this trip. I'm dying to get out of the city.[1]

ARNOLD: Yeah. It's a shame that we can't go camping for a whole week.

MOLLY: A weekend is **enough time for me to get all the fresh air I need for a lifetime.**

YOLANDA: Oh, Molly. Camping is **such fun that you won't want to come back.** You'll see.

MOLLY: Jack, where are we going to sleep? There isn't **enough space in that tent for all of us to fit.** Maybe I shouldn't go.

JACK: Don't worry. It'll probably be **warm enough to sleep out** under the stars.

MOLLY: Oh, no! There are **too many mosquitoes for us to sleep outdoors!**

YOLANDA: There aren't that many in September. Try your pack[2] on and see how it feels.

MOLLY: Okay, help me put it on. This pack is **too heavy for me to carry.** I can't walk!

ARNOLD: What do you have in there, Molly? Oh, no! There are **enough sandwiches here for a month.**

YOLANDA: And all these pots and pans! This is **too much equipment to take for such a short trip.** You can't take all these shoes and a pillow, too!

MOLLY: But I have to take comfortable shoes.

ARNOLD: Okay, okay. But you'll sleep all right without a pillow. Think of the great explorers, Molly. They didn't take pillows. They had **so many hardships that it's a wonder they didn't give up.**

YOLANDA: That's right. And they ran into all kinds of wild animals.

JACK: I'll be surprised if we even see a rabbit.

MOLLY: That's good. And I don't want to get lost.

---

1. *I'm dying to get out of the city:* an expression. *Dying to* means want to do something a lot.
2. *pack:* the bag a camper carries equipment in. Usually the pack is carried on the back. It is also called a *backpack.*

ARNOLD: Jack's bringing **such good maps that we can't get lost.**

JACK: Look, let's get going. We have very few opportunities to get out of the city, and we're wasting time.

MOLLY: I've never climbed a real mountain. I'm afraid I'll get out of breath **so fast that I'll have to rest every five minutes.**

YOLANDA: You don't have to be the first to get to the top of the mountain. We aren't going to discover the mountain. We just want to climb it.

Part 1   Too and Very

Explanation

Very emphasizes or intensifies a quality. It makes the quality stronger. *Too* has an entirely different meaning from *very. Too* has the meaning of excess. Notice the difference in these two sentences:

This pack is *very* heavy, but I think I can carry it.
This pack is *too* heavy. I can't pick it up. No one can carry it.

Part 2   Too . . . To

A. *Too* with Adjectives and Adverbs

Explanation

When we use *too* before an adjective or adverb, we mean there is an excess of the quality. This is usually followed by an infinitive expressing result.

Subject + verb + *too* + adjective / adverb + infinitive.

This pack is too heavy to carry.

Examples

During the nineteenth century people believed it was impossible to reach the North Pole. Even Greenland was **too far north to explore.** Robert Peary (1856–1920) was an admiral in the U.S. Navy. He led several expeditions to Greenland and the Arctic. He wasn't successful in reaching the North Pole, which was his main objective, until 1909. The Arctic Sea was **too icy to navigate** safely. The men on the expedition found the weather was **too harsh.** The explorers had to turn back several times. But Peary was **too adventurous to give up** for long.

B. _Too_ with Quantifiers

Subject + verb + too + $\begin{matrix} little \\ much \end{matrix}$ + mass noun + infinitive

This is too much equipment to take.

Subject + verb + too + $\begin{matrix} many \\ few \end{matrix}$ + count noun + infinitive

There are too many mosquitoes to sleep outdoors.

Examples

In 1909 Robert Peary took an assistant and four Eskimos on the final expedition. They had **too much equipment to carry**, so they left a lot behind. They wanted to move very quickly. Peary said they traveled 134 miles in eight days and reached the North Pole on April 6, 1909.

Another explorer, Dr. Frederick Cook, claimed he had reached the North Pole in 1908. There was a bitter argument. Some people said they didn't believe Peary's claim of 134 miles. They said that was just **too many miles to cover** in eight days. There was **too little information to prove** absolutely which explorer got to the North Pole first. In 1911 the U.S. Congress decided to recognize Peary's claim. Cook died a bitter man.

C. _Too_ with Adjective + _For_ (Someone)

Subject + verb + too + $\begin{matrix} adjective \\ adverb \end{matrix}$ + for (object) + infinitive

This pack is too heavy for me to carry.

Examples

Most people thought the expedition was **too dangerous for the explorers to bring** their wives.

Sometimes the infinitive is omitted:

The weather was **too cold for them** (to go).

Part 3   Enough

A. *Enough* with Adjectives

> Subject + verb + (not) + adjective/adverb + enough + [for (object)]
>
> *It will be   warm enough for us*
>
> + infinitive
>
> *to sleep outdoors.*

Explanation

We use an adjective or adverb followed by *enough* to show something is possible because there is a sufficient amount of the quality. This is usually followed by the infinitive form of the verb.

Examples

In 1803 much of the United States was still unexplored. President Thomas Jefferson was **perceptive enough to recognize** the importance of this unexplored territory. He appointed Meriwether Lewis and William Clark to head an expedition to the Far West and spoke **persuasively enough to convince** Congress to finance the entire project. Congress decided the expedition was **important enough to support.**

Lewis and Clark started to train the men in their party in 1803. The expedition was dangerous. They left from St. Louis in 1804.

B. *Enough* with Nouns

> Subject + (not) + enough + count noun/mass noun + [for (object)] + infinitive
>
> *A weekend is enough time for me to get some fresh air.*

Explanation

Enough is used before a noun to show there is a sufficient amount or number of something for something to happen or for someone to do something.

Examples

The Lewis and Clark expedition had a remarkable guide, the Indian woman Sacajawea. She gave them **enough horses for them to continue** across the High Rockies. They crossed the Continental Divide and reached the Pacific Ocean. On the return trip they didn't have **enough time to explore** everything, so they split into two groups. They traveled down two different rivers and met later on the Missouri River.

NOTE: Sometimes we see this pattern:

Subject + (not) + noun + enough + infinitive.

A weekend is time enough to get some fresh air.

This pattern is less common, especially in spoken English.

Exercise 1   Too and Very

Directions

Some of the following sentences are incorrect in the use of *too* and *very*. Put an X next to any sentence that is incorrect. Then rewrite it correctly.

1.   Many explorers in the nineteenth century were too courageous. They traveled to dangerous and remote parts of the globe.

Many explorers in the nineteenth century were very courageous.

2.   Their voyages were often too dangerous for their wives to travel with them.

Correct.

3.   Often weather conditions at sea were very severe for the ships to travel safely.

4.   Sometimes there wasn't much food, and people became very hungry.

5.   Sometimes the food was very spoiled to eat, so the men almost starved.

6.   A few explorers were too adventurous and traveled into places where no one had ever been before.

7.   Some were too eager to discover new waterways for ships, so they looked for routes connecting different oceans.

8.   Their days were often very full of excitement for them to sleep at night.

9.   They were too brave. When they came home, they became too famous because they had accomplished great things for their country.

Exercise 2   Too . . . To

Directions

Read the following sentences. Then complete the sentence using:

$$too + \left\{ \begin{array}{c} \text{adjective} \\ \text{adverb} \end{array} \right\} + to \quad \text{(or)} \quad too \left\{ \begin{array}{c} \text{many} \\ \text{much} \\ \text{little} \end{array} \right\} + noun + to$$

Practice this exercise orally in class before you write it.

1. Lewis and Clark were about to cross the Missouri River. There were a lot of rapids. It was very dangerous. They decided to look for another place to cross because the river was

   too dangerous to cross at that point.

2. The High Rockies are covered with snow all winter. Most of the snow melts by April. The explorers couldn't get across in January. There was

   _____

3. Some of the land was very difficult to travel over. There were areas that were very rocky and treacherous. Some places were

   _____

4. The explorers wanted to investigate many areas of the Far West, but they had little time before winter came. They couldn't investigate everything. They had

   _____

5. They encountered many Indians. Many of them were hostile. The expedition could not travel safely in many areas. There were

   _____

6. In the winter there was a lot of extremely cold weather. They couldn't hunt in this cold weather for very long. There was

   _____

7. In winter they couldn't cross the Rockies. They wanted to get back to St. Louis as soon as possible, but winter came very quickly. Winter came

   _____ for them _____

Directions

Combine the following sentences into one sentence using *enough* +
infinitive. Some sentences will be affirmative; others will be negative. In
sentences 5 and 6 you need to add *for* + object.

Many Americans went out West to search for gold in the great Gold Rush of
1849.

1. Many people weren't very strong. They didn't survive the long and
   difficult journey West.

   *Many people weren't strong enough to
   survive the long and difficult journey West.*

2. The men who made it to California were very strong. They survived
   terrible hardships on the trip out.

   _____

3. A few found gold quickly. They were able to bring their families out
   West right away.

   _____

4. Others didn't have much money. They couldn't buy the equipment they
   needed.

   _____

5. There weren't many women out West. Not all of the miners could find
   wives.

   _____

6. There wasn't a lot of gold. Not everybody became rich.

   _____

7. The miners had to buy a lot of supplies. The supplies had to last through
   a long hard winter on the trip to California.

   _____

8. They had to take pack horses with them. The horses carried all their supplies and equipment.

_____

9. There were very few lawmen. They couldn't protect everyone from outlaws.

_____

Exercise 4   Enough or Too

Directions
Make questions from the following phrases. Then ask a classmate the questions and discuss your opinions. Use enough + infinitive (or) too + infinitive in both your questions and answers.

1. (a sixteen-year-old) (immature) (get married)

   Is a sixteen-year-old too immature to get married?

2. (a sixteen-year-old) (responsible) (have children)

   Is a sixteen-year-old responsible enough to have children?

3. (A sixteen-year-old) (old) (vote)

   _____ ?

4. (A fourteen-year-old) (mature) (drive a car)

   _____ ?

5. (A thirteen-year-old) (young) (smoke)

   _____ ?

6. (Fifteen thousand dollars a year) (money) (live on in a big city)

   _____ ?

7. (Ten thousand dollars a year) (money) (support a family these days)

   _____ ?

8. (Five thousand dollars) (money) (make a down payment on a new house in your hometown)

_____ ?

9. (A person who has had three drinks) (drunk) (drive)

_____ ?

10. (A person who is sixty-five) (young) (retire)

_____ ?

Part 4   So ... That

A. So with Adjectives and Adverbs

Look at these two sentences:

Thomas Edison's family was very poor.
Edison had to work from the time he was a boy.

These sentences can be combined with *so* + adjective + *that*:

Edison's family was so poor that *he had to work from the time he was a boy.*
    (main clause)   (result clause)

Explanation
We use this pattern to show that the clause after *that* is the result of the main clause:

Subject + verb + so + adjective / adverb + that
Mt. Marcy is so high that you can see for miles.

Examples
Thomas Alva Edison (1857–1937) was a famous American inventor. His family was **so poor that** Edison had to work from the time he was quite young. He only went to school for three months in his entire life, but he was obviously very bright. Whenever he worked with any kind of machine, he immediately thought of ways to improve it. When he was working as a telegraph operator, he developed an automatic telegraph system. It was a great success. It worked **so efficiently that** it could send four messages simultaneously.

B. <u>So . . . That</u> with Quantifiers

Explanation

So . . . that may also be used with quantifiers:

Subject + verb + so $\begin{Bmatrix} \text{few} \\ \text{many} \end{Bmatrix}$ + plural count noun

There are so many mosquitoes that they won't be able to sleep.

Subject + verb + so $\begin{Bmatrix} \text{little} \\ \text{much} \end{Bmatrix}$ + mass noun

They'll have so much fun that they won't want to come back.

Examples

Edison went to school for only three months in his entire life. He had **so little formal education that** he had to teach himself almost everything. Yet he invented **so many things that** he is considered one of the greatest inventors of all time. By his death he had 1,300 patents from his inventions. One of the most famous was the first electric light with a carbon filament. He did **so much work** in the field of electricity **that** his name is used by many utility companies today. He designed the first electric power plant in the world in 1881. **So few people** have accomplished as much as Edison did **that** it is truly appropriate to call him a genius.

C. <u>So Much That</u>

Look at these two sets of sentences:

Edison worked *a lot*. Sometimes he didn't get to bed until morning.
Edison worked **so much that** sometimes he didn't get to bed until morning.

People admired Edison's work *a lot*. They decided to preserve his laboratory intact.
People admired Edison's work **so much that** they decided to preserve his laboratory intact.

Explanation

A lot is an adverb that tells how much Edison worked. If we want to add a result clause, we change *a lot* to *so much that*.

Part 5 Such . . . That

Explanation

We also make result clauses using nouns. Use these patterns:

---

such a(n) + adjective + singular count noun + that

Edison was such a brilliant inventor that he obtained 1300 patents in his lifetime.

such + adjective + { mass noun / plural count noun } + that

He achieved such fame that his laboratory is now a museum.

We do not always use an adjective before the noun.

Examples

Thomas Edison was **such a brilliant inventor that** he came up with new ideas almost every year. In 1877 he invented a telephone transmitter for Western Union Telegraph Company. In 1878 he designed the first successful phonograph. He was **such a genius that** he could imagine what was inconceivable to other people, and he had **such skill** as a craftsman **that** he could build the things he imagined. He designed **such wonderful inventions that** he changed the way people lived their daily lives.

Exercise 5 So . . . That

Directions

Combine the following sentences into sentences with *so . . . that*. Look at part 4 to review all the patterns with *so*.

Helen Keller (1880–1968) was blind and deaf. She made a very important contribution by showing people that the handicapped were teachable and that they could be valuable members of society.

1. From the age of two, Helen Keller was badly handicapped. She couldn't see or hear anything.

   From the age of two, Helen Keller was so badly handicapped that she couldn't see or hear anything.

2. She was very isolated from other people.
She became emotionally disturbed.

_____

_____

3. She became very wild.
Her parents couldn't manage her.

_____

_____

4. They thought Helen was very difficult to teach.
Nobody could reach her.

_____

_____

5. At that time there were very few people who knew how to teach the
blind and the deaf.
Helen's parents had no one to turn to for help with Helen.

_____

_____

6. They hired a special teacher for the blind.
At first she made very little progress with her student.
Helen's parents became discouraged. (Combine only the second and
third sentences.)

_____

_____

7. The teacher, Anne Sullivan, had a lot of faith in the human spirit.
She refused to give up.

_____

_____

8. Ann Sullivan had been blind herself.
   She had suffered a lot as a child.
   She understood how Helen felt. (Combine only the second and third sentences.)

   _____

   _____

9. Ann Sullivan was extremely patient, and she tried many different approaches.
   Helen began to respond to her teaching.

   _____

   _____

10. Helen wanted to learn very badly.
    She mastered sign language very quickly.

    _____

    _____

11. Helen loved Anne Sullivan a lot.
    They remained close friends for the rest of their lives.

    _____

    _____

12. Helen Keller also learned how to talk.
    She lectured in many places.
    People all over the world were influenced by her. (Combine only the second and third sentences.)

    _____

    _____

13. She eventually learned to write beautifully.
    Her autobiography and several other books became classics.

    _____

    _____

14. She spent a lot of time and energy teaching people about the
    handicapped.
    People all over the world were impressed by her dedication.

    _____

    _____

Exercise 6   Such . . . That

A.   Combine the following sentences using *such + that.*

   Mount McKinley is the highest mountain on the North American continent. It is in Alaska. By 1905 no one had ever reached the top of Mount
McKinley.

   1.   Frederick A. Cook was an ambitious man.
        He decided to lead an expedition to the top of Mount McKinley.

   Frederick A. Cook was such an ambitious man that he decided to lead an expedition to the top of Mt. McKinley.

   2.   It was a very treacherous mountain to climb.
        The men in his party could not reach the summit.

        _____

        _____

   3.   There were terrible blizzards on the mountain.
        Most of the men suffered from frostbite.

        _____

        _____

   4.   The men had difficulty with the slippery rocks.
        Many of them wanted to turn back.

        _____

        _____

B. Combine the following sentences. Choose between *so . . . that* and *such . . . that*.

5. Many people in Cook's party decided to leave.
   Cook was left with only one companion.

   _____

   _____

   Later Cook claimed that he and his companion continued the
   climb. He said that they successfully reached the summit of
   Mount McKinley.

6. There was very little evidence.
   People did not believe Cook.

   _____

   _____

7. In 1907 Cook set out on a very long expedition to the Arctic.
   He didn't return for two years.

   _____

   _____

   In 1909, both he and Peary claimed to be the first man to reach
   the North Pole.

8. They had a very bitter argument.
   It became the sensational story of the time.

   _____

   _____

9. Peary was very angry.
   He accused Cook of lying.

   _____

   _____

10. Later Cook got into a lot of trouble in an oil scheme.
    He went to jail for five years.

    _____

    _____

11. The public was very hostile to Cook.
    Hardly anyone believed his claim about Mount McKinley or
        about the North Pole.

    _____

    _____

12. Very few people believed Cook was the first man to reach the
        North Pole.
    He died a very disappointed man.

    _____

    _____

Exercise 7   So ... That, Such ... That

Directions
Make sentences with *so ... that* or *such ... that*.

1. Muhammad Ali is very famous.

   *Muhammad Ali is so famous that people
   all over the world know his name.*

2. Sophia Loren is a very beautiful woman.

   _____

3. Aristotle Onassis was a very rich man.

   _____

4. Albert Einstein was a genius.

   _____

5. Alexander the Great was a great general.

   _____

6. Shakespeare was a great writer.

   _____

7. The families of Romeo and Juliet hated each other.

   _____

8. Don Juan was a great lover.

   _____

9. Joan of Arc was a brave woman.

   _____

10. Orpheus loved Eurydice.

   _____

11. King Midas loved gold.

   _____

12. Omar Khayyam wrote beautiful poetry.

   _____

13. Caviar is very expensive.

   _____

14. Learning English is very difficult.

   _____

15. The Great Pyramids of Egypt are fascinating.

   _____

16. Russia is a very big country.

_____

17. There are many different dialects of Chinese.

_____

Exercise 8 *So . . . That*

Directions
Make sentences using the pattern:

   Some people are *so* + adjective + *that* . . . .

What problems do the following people sometimes have?
Example

1. people who are very tall

   Some people are so tall that they can't fit into a sports car comfortably.

2. people who are very short

_____

3. people who are very beautiful

_____

4. people who are very jealous

_____

5. people who are very shy

_____

6. people who are very clumsy

_____

Exercise 9   So $\left\{ \begin{array}{c} \underline{\text{Much}} \\ \underline{\text{Many}} \\ \underline{\text{Few}} \end{array} \right\}$ + Noun + $\underline{\text{That}}$

Directions

What complaints do people often have about large, overcrowded cities?
Make sentences using the above pattern.

   crime   pollution   noise   parking spaces   people   garbage   strikes

Example

1. *There's so much crime in many large cities that people are afraid to walk on the streets at night.*

2. _____

   _____

3. _____

   _____

4. _____

   _____

5. _____

   _____

6. _____

   _____

7. _____

   _____

Expressing Your Ideas: Speaking and Writing

A. Personal Questions

1.   Talk about a time you succeeded in doing something that surprised
     other people or a success that was so unexpected that you even sur-
     prised yourself: for example, a time you won a special award or schol-

arship, a time you figured something out, a time you overcame some obstacles and accomplished something that seemed remarkable to you.

2. What are some of the things that you are dissatisfied with? For example, what's wrong with your apartment, your school, your job, your family, or your country? Talk about what is lacking or what there is too much of.

3. Think about a time in your life when you weren't old enough to do the things you wanted to do. Talk about the things you wanted to do and what prevented you.

B. Discussion Questions on Exploration and Achievement

1. Why do people go exploring?

2. What do you know about the explorers of the eighteenth and nineteenth centuries? Why do you think governments supported their exploration? What was the importance of the discoveries the explorers made?

3. Some people explore new territories and others explore new ideas in the field of science or engineering. For example, Thomas Edison and Alexander Bell made discoveries that changed the course of history. Talk about a discovery or invention that you think was important in changing history.

4. Who are some of the great explorers and inventors of your country? Tell what they did and the importance of each discovery and invention.

5. Talk about a famous person who had to overcome many obstacles to accomplish his or her goal. What things did this person lack? How did the person overcome these obstacles? For example, Columbus didn't have enough money to finance his trip by himself. He had to get money from the king and queen of Spain.

6. Do you think discoveries and inventions happen because of the particular needs of people at a particular time in history, or do you think they happen because of the genius of a particular person? Give reasons for your answer.

Chapter
16 The Simple Perfect Tense

I now thee wed.

Theme: *Love and Marriage*

Grammar: *Present Perfect with Questions with* Ever *and* How Many
Times; with Statements with Always/Never; *with*
Unstated Past; with Superlative

Dialogue

SANDRA: Guess what?[1] I have wonderful news. Jeff and I are engaged!

YOLANDA: What! You . . . engaged?

SANDRA: What's the matter? Aren't you going to congratulate me?

YOLANDA: Of course I'm happy for you. I'm just . . . surprised.

SANDRA: I know this is all very sudden. I know you think we're very
young, but we really love each other.

YOLANDA: Yes, I'm sure you do.

SANDRA: I **haven't told** anyone **yet. This is the first time I've spoken** about
it. Will you come with me when I break the news[2] to
Mom and Dad?

YOLANDA: Yes . . . but are you sure you know what you're doing? I**'ve never
met** Jeff. Who is he?

SANDRA: **He's the most wonderful person I've ever known.**

YOLANDA: Where did you meet him?

SANDRA: I met him in biology class last semester.

YOLANDA: Oh, he's a student. **Has he finished** college **yet?**

SANDRA: He **hasn't graduated**, but he**'s already finished** most of his
courses.

YOLANDA: How will you support yourselves?

SANDRA: We**'ve already discussed** that. I'm going to work until he finishes
school.

YOLANDA: Sandra, you**'ve never been** on your own.[3] **Has he? Has he
ever worked** before? **Has** he **ever lived** alone?

SANDRA: No, he **hasn't**, but that's not important. What matters is that
we're in love.

YOLANDA: How do you know you're really in love? You **haven't had** much
experience with men. How many guys **have** you **gone out** with?[4]

SANDRA: Well, not that many. **Jeff's the first one I've ever fallen in love
with.** I feel as if I**'ve always known** him.

---

1. *Guess what?:* We often say this when we have interesting news and want to get
someone's attention.
2. *to break the news:* to tell someone something important that may be upsetting.
3. *to be on your own:* to be independent and totally responsible for yourself.
4. *to go out:* to date someone.

YOLANDA: I know, I know. Love makes the world go round. But **so far** you **haven't convinced** me that you know what you're doing. Why don't you wait for a while?

SANDRA: I thought about waiting. But I don't want to wait. I'm just too excited. They say sometimes you have to follow your heart.

YOLANDA: They also say, "Look before you leap."[5]

The simple present perfect tense is formed in this way:

STATEMENTS

I
you   + have (not)   + the past participle
we
they

he
she + has (not)   + past participle
it

Jeff hasn't   graduated from college yet.

QUESTIONS
(question word) + have / has + subject + past participle

Has Jeff ever lived alone?

This tense is called the simple present perfect tense because it expresses a connection between the present and the past. The word *perfect* here means a completed action. In this chapter we are going to show some clear categories where we use the simple present perfect tense.

Part 1   *Ever, How Many Times, Always, Never*

A. Questions with *Ever* and *How Many Times*

Explanation

When we want to ask if something has happened at any time between a time in the past and the present, we use the simple present perfect tense

---

5. *Look before you leap:* This saying means, "Think before you act."

and *ever*. When we want to know the number of times something has happened, we use *how many times* with the present perfect tense. In addition to *how many times*, we also use *how many people, events, things,* etc.

Examples

SANDRA: **Have** you **ever been** in love, Yolanda?

YOLANDA: Yes, I **have.**

SANDRA: When was the last time that you were in love?

YOLANDA: I was really crazy about a guy from the office last year, but it didn't work out.

SANDRA: **Has** Arnold **ever mentioned** marriage to you?

YOLANDA: No, he **hasn't.** I only met him a few months ago.

SANDRA: **How many guys have** you **gone out** with, Yolanda?

YOLANDA: **I've gone out** with a lot.

SANDRA: Really, **how many times have** you **gotten** serious about a relationship?

YOLANDA: Only a couple of times up to now. My first love was my high-school sweetheart. That was over a long time ago.

B. Did You Ever/Have You Ever

Explanation

There is a difference between the questions *did you ever* and *have you ever*. If we are asking about a specific period of time in the past that is finished or completed, we must ask the question in the past tense (*Did you ever . . .?*) If we are asking about an action that took place between some time in the past and now, we use the present perfect (*Have you ever . . .?*)

Examples

SANDRA: When you were in high school, **did you ever** *think* about marrying the boy you loved?

YOLANDA: No, I **didn't.** I thought we were too young at the time.

SANDRA: **Have you ever** *wanted* to get married?

YOLANDA: No, I *haven't.* But who knows?

C. Always/Never

Explanation

When we want to talk about something that began at a time in the past and has never stopped up to this moment, we use *always* with the simple present perfect tense. We use *never* with the simple present perfect tense to express the opposite meaning.

Examples

SANDRA: You and I are really very different people. A career *has* **always** *been* very important to you. I've **always** *wanted* to get married and have a family. I've **never** *been* very serious about a career.

YOLANDA: Marriage *has* **always** *frightened* me a little bit. I've **never** *thought* I could spend my life with one person.

Exercise 1   Ever

A. Ask questions using the simple present perfect tense with *ever*. Use the words in parentheses as a guide for your questions. Ask a partner these questions.

Example

1. (be in love)

   Have you ever been in love?

2. (be engaged)

   _____?

3. (meet the person of your dreams)

   _____?

4. (fall in love at first sight)

   _____?

5. (read *Romeo and Juliet*)

   _____?

B. First ask a partner a question with *have you ever*. If the answer is yes, ask questions with *how many times* or *how many* (people, places, events) using the simple present perfect tense.

1. (be on a blind date)

   Have you ever been on a blind date ?
   How many times have you been on a blind date ?

2. (make a mistake in love)

   _____?

   _____?

3. (men or women . . . propose to you)

    _____?

    _____?

4. (go to a fortune teller)

    _____?

    _____?

5. (men or women . . . be serious about)

    _____?

    _____?

C. Ask questions using the following phrases as guides. Ask the first
    question in the simple present perfect tense with *ever*. Then ask a
    question beginning with *when*. You must use the simple past with *when*.

1. (write a love letter)

    Have you ever written a love letter ?

    When *did you last write a love letter* ?

2. (buy flowers for someone you loved)

    _____?

    When _____?

3. (fight with your parents over the person you loved)

    _____?

    When _____?

4. (dream about a sweetheart)

    _____?

    When _____?

5. (promise to love someone forever)

_____?

When _____?

Exercise 2   Always/Never

A.   Ask questions using *always* in the simple present perfect tense. Use the information in parentheses. Then answer the questions in complete sentences using *always* and *never*.

Example

1. (women . . . have a greater desire to get married than men)

   Have women always had a greater desire to get married than men?

   _____

2. (Throughout human history women . . . be more faithful than men)

   _____?

   _____

3. (Over the centuries men . . . be the providers for their families)

   _____?

   _____

4. (men . . . want to have relationships with more than one woman)

   _____?

   _____

5. (Throughout history couples . . . be able to get divorced easily)

   _____?

   _____

B. For the rest of this exercise, do not ask questions. Make statements in the simple present perfect tense with *always* or *never*.

1. (Throughout history men . . . be as eager to get married as women)

   _____

2. (Women . . . be the ones who stay home with the children)

   _____

3. (Men . . . be the ones to go out and hunt or work)

   _____

4. (Society . . . reject marriage as an institution)

   _____

5. (From the beginning of time . . . be a battle of the sexes)

   _____

6. (Over the centuries love . . . be an inspiration to great writers)

   _____

7. (Marriage . . . necessary to preserve society)

   _____

C. Do you think the above statements are really true or are some of them stereotypes? Do any of them make you angry? Discuss with a partner what he or she thinks about the above statements. Write down his or her answers and the reasons for these answers.

D. Can you think of any other stereotypes that people have always believed about men and women? Write them down. What is your opinion? Are these stereotypes disappearing now? Are men and women becoming more alike?

E. Think of a person you know who has always had certain annoying characteristics. Describe the annoying characteristics. Has this person always annoyed you? What has he or she done that has bothered you? Tell about one specific time or incident to explain what this person is like.

Part 2   Unstated Past

A. Unstated Past with No Time Marker

Explanation

Sometimes we talk about an event in the past but don't want to mention the definite time when the event took place or don't think the specific time is important. In this case, we use the simple present perfect.

Examples

Marriage patterns in the United States **have changed** a great deal. Sociologists **have studied** this change and **have found** that 96 percent of all Americans get married. Almost 40 percent of these couples get divorced. Many of these people get married again.

We cannot use the simple present perfect when we use a past tense time expression such as *a week ago, yesterday, last year, in 1965*. We must use the simple past tense. We can't ask a *when* question about the past with the present perfect.

Examples

In 1968 the divorce laws **changed** radically in New York. It **was** very difficult to get a divorce before that time. Now it is much easier.

B. *So Far, Up to Now, As of Now*

Explanation

When we talk about actions between some nonspecific time in the past and the present moment and we want to show that related actions may still happen in the future, we use the simple present perfect tense with these expressions: *so far, up to now,* and *as of now.*

Examples

Statistics show that the American family is in trouble. Many sociologists have criticized the nuclear family,[6] but **up to now** most Americans haven't accepted other alternatives. The younger generation has experimented a great deal. **So far** they have tried many different family structures, such as communal living and open marriage.[7]

C. *Already, Yet, Still*

1. ALREADY

Explanation

When we want to emphasize that an action was completed at some unstated time before the present moment, we use *already* with the simple present perfect in affirmative statements. We usually place *already* between *has* or *have* and the past participle. It is also possible to place *already* at the end of the sentence.

---

6. *nuclear family:* consists of the mother, the father, and the children.
7. *open marriage:* in which the husband and wife agree to date other people.

Example

The way children are cared for is changing in many countries. In fact, it *has* **already** *changed* a great deal in countries such as the Soviet Union and Israel. For example, the governments of these countries have set up day-care centers run by the state.

2. YET, STILL

Explanation

We use *yet* and *still* in negative sentences with the simple present perfect when we want to emphasize that an action has not yet happened up to the present moment, but we expect the action to be completed at some time in the future. We usually place *yet* at the end of the sentence. *Still* almost always comes after the subject of the sentence.

Examples

In the United States many women's groups have asked the government to build more day-care centers for working mothers. The government **still hasn't done** much in this area. Some mothers support day-care programs, but other mothers **haven't accepted** this idea **yet.**

3. QUESTIONS

We use *already* and *yet* in questions in order to find out if the action has happened before the present moment. *Yet* comes at the end of the question. *Already* comes after the subject or at the end of the question.

Examples

Have many European countries *built* day-care centers **yet?**
    Yes, Sweden and France have, for example.

How many communities in the United States *have* **already** *organized* an efficient day-care system?
    A few have.

Exercise 3   Unstated Past

Directions

Fill in the blanks with the correct form of the simple present perfect tense.

The American family ___*has gone*___ through many changes in recent
                        (go)

years. One of the reasons for this is the increase in divorce. The divorce

rate _____ to the point where one of every two marriages ends
        (rise)

in divorce. The increase in divorce _____ millions of families
                                        (create)

with only one parent.

Divorce is not the only reason that the family _____. Another
                                                      (change)

change in the family has to do with the fact that the number of working

mothers _____ sharply in the past decade. More than 50
                   (increase)

percent of married women with school-age children _____ the
                                                       (join)

work force. More and more mothers need to work because the cost of rais-

ing a child _____ up in recent years.
                   (go)

Exercise 4   Present Perfect/Past Tense

A. Fill in the blanks with the correct tense. Choose between the simple
present perfect and the simple past tense.

One problem connected with divorce is the question of who will get

custody of the children. Up to now mothers *have almost always kept*
                                                        (almost always/keep)

the children. At least up to now, most people, including judges,

_____ that mothers are closer to the children and are
            (feel)
better able to raise them. Because of this, traditionally judges

_____ children to the mother in most cases.
            (give)

    There _____ a famous case in custody rights in 1975. In
                    (be)
this case, Dr. Lee Salk, a famous child psychologist, _____
                                                      (want)
to keep his children after he _____ a divorce. The mother
                              (get)
also _____ them. The unusual part of this case
         (want)
_____ that the judge _____ the children what
        (be)   (ask)
they _____. In the end, the judge _____ the
        (want)   (award)
children to their father. He partly _____ his decision on
                                    (base)
what the children _____.
               (want)

This case marks a change in the way the legal profession is thinking about custody cases nowadays. In the past few years the courts

_____ to listen to the desires of children and fathers.
    (start)

Judges explain that the father's role is changing in the family and that in some cases he may be closer to the children and better able to care for them.

B.   Discuss or write about a recent change you have noticed in family life. Then give a specific example to explain your idea.

Exercise 5   *Present Perfect:* Already, Yet, So Far, Still

A.   Here the dialogue between Yolanda and her sister continues. Use the simple present perfect whenever it is possible. Use the simple past only when it is not possible to use the present perfect. When you see *already, yet, so far,* or *still* at the end of a sentence, decide where to place these words in the sentence.

YOLANDA: Have you told Jeff's parents yet?

SANDRA: We _____ **'ve already spoken** _____ to his mother (already).
                  (speak)

          We _____ her two days ago. We
                  (tell)

      _____ his father (yet). We know he'll be upset
      (negative, tell)

      because Jeff _____ school (still).
                (negative, finish)

YOLANDA: What _____ his mother _____ when
                          (say)

          you _____ her?
              (tell)

SANDRA: She _____ very surprised. She thinks we
              (be)

      _____ enough about life (yet). She says Jeff
      (negative, learn)

      _____ out on his own (yet).
      (negative, be)

YOLANDA: _____ you _____ on the date for the wedding?
                    (decide)
(already)

SANDRA: No, we _____. We _____ our
                    (negative)   (change)
minds a hundred times (already).

B. Continue the dialogue by writing questions and answers with *already*, *yet*, *so far*, *still*. Use these ideas or add your own ideas to make questions:

    find an apartment
    have a blood test
    get a marriage license

Exercise 6 / Present Perfect/Simple Past

Directions
A. Fill in the blanks with the correct tense. Choose between the simple present perfect tense and the simple past tense.

ARNOLD: What's the latest news on your sister? Is she still planning to get

married? _____ you _____ her yet
                              (convince)
that she's making a mistake?

YOLANDA: No, I _____. We _____ about it several
                    (negative)   (talk)
more times. She's sure she's doing the right thing. I don't know

though. I just feel upset about it. My sister and I

_____ very close. She _____ this kind
        (be/always)   (make/never)
of snap decision[8] before. No matter what I say, she just won't

listen to me.

ARNOLD: _____ you _____ about why this makes you feel so upset?
                    (think/ever)
YOLANDA: Well, I don't know why . . . . She's so young . . . .

---

8. *snap decision*: a decision made without careful thought.

ARNOLD: She's twenty years old. That's not so young.

YOLANDA: She _____ so level-headed.[9] She _____
(be/always)   (be/never)
impulsive before.

ARNOLD: It's *her* life, Yolanda. You can't decide for her.

YOLANDA: I just don't understand it. Up to now she _____ my
(take/always)
opinion very seriously.

ARNOLD: _____ you _____ you could be . . . jealous?
(think/ever)

YOLANDA: Jealous!

ARNOLD: Just a little?

YOLANDA: I don't think so . . . maybe. . . .

ARNOLD: Sometimes I think . . . well, you know . . . maybe we—you and

I—should try . . . living together.

YOLANDA: Living together?

ARNOLD: Why not? We _____ to know a lot about each other
(get)
over the past few months.

YOLANDA: I _____ like living with anyone before, but. . . .
(feel/never)

ARNOLD: It could be really exciting. . . .

B. It is the next day. Yolanda and Arnold are talking about this again.
    Write a continuation of the dialogue above.

---

9. *level-headed*: a very practical person who thinks about each decision very
carefully.

Part 3 Expressions that Require the Simple Present Perfect

A. In the $\left.\begin{matrix} last \\ past \end{matrix}\right\} \left.\begin{matrix} two \\ three \\ four \end{matrix}\right\} \left.\begin{matrix} days \\ weeks \\ months \\ years \end{matrix}\right\}$

The expression *in the last six weeks* means that an action took place at some unstated time between six weeks ago and now.

B. This is the $\left.\begin{matrix} first \\ second \\ third \end{matrix}\right\}$ time that something has happened.

Example

In the past forty years the American family *has changed* greatly. There are many possible reasons to explain this change. For example, **this is the first time in history** that so many women *have worked* outside the home.

Exercise 7   This Is the First Time/In the Past Few Years

A. In this exercise describe a situation in your own country. Use the expression *this is the first time in the history of my country.*

Example

1. *This is the first time in the history of the United States that there have been so many single-parent families.*

2. This is the first time in the history of my country _____

   _____

3. _____

   _____

4. _____

   _____

B. Now talk about how your country has changed or developed. Use the expression *in the last fifty years* or *in recent years*.

Example

1. *The family has changed a great deal in the United States in the last fifty years.*

2. _____

_____

3. _____

_____

4. _____

_____

Part 4   The Simple Present Perfect with the Superlative

Explanation

We often use the simple present perfect tense with the frequency adverb *ever* in a clause that follows the superlative.

Examples

YOLANDA: Sandra, tell me more about Jeff.
SANDRA: Well, he's the most exciting guy that[10] **I've ever gone** out with.
YOLANDA: Really, and what does he look like?
SANDRA: Oh, he has the bluest eyes and the sexiest smile **I've ever seen**.
YOLANDA: I can't wait to meet him.

Exercise 8   The Superlative and the Present Perfect

Directions

Fill in each blank with the superlative of the adjective in parentheses and put the verb in the present perfect.

(YOLANDA and ARNOLD are going to dinner and then to a discotheque tonight. They are both wearing new clothes and they are very excited about the evening.)

---

10. It is not necessary to use *that*.

ARNOLD: Yolanda, you look beautiful. That's *the sexiest dress*
(sexy dress/ever/wear)

that *you have ever worn* .

YOLANDA: Thanks. That's _____ that I
(nice thing/hear)

_____ all day. You don't look too bad yourself.

ARNOLD: Okay. Let's go. We're _____ that
(great couple/ever/see)

New York City _____ .

(At dinner.)

YOLANDA: Arnold, this is _____ that I
(good meal/ever/eat)

_____ . This was really fun.

ARNOLD: Yes. Except for the music. It's _____ that
(bad music/ever/hear)

I _____ .

Exercise 9   *Superlative with the Present Perfect*

Directions

Get together with a partner. One of you can ask questions with the superlative and the present perfect. The other student should answer using the same pattern. Later, switch roles.

Example

1. (good movie)   (ever see)

   STUDENT A: What's the best movie that you've ever seen?

   STUDENT B: _____ is the best movie I've ever seen.

2. (high mountain)   (climb)
3. (good restaurant)   (eat in)
4. (beautiful place)   (visit)
5. (interesting book)   (read)
6. (good teacher)   (had)
7. (cute man or woman)   (kiss)
8. (dynamic person)   (meet)
9. (famous leader of your country) (have)

10.	(big lie)	(tell)
11.	(reckless thing)	(do)
12.	(embarrassing experience)	(have)
13.	(dumb thing)	(do)

Expressing Your Ideas: Speaking and Writing

1. Talk about love, courtship, and marriage in your country. What do you think is a good age to get married? How long do people date each other before they get married? Do people get engaged? How long is that engagement period? Do people ever live together before they get married? Have attitudes toward living together changed in the past ten or fifteen years? What do you think about living together without getting married? What do couples have to do to get married? Is there a religious and a civil ceremony? Describe wedding customs in your country. If you are married, talk about your own courtship and wedding. Where do people go for their honeymoon in your country?

2. Has the structure of family life in your country changed in recent years? What changes have taken place? In your opinion, what is the most serious change that has taken place? For example:
   a. Have families gotten smaller? Why? Is it because more women have begun to work? If the family hasn't gotten smaller, has it stayed the same? Why?
   b. Have attitudes toward working mothers changed? Have men begun to take more responsibility for child care and housework? Have people's attitudes toward birth control changed in the past ten or twenty years? How?

3. In the United States, divorce has become more acceptable in recent years. Is this true for your country? Is it very difficult to get a divorce? Has the rate of divorce risen? Why? Do divorced people usually get married again? What are some of the emotional problems that divorced people face? When there is a divorce, who usually gets custody of the children? What are the problems that divorced parents face? Who do you think is better suited to raise the children: the mother or the father? Why?

17 The Present Perfect Continuous and the Simple Present Perfect

Quilting.

Theme: *Changes*

Grammar: *Present Perfect Continuous; Simple Present Perfect with the Expressions:* How Long, For/Since, *and* Recently/Lately

---

Dialogue

YOLANDA: Oh, Jack! We're over here.

JACK: I'm sorry I'm late. **How long have** you **been** here?

ARNOLD: **We've been waiting for about thirty minutes.** We got here at 6:00. Where have you been?

JACK: I was finishing a pot in my pottery class. It took me a really long time to clean up.

ARNOLD: Your pottery class? **How long have** you **been taking** a class in pottery? You've never mentioned it before.

JACK: I just registered for the class last week. I needed a break from all my science classes.

YOLANDA: What a great idea!

JACK: Yes, it is. **I've been having** a really good time. I've never tried to do anything creative before.

YOLANDA: Hey, where's Molly? Isn't she coming?

JACK: No, she's still working on that old oak table. **Since she got her own apartment,** she**'s been spending** all of her free time fixing up the place.

YOLANDA: Is she still working on that table? She**'s been trying** to get the paint off **since 8:00 this morning.** I know, because I called her then.

ARNOLD: She's refinishing a table?

YOLANDA: She just learned how. She's read several books on it.

JACK: She**'s been running** around to antique stores and reading "do-it-yourself" books and not much else. She **hasn't been going out** much **recently**—at least not with me.

YOLANDA: When the apartment's finished, things will get back to normal.

JACK: I don't think she'll ever be finished.

YOLANDA: I think she's much happier now than when she was living at home.

ARNOLD: You can take some credit for that. You helped her make up her mind,[1] and she**'s been acting** like a new person **ever since.**

---

1. *to make up (your) mind:* to decide to do something.

Part 1   The Present Perfect Continuous

A. Use of the Present Perfect Continuous

Explanation

We use the present perfect continuous tense when we talk about an action that began in the past and is still going on in the present. This is not a completed action, but a continuing action. The present perfect continuous is formed in this way:

Subject + $\dfrac{has}{have}$ (not) + been + base form + ing

Molly hasn't been going out much recently.

Examples

Molly **has been fixing up** her apartment for several days. She also **has been painting** the apartment herself.

In this example notice that the sentences in the present perfect continuous show an unfinished and continuing action. When we talk about a physical action that began in the past and is still continuing (actions such as waiting for someone, talking on the phone, dancing, painting, etc.), we use the present perfect continuous.

B. Contrast of Simple Present Perfect and Present Perfect Continuous

Examples

So far Molly **has cleaned** the floors and the windows, but she **hasn't put up** curtains yet. As of now, she**'s painted** the living room, but she **hasn't finished** the kitchen.

Explanation

Notice that the sentences in the simple present perfect (*has cleaned, hasn't put up, hasn't finished*) do not refer to an action that is continuing now. When we use the simple present perfect here, it means the action is completed.

C. Time Expressions

Explanation

1. We often ask questions beginning with *how long* in the present perfect continuous. When we answer these questions, we use the following time expressions:

   for + a certain period of time: *for a few minutes, for two weeks, for several months* since + a specific date or time: *since 3:00, since yesterday, since 1977*

since + a clause: *since I left home, since I came here*

other time expressions: *all morning, all day, all week*

2. We often ask questions and make statements in the present perfect continuous by using the time expressions *lately* and *recently*.

Examples

YOLANDA: Molly, what are you doing? It's already 2:00. Aren't we going shopping?

MOLLY: I know it's 2:00. Everything takes twice as long to do as I expect.

YOLANDA: **How long have you been painting** those cabinets?

MOLLY: I started at 8:00 this morning.

YOLANDA: You mean you*'ve been painting* **for six hours**!

MOLLY: I really don't know what I'm doing. I've never painted before. Have you? Besides, nothing has gone right today. The man from the phone company still hasn't come. I*'ve been waiting for him* **all day**.

YOLANDA: What's that strange noise I hear?

MOLLY: Oh, that! That's the toilet. It*'s been running like that* **since last night**. Not only that, but the refrigerator *hasn't been working* properly **since I moved in**.

YOLANDA: Well, those things can be fixed. Just call the super.

MOLLY: I don't know. Maybe I've made a mistake. I*'ve been thinking* things over **lately**. Maybe I shouldn't have moved into this apartment. It needs too much work.

YOLANDA: It's not that bad. Your apartment will be great in another few days.

MOLLY: Maybe. All I know is that I moved in here last month, and I*'ve been having* nothing but headaches **ever since**.

YOLANDA: But don't forget that you've been having a lot of fun, too.

D. Clauses with <u>Since</u> and <u>Ever Since</u>

Explanation

We can use *since* clauses in two ways. This is the most common pattern:

Molly's been having a lot of problems *since* she moved into an apartment.

Here is a more emphatic way of expressing the same idea:

Molly moved away from home last month, and she's been having nothing but headaches *ever since*.

Part 2   Simple Present Perfect and
Present Perfect Continuous

A. Cases in which There Is Little Difference in Meaning

Explanation

In the first part of the chapter we studied one case when we almost always use the present perfect continuous:

Molly has been painting her apartment since 8:00 this morning.

She started to paint at 8:00, and she is still painting at this moment. In this case we don't usually say, "She has painted." When we talk about an action that has been continuing over a period of days, months, years, and which is not necessarily happening at the present moment (the moment of speaking) but is happening nowadays, we can use either the present perfect or the present perfect continuous. When we use the present perfect continuous, we are emphasizing the continuous nature of the action.

Examples

Recently more and more young Americans **have been leaving** home. These young people **have been trying** to establish their own life-style away from parental influence. This trend has resulted in a major change. For the last twenty years the number of households **has been increasing** in large American cities. This means that the number of available apartments to rent **has been shrinking** since the early 1960s.

All the verbs that are in the present perfect continuous can also be written in the simple present perfect. Here the idea of continuous action is not as strong:

Recently more and more young Americans **have left** home. These young people **have tried** to establish their own life-style. For the last twenty years the number of households **has increased** in large American cities.

B. Special Cases in which Meaning Changes

Explanation

With some verbs the meaning of the sentence changes completely when we use the simple present perfect or the present perfect continuous. With these verbs, the simple present perfect clearly indicates a completed action, and the present perfect continuous indicates an action that began in the past and continues up to now. When we want to use the time expressions that tell *how long* with these verbs, we can only use the present perfect continuous.

Here are some common examples:

grow (a beard)	build (a bridge, a road)
write (a novel)	pay for (purchases in installments)
paint (a picture, a house)	

Look at the following groups of sentences:

Arnold *has been growing* a beard for the last three weeks.
(The beard isn't complete. It needs two more weeks.)
Arnold *has grown* a moustache.
(The moustache is complete.)

Jack *has been building* a telescope since last September.
Jack *has built* a radar unit.

Molly *has been reading* a book about home repair.
Molly *has read* several books about interior design.

Part 3   Special Verbs which Require the
Simple Present Perfect

Explanation
We do not use the present perfect continuous with certain verbs when we
want to express an action which began in the past and continues into the
present. With these verbs we have to use the simple present perfect. Here
is a list of some common verbs which require the simple present perfect, not
the present perfect continuous. Most of these verbs are on the list of stative
verbs in chapter 4.

· know	belong	perceive	· prefer
· understand	contain	suppose	love
owe	equal	· believe	· like
possess	resemble	· decide	seem
· be	tend	conclude	realize
have²			

Examples
Arnold **has known** Yolanda for nine months. They have been getting more
serious about their relationship recently. Arnold **has loved** her since the
day he met her.

NOTE: The correct form is *has known* and *has loved*, not *has been
knowing* or *has been loving*.

---

2. *have* with the meaning of possession: I *have* a car.

Exercise 1   Time Expressions

Directions
Choose the correct time expression for the following sentences. Choose among *for, since, ago, when, in, ever since.* Finish the sentence using the information in parentheses.

1. Molly has lived in New York / (1965)

    Molly has lived in New York since 1965.

2. Arnold wrote his first song / (1968)

    _____

3. Arnold has been playing the guitar / (1965)

    _____

4. Arnold played his first job in a night club / (three years)

    _____

5. Yolanda has been living on her own / (she got a job as a lawyer)

    _____

6. Jack has been studying astronomy / (three years)

    _____

7. Jack was accepted into graduate school / (a year)

    _____

8. Jack, Arnold, Yolanda, and Molly have been friends / (quite a while)

    _____

9. Yolanda and Arnold have been going out / (they met last autumn)

    _____

10. Molly started to jog / (she's been feeling better)

    _____

Exercise 2 Present Perfect Continuous: _How Long_, _For_, _Since_

Directions
Ask questions with _how long_. Answer the questions, using _for_ or _since_.

1. Samuel Barber is a famous American composer.

   How long _has Samuel Barber been composing music_?
   He's been composing music since the early 1930s.

2. Bjorn Borg is a famous tennis player.

   How long _____ professionally?

   _____ 1974.

3. Baryshnikov is a famous Russian dancer who became a United States resident.

   How long _____ in America?

   _____ 1974.

4. Van Cliburn is a famous pianist. He began his career when he won a Moscow competition.

   How long _____ professionally?

   _____ the 1950s.

5. Pavarotti is a famous singer at the Metropolitan Opera of New York.

   How long _____ with the Metropolitan?

   _____ 1968.

6. The Dallas Cowboys are a famous football team in the United States.

   How long _____?

   _____ the early 1960s.

Exercise 3 Present Perfect Continuous and Simple Present Perfect with Stative Verbs

Directions

Ask your partner information about himself. Use the present perfect continuous whenever possible, but remember that some of the verbs can be used only in the simple present perfect.

1. Do you drive?

   How long _*have you been driving*_ ?

   How long _*have you owned*_ your car?
   (own)

2. Do you play an instrument?

   How long _____?

3. Do you have a hobby?

   How long _____?

4. How long _____ your best friend?
   (know)

5. How long _____ interested in learning English?
   (be)

6. a. _____ care of yourself recently?
   (take)

   b. _____ enough sleep lately?
   (get)

   c. _____ the right food or
   (eat)

   _____ a lot of junk food?
   (eat)

   d. _____ too much?
   (eat)

   e. _____ too much recently?
   (drink)

   f. _____ enough exercise?
   (get)

   g. Do you smoke?

   How long _____?

How much _____ lately?

_____ to cut down recently?
(try)

7. What _____ since you graduated from
(do)

high school (college)?

_____ came to the U.S.?

8. Are you married? If not, do you have a girl friend? boy friend?

_____ your $\left\{\begin{array}{l}\text{wife} \\ \text{husband} \\ \text{girl friend} \\ \text{boy friend}\end{array}\right\}$ since you first met him/her?
(love)

Exercise 4   *Ever Since*

Directions
Finish these sentences. Use the present perfect continuous and put *ever since* at the end of your sentences.

1. Borg dropped out of high school in the ninth grade to play tennis, and

    he's been playing professional tennis ever since.

2. Baryshnikov defected to the United States from the Soviet Union in

    1974, and _____

3. Van Cliburn won the Moscow competition in the 1950s, and he _____

    _____ professionally _____

4. Clint Eastwood made his first film in the 1950s, and he _____

    _____

5. The Bee Gees are a famous English rock group. They started singing

    when they were children, and they _____

6. I got my driver's license when I was _____, and I _____

   _____

7. I started to smoke at _____, and I _____

   _____

8. I first became interested in _____ _____ years

   ago, and I _____

Exercise 5 Contrast of Present Perfect Continuous and Simple Present Perfect

Directions
In this exercise use only the present perfect and the present perfect continuous. Use the present perfect continuous wherever possible. Use the simple present perfect only when necessary.

MOLLY: Jack, I really like this pot you made. Maybe someday you'll be good

enough to sell your work.

JACK: Yeah. Lots of people make their hobbies into real professions. One

of my professors in art history left the university a few years ago,

moved to the country, and he _has been making_ jewelry there
                                        (make)
ever since.

MOLLY: That's an interesting change. But can he make a living doing that?

How _____ himself since he left his job at the
         (support)
university?

JACK: He _____ several crafts fairs so far, and he
           (enter)
_____ to get department stores to carry his work. His
      (try)
shop is doing well, too.

MOLLY: _____ a show of his own?
         (ever/have)

JACK: Yes, he _____. He had a major show in New York just

after he left the university.

MOLLY: How long _____ jewelry?
(make)

JACK: Since he took a night course in jewelry making about ten years ago.

MOLLY: _____ his family _____ their new life in
(enjoy)

the country since they moved?

JACK: Yes, so far they _____. They _____ too
(negative, become)

bored yet. They all keep very busy. His wife _____ a
(write)

book on changing careers. She _____ most of the text,
(write)

but she _____ a conclusion yet.
(negative, write)

Exercise 6   Integration

Directions
Fill in the blanks with the correct tense. Choose among the simple present,
present continuous, simple past, simple present perfect, and present perfect
continuous.

(MRS. EMERSON lives across the hall from MOLLY. JACK and MOLLY have come to
visit her.)

MOLLY: Hello, Mrs. Emerson. I hope we didn't interrupt you?

MRS. EMERSON: No, not at all. I *am not doing* anything special right
(negative, do)

now. I just sat down to read.

MOLLY: What _____ ?
(read)

MRS. EMERSON: *War and Peace* by Tolstoi.

JACK: That's such a long book. How long _____ it?
(read)

MRS. EMERSON: For about six months. It'll take me forever to finish it.

_____ _War and Peace?_
(ever/read)

JACK: Yes, I _____ it when I _____ in
(read)   (be)

high school.

MRS. EMERSON: Don't tell me how it ends. I wish I had more time to read,

but I have so many things to do. Right now I _____
(try)

finish this patchwork quilt before my grandchild is born. I

_____ on it a lot recently.
(work)

MOLLY: It's exquisite. Where _____ you _____
(get)

the pieces of material to make it?

MRS. EMERSON: My daughter _____ them to me regularly for
(send)

several years.

JACK: It really is beautiful. How long _____ quilts?
(make)

MRS. EMERSON: I _____ my first one when I _____
(make)   (get)

married, and I _____ them ever since. Each of
(make)

my grandchildren _____ one.
(have)

MOLLY: How many _____ altogether over the years?
(make)

MRS. EMERSON: I couldn't count them.

MOLLY: These quilts are lovely. You could sell them for a lot of

money.

JACK: Yeah, you could. Prices _____ sky high in the
(go)

past five or ten years.

MOLLY: Quilts are such an American art form. Women

_____ them since colonial times.
(make)

MRS. EMERSON: It's an art form I _____.
(always/love)

Exercise 7   Integration

Directions
A TV host is interviewing a famous woman author who is eighty-five years old. He is asking her about the changes she has seen in her lifetime. Fill in the blank with the correct form of the simple present, present continuous, simple past, simple present perfect, and present perfect continuous.

HOST: I'd like to ask you some questions on changes that you

_____ in your lifetime. What is the biggest change
(see)

that you _____ in your lifetime in the way people
(notice)

live?

AUTHOR: That's a difficult question to answer. I guess it would be the

change in the younger generation. Young people _____
(change)

a lot recently. In my day, young people _____ very
(be)

different.

HOST: In what way _____?
(change)

AUTHOR: To my way of thinking, they _____ too casual and
(become)

much too liberal in language, in dress, in attitude in general. I

guess I'm just old-fashioned.

HOST: Would you give me an example of what you mean?

AUTHOR: Here's a small example. For the last ten years, since my youngest

granddaughter _____ high school, students
(leave)

_____ blue jeans and T-shirts to school. I understand
            (wear)

that even some women teachers _____ pants in the
                                        (wear)

classroom recently. In my day, they _____ you out of
                                            (kick)

school when you _____ properly.
                    (negative, dress)

HOST:　What you're saying is true. Even professors at the universities

_____ in blue jeans nowadays.
        (lecture)

AUTHOR:　Of course, life-styles with the younger generation _____
                                                                    (be)

completely different from what I _____ up with. It
                                        (grow)

seems to me that for the last ten or fifteen years young people

_____ to start dating at an earlier and earlier age.
        (tend)

They start dating at thirteen, and, as you know, today many

couples _____ together without being married. That
                (live)

_____ unthinkable in my day.
        (be)

HOST:　If it's not too personal, I'd like to ask another question. What is

the biggest change that you personally _____?
                                            (experience)

AUTHOR:　That is another difficult question. I suppose I would say getting

married was the biggest change.

HOST:　How long ago _____?
                        (get married)

AUTHOR:　I _____ married sixty years ago. My husband and I
                (get)

_____ happily together ever since.
        (live)

HOST:　Congratulations. It's nice to meet someone who _____
                                                            (be)

married for so long and _____ still happy.
                            (be)

Expressing Your Ideas: Speaking and Writing

1. Have you made any changes in your life recently? What have you been doing since this change took place?

2. Choose a person that you know about whose life-style has changed. What change took place in the person's life? What was his life like before? What has he or she been doing since the change took place?

3. Do you have a particular hobby? Have you ever had one? How long have you been interested in this? How did you become interested in it? Why do you enjoy it? Why are some hobbies important to people? What are some typical hobbies that people in your country enjoy?

4. Have people's eating habits been changing in recent years in your country? Has the quality of food changed in your lifetime? Has agriculture been mechanized? In recent years have people been using processed food, such as canned food, frozen food, or specially prepared TV dinners? How do you feel about this change?

5. Have styles in fashion been changing much in recent years? Do people dress very differently nowadays from the way they did ten or fifteen years ago? How do you feel about this change?

6. How has the younger generation been changing in your country? Is the sense of morality with the younger generation different today from what it was twenty years ago? In what ways? Why has this change been taking place in your opinion?

7. Do people in your country return to college to take courses after they have retired or after they have been working for a number of years? Do they return to get a degree or just to take courses of special interest?

The Past Perfect Tense, Past Perfect Continuous Tense, and the Future Perfect Tense

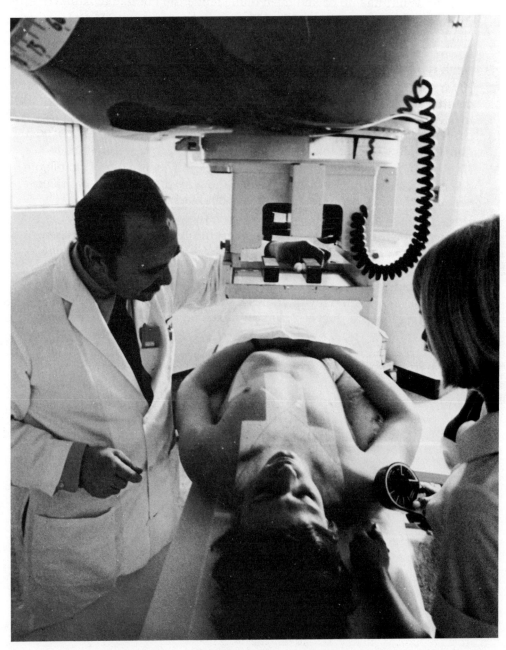

A patient receiving radiological treatment for cancer. (*Wide World Photos*)

Theme: Medicine

Grammar: Past Perfect, Past Perfect Continuous, and Future Perfect

---

Dialogue

YOLANDA: You'll never believe this. You know my girl friend Betty, the one who's expecting?[1] She just got her first baby picture.

ARNOLD: What do you mean, baby picture? She hasn't had the baby yet.

YOLANDA: I know. That's the exciting part. Doctors took a picture by sonar.[2] When the picture was finished, they found out that Betty was expecting triplets! They were really surprised. **Up to that point, they hadn't suspected** anything unusual.

ARNOLD: A picture by sonar! Modern medicine is really amazing. How did Betty take the news about triplets?

YOLANDA: She nearly passed out.[3] But **by the time she saw her husband, she had calmed down** enough to prepare him for the shock.

ARNOLD: What did he do when he found out?

YOLANDA: When Betty broke the news,[4] he nearly fainted.

ARNOLD: She obviously **hadn't prepared** him enough.

YOLANDA: How could anyone be prepared for news like that? They **had** only **been thinking about** having a child for a couple of months **when Betty got pregnant.**

ARNOLD: Just think, **by this time last year**, they **hadn't** even **decided** to have children, and **by the end of this year**, their family **will have doubled** in size.

YOLANDA: More than doubled.

ARNOLD: At least they know ahead of time. Ten years ago no one **had heard** of pictures by sonar, and now they're becoming commonplace.

YOLANDA: When our kids are ready to have children, I wonder what else doctors will be able to do?

ARNOLD: Who knows? **By that time**, maybe they**'ll have** already **developed** ways to correct birth defects.

YOLANDA: Maybe they'll be able to control the genetic make-up of children.

ARNOLD: If scientists do all that, they**'ll have gone** too far.[5] In my opinion, we should leave nature alone.

---

1. *expecting*: expecting a baby.
2. *sonar*: a device that can locate an object by means of sound waves.
3. *to pass out*: to faint.
4. *to break the news*: to tell someone something that will be surprising or shocking.
5. *to go too far*: to go beyond the limits of what is right.

The Past Perfect, Past Perfect Continuous, and Future Perfect Tenses   **293**

Part 1   The Simple Past Perfect Tense and the Past Perfect Continuous Tense

A. The Simple Past Perfect

Explanation

We use the past perfect tense to talk about an action that took place before another action in the past. These two past events should be clearly mentioned or implied. If we are talking about only one event in the past, we use the simple past tense. Don't make the mistake of using the past perfect tense in this case. The past perfect tense is only used *in relation to* another past time. We form the past perfect tense in this way:

> subject + *had* + (*not*) + past participle
>
> *Betty's doctor hadn't suspected anything unusual before they took pictures by sonar.*

Here are some cases that usually require the past perfect tense:

1. *BY* . . . /*BY THE TIME* . . .

When we use a phrase with *by* or a clause with *by the time* in a sentence about the past, we usually use the past perfect in the main clause. In this case, *by* and *by the time* mean *before*.

Examples

Louise Brown is one of the most famous babies in history. In fact, *by the time she was born in 1978*, she **had** already **become** the subject of intense interest. Newspapers called her the world's first test-tube baby. *By the time of her birth*, one London newspaper **had paid** thousands of dollars for the rights to her story and pictures.

By the end of 1979 a woman in India **had given** birth to a test-tube baby.

2. *WHEN CLAUSES*

There are two different kinds of *when* clauses about the past. We often use the simple past tense in the main clause and in the *when* clause about an event in the past. In this case we mean the action in the main clause happened after the action in the *when* clause. *When* means *after*.

Examples

When Mr. and Mrs. Brown **discovered** they couldn't have children, they **went** to Dr. Steptoe of Oldham Hospital in London. Dr. Steptoe and his associate Mr. Edwards promised to try to help.

Very often we use the past perfect tense when we use a *when* clause in a sentence about the past. When we do this, we mean the action in the main clause (in the past perfect) happened before the action in the *when* clause (in the past tense). *When* means *before* in this case.

Examples

When the Browns **came** to Oldham Hospital, Steptoe and Edwards **had had** some success in placing embryos in the bodies of women. However, none of these embryos **had lived** for a long time.

3. PAST PERFECT TENSE WITH CERTAIN ADVERBS

Many uses of the past perfect are parallel to those of the present perfect tense. The following expressions usually require the past perfect tense when we are talking about an action that took place before another action in the past:

still	earlier	from the time that
already	up to + specific past time	That was the first time
yet	for + period of time	that I _____.
before	since + specific past time	

Examples

Mr. and Mrs. Brown were eager to accept the help of Steptoe and Edwards. They **had tried** to adopt a child for two years *before* with no success. They felt that was their last chance. In a complex process, Steptoe and Edwards placed an egg cell from the mother and sperm cells from the father in a glass container. Life began. *This was not the first time human life* **had begun** outside a woman's body. Seventeen years *earlier*, an Italian scientist **had performed** the same experiment. *Up to 1978*, however, test-tube embryos **hadn't developed** into a full-grown baby.

Subject   *had*   (not)   past participle

    ↑   ↑   ↑

 (*still*) (*already*)   (yet
                         before
                         earlier)

NOTE: *Still* and *yet* are used only in negative sentences in the perfect tenses. *Yet* is also used in questions.

B. The Past Perfect Continuous Tense

Explanation

We use this tense when we mean that an action continued over a period of time up to a certain time in the past. It is often used to express the amount of time (how long) an action continued before a time in the past.

Subject + had (not) + been + base form + ing

The Browns had been trying to have a baby for years when they went to Steptoe and Edwards.

Examples

Steptoe and Edwards **had been experimenting** for a number of years when the Browns came to them. They **had been working** together since the sixties.

C. Questions for Simple Past Perfect and Past Perfect Continuous

Past Perfect: *Had*	(not)	subject	adverb (ever, already)	past participle
Past Perfect Continuous: *Had*	(not)	subject		been + base form + ing

Examples

YOLANDA: Arnold, isn't the story of baby Louise just amazing?

ARNOLD: Yeah, it is. It's medical history. **Had** doctors ever **tried** anything like that before Steptoe succeeded?

YOLANDA: No, they hadn't, not really. They had succeeded with animals. But Louise is one of the first attempts with human life, as far as I know.

ARNOLD: It's fascinating. How long **had** Steptoe **been trying** to do this before Louise?

YOLANDA: I don't know, but he's been interested in that area of medicine since the sixties, I think. **Had** you ever **heard** of him before?

ARNOLD: No, I never had.

Exercise 1   The Past Perfect Tense

A. Fill in the blanks with the past perfect tense. Use the verb in parentheses.

1. Before the mid nineteenth century, no dentist _had ever used_
   _____
   (ever/use)

   anesthesia.

2. Before 1893, no doctor _____ on the heart.
   (ever/operate)

3. 1967 was an important year in medicine. That was the first time a

   doctor _____ a heart transplant.
   (ever/perform)

4. Before the 1930s no doctor _____ on the brain.
   (ever/operate)

5. Before the 1960s, no one _____ a picture of an unborn
                                      (ever/take)
   child inside the mother's body.

6. As of 1961, doctors _____ in starting human life
                              (negative, succeed)
   outside the mother's body.

Write four more sentences of your own if you know of other medical or
scientific advances.

7. Before _____, _____.

8. Before _____, _____.

9. As of _____, _____.

10. _____ was an important year. That was the first time that

    _____ ever _____.

B. Describe one medical discovery that you know about. Tell what had not
   been possible previous to this discovery.

Exercise 2   Personal Questions in the Past Perfect Tense

Directions
Answer the following questions about yourself using the past perfect tense
and the past tense. Use complete sentences.

1. What had you accomplished by the time you got home last night? (Write

   two sentences.)

   _____

   _____

   _____

2. Where did you go on your last vacation?

   _____

Had you ever been there before?

_____

What did you do that you had never done before?

_____

What did you see that you had never seen before?

_____

_____

3. When did you come to this country? What had you heard about the
    American life-style? How much of what you had heard turned out to be
    true? Not to be true? Give several examples.

    (Write on a separate sheet of paper.)

Exercise 3   Contrast of Past and Past Perfect

A. Choose between the simple past tense and the past perfect tense. Use
    the verb in parentheses.

    Albert Schweitzer is one of the most famous names in the history of

medicine. He ___*decided*___ to become a doctor when he
                  (decide)

___*was*___ thirty years old. By this time he *had established*
     (be)   (establish)
himself in two other careers, in music and theology. In fact, he

_____ two books: one on the life of Jesus and the other on
  (already/publish)
the works of Bach. Even though he _____ famous in these
                                        (become)
fields, he _____ them up in order to become a doctor and
               (give)
help the sick of Africa. It _____ him seven years to complete
                               (take)
his medical studies. So at the age of thirty-seven, he _____
                                                            (arrive)

in Equatorial Africa to begin his service. When he _____,
                                                    (arrive)
no one _____ a hospital yet, so he _____ his
              (build)   (receive)
first patients in a house where chickens _____ before. Con-
                                               (live)
ditions did not remain so difficult, however. Schweitzer _____
                                                              (use)
his own money, which he _____ in Europe from organ recitals
                              (earn)
and lectures, to build a hospital. His success in Africa was so impressive

that he _____ the Nobel Peace Prize in 1952. In his accep-
            (receive)
tance speech, he _____ about the problems of peace in the
                      (speak)
world. Peace and respect for life _____ concerns of his
                                         (be)
from the time he was a young boy. His philosophy is sometimes simply

called "reverence for life." By the time he _____ in 1965, he
                                                  (die)
_____ over fifty years of his life treating the sick of Africa.
    (spend)
After his death, his daughter _____ at the Schweitzer
                                    (remain)
Hospital to carry on his work.

   Although he is regarded as an authority in many fields, his greatest

contribution is perhaps his life itself, an example of devotion to the sick

and poor. When Larimer Mellon, a member of a very wealthy American

family, _____ about Schweitzer, he _____ to
             (hear)   (decide)
follow his example. He _____ his medical degree when he
                            (receive)
_____ in his forties. Then he _____ with his
    (be)   (go)
wife to Haiti, where he _____ the Albert Schweitzer
                             (found)
Hospital.

B. Talk about a famous person or someone you know about who is no longer living. Tell about this person's life. Try to use *by the time* and *when* clauses.

C. Describe an event in your past which changed your way of living or thinking. What had your life been like before this event? What was it like afterwards?

Exercise 4   <u>When</u> Clauses with the Simple Past Tense and the Past Perfect Tense

Directions

First read the following sentences about Marie Curie. They are in chronological order.

1. Marie Curie was born in Warsaw in 1867.
2. She went to Paris in 1891 to study at the Sorbonne. She met her husband, Pierre Curie, there.
3. She married Pierre Curie in 1895.
4. They started to work together in 1897.
5. They discovered radium in 1898.
6. Marie and Pierre shared the Nobel Prize in physics with another French scientist in 1903.
7. Pierre died in an accident in 1906.
8. Marie took over his teaching position at the Sorbonne a few years later.
9. She was the first woman professor there.
10. In 1910 she isolated pure radium.
11. She received the Nobel Prize for chemistry in 1911.
12. She died in 1934 from leukemia, an illness probably caused by excessive radiation from her experiments.

A. Ask questions about the life of Marie Curie. Each question begins with a *when* clause. In your questions, use the past perfect tense. Answer the questions.

Example

1. When Marie married Pierre, how long *had she been*
   *in Paris*_____?
   She'd been there for four years.

2. When Marie and Pierre received the Nobel Prize in 1903, _____

_____?

_____

3. When Pierre died in 1906, _____

_____?

_____

4. When Marie Curie took over her husband's position at the Sorbonne,

_____?

_____

5. When she won the Nobel Prize in chemistry in 1911, _____

_____?

_____

6. When she died in 1934, _____

_____?

_____

B. Write sentences using *when* clauses about Madame Curie's life. Use the simple past tense in the *when* clause. In the main clause, use either the simple past tense or the past perfect tense.

1. *When Madame Curie left Warsaw, she went to Paris to study.*

2. *When Marie and Pierre started to work together, they had been married for a year.*

3. _____

_____

4. _____

   _____

5. _____

   _____

6. _____

   _____

7. _____

   _____

8. _____

   _____

Part 2   The Future Perfect Tense

Explanation

We use the future perfect tense to talk about an action that will be completed before another action in the future. This tense is used only in relation to another time in the future.

> subject + *will* + *have* + past participle
>
> *Researchers will have discovered many cures by the year 2000.*

Here are some cases where the future perfect tense is usually required:

A. By. . ./By the Time. . .

By and *by the time* mean *before* in these cases.

Examples

Many experts in the medical field predict vast changes in medicine, even in a simple doctor's visit. By 1990 some doctors **will have turned over** most of their work to machines. In the future, people will be examined painlessly by many different machines, and the results will be sent to a central computer. By the time the patient is dressed again, the computer will have analyzed all the tests and **will have sent** its suggested treatments to the doctor.

B. <u>When</u> Clauses

Examples

No one knows where scientific research will lead. One thing seems certain.
(1) Whenever doctors make a discovery in medicine, they **will want** to put
this discovery into practice. This alarms many people, who make terrible
predictions about what the future holds for us. (2) They say, for example,
when today's children are ready to have children, maybe researchers **will
have developed** ways to "grow" children in a laboratory. They hope that
before research goes this far, the government **will have stepped in** to stop it.

In sentence (1) we mean that *after* doctors make a discovery, they will want
to put it into practice. In sentence (2) we mean that scientists will develop
ways to "grow" children in a laboratory *before* our children are ready to
have families.

C. Future Perfect Tense with Certain Adverbs

When we use adverbs such as *before, still, yet, already, earlier, previously*
to talk about an action that will take place before another action in the
future, we usually use the future perfect tense.

Examples

Some people see the year 2000 as a turning point. Certainly by that time
scientists **will have already perfected** many artificial organs. For example,
they **will probably have discovered** how to perform eye transplants by then.
When a person loses the use of an eye or another organ of the body, a
doctor will be able to replace it with an artificial one. It is possible that
doctors **still won't have conquered** heart disease, but everyone hopes that
they **will have come closer** to finding a cure for it.

Subject + *will* (not) + *have* + past participle		
↑	↑	↑
(adverb)	(adverb)	(adverb)
(*still*)	(*already*)	(*yet, before, earlier, previously*)

NOTE: *Still* and *yet* are used only in negative sentences in perfect tenses.
Notice their different positions in the sentence.

D. Questions

Will + subject + *have* + past participle?

Will researchers have discovered a cure for
cancer by the turn of the century?

Examples

ARNOLD: You know, with all the warnings about the danger of heart disease, I should really watch my diet more closely.

YOLANDA: Yes, you eat too much junk food. It's high in cholesterol. If you continue like this, you'll be a perfect candidate for heart trouble when you're fifty.

ARNOLD: That's true, but a little scary. But anyway, that's a long way off.

YOLANDA: But be realistic. Don't wait until you're fifty to do something. Medicine can't cure everything. **Will** doctors **have discovered** a way to cure heart disease by then? **Will** they **have developed** an artificial heart by that time? An ounce of prevention is worth a pound of cure.[6]

Exercise 5   The Future Perfect Tense

A. Fill in the blanks with the future perfect tense. Use the verb in parentheses.

1. By the year 2000, perhaps scientists *will have found* a cure for
    (find)
    cancer.

2. By this time, maybe they _____ how life begins.
    (discover)

3. By the time our grandchildren are born, maybe researchers

    _____ many strange new forms of life.
    (develop)

4. By the time our grandchildren are born, maybe scientists

    _____ how to clone people.
    (learn)

5. By this time, scientists _____ many revolutionary
    (certainly/make)
    discoveries.

    Write some predictions of your own using the sentences above as models.

---

6. *An ounce of prevention is worth a pound of cure*: It's easier to prevent an illness by taking care of yourself than it is to cure the illness later.

6. Have scientists discovered how to help the deaf to hear and the

   blind to see?

   No, but perhaps by the year 2000, _____

7. Have doctors developed an artificial heart?

   No, but perhaps by the year 2000, _____

8. By the time _____, _____

9. By the time _____, _____

10. By the time _____, _____

B. By the time your grandchildren are grown, what changes do you think
   will have taken place in your family, in your hometown, and in your
   country?

Exercise 6   Integration

Directions
Fill in the blanks with the correct tense, using the verb in parentheses.
Choose among the present perfect, past, past perfect, present, future, and
future perfect.

DOCTOR: _____*Have*_____ you _*ever had*_ a complete physical
                    (ever/have)
             examination before?

ARNOLD: No, I _____. This is the first time I _____
                       (negative)   (take)
             so many tests.

DOCTOR: Of course, I think everyone should have a complete checkup once

             a year. Now I need some information about your medical history.

             Which childhood diseases _____ you _____ ?
                                                   (have)

ARNOLD: Oh, I _____ all of them. In fact, by the time I
(have)

_____ eight years old, I _____ measles,
(be)   (have)

mumps, and chicken pox.

DOCTOR: How old _____ you when you _____
(be)   (come)

down with the measles?

ARNOLD: Five. I remember because it was just before I _____
(start)

school. I _____ from the chicken pox when I
(just/recover)

_____ measles. I _____ the first two
(catch)   (miss)

weeks of school.

DOCTOR: I see. And when _____ you _____
(get)

the mumps?

ARNOLD: Oh, that _____ just before the second grade. I
(be)

_____ them first, and then I _____ them
(get)   (give)

to my sister. She _____ sick for a month.
(be)

DOCTOR: I notice that you wear contact lenses. How long _____
(wear)

you _____ them?

ARNOLD: I _____ them for the past two years. When I
(wear)

_____ them, I _____ glasses for ten
(get)   (wear)

years.

DOCTOR: Do you smoke?

ARNOLD: I'm afraid so. About a pack a day.

DOCTOR: How long _____ you _____ so much?
(smoke)

ARNOLD: Since high school. When I _____ from high school, I
(graduate)

_____ a cigarette, even though most of my friends at
(never/touch)

that time _____. But I _____ a lot since
(smoke)   (smoke)

I _____ to perform.
(start)

DOCTOR: You know how dangerous it is. All I can do is to recommend that

you stop or at least cut down.

ARNOLD: I _____ to cut down before, but I can't. I promise I
(try)

_____ to stop.
(try)

DOCTOR: You seem to be in relatively good health. I _____ only
(find)

one thing wrong so far. Your cholesterol level is too high. I want

you to follow the diet that the nurse _____ you when
(give)

you _____.
(leave)

ARNOLD: Diet? I _____ on a diet before. ____I____
(never/be)   (have to)

change my eating habits from now on? I play rock music. I don't

have time to eat right.

DOCTOR: If you _____ to take care of yourself, you
(want)

_____ change. This diet is very detailed. It tells you
(have to)

what you can eat and what you absolutely cannot eat. It doesn't

tell you how much. That's up to you. Now, by the time I

_____ you next, I hope that your cholesterol level
(see)

_____ down.
(go)

ARNOLD: See you again? When _____that_____?
(be)

DOCTOR: Four weeks from now.

ARNOLD: All right. I _____ . Maybe by this time next month,
         (try)

         I _____ my taste for junk food and maybe I
             (lose)

         _____ smoking altogether.
             (stop)

Expressing Your Ideas: Speaking and Writing

1. Talk about the system of medical care in your country. Is there a government sponsored health care system? Who pays for major medical expense: the government, the employer, or the individual? Is everyone entitled to the same benefits? What is the major problem that the health care system faces?

2. What is the status of doctors in your country? Do they enjoy a high standard of living? Do you think that doctors charge too much for their services?

3. Researchers are currently working on methods of altering or determining the genetic make-up of human beings. In the future they may be able to determine the sex, intelligence, and appearance of people. Should they be allowed to continue this research? Who should control this research: the government, private industry (pharmaceutical companies, chemical companies), citizens' committees, or anyone at all? If researchers ever succeed in this area, what might some of the problems be?

4. With modern medical technology, it is possible for doctors to freeze a person's body just before death. After doctors have found new medical cures and can extend the life span, a frozen body will be brought back to life. What is your opinion of this process? Would you do this if you had the opportunity? How do you think you would feel when you woke up?

5. Some people have agreed to donate certain organs of their body to medical science after they die. How do you feel about these organ banks? Would you leave your eyes, heart, or kidneys for use by someone else after your death? Why or why not?

6. Louise Brown was the world's first test-tube baby. What do you think of this new technique? Do you think it is ethical or not? Explain. If you couldn't have children any other way, would you use this method? If it were possible to "grow" a baby in the laboratory for nine months, would this be ethical? What questions would this raise for society?

7. In the United States today, men can donate or sell their sperm to a sperm bank. When a couple can't have children because the husband is infertile, they can use the services of a sperm bank. What do you think of this? Has science gone too far or not?

8. In California, there is now a special bank that accepts only the sperm of Nobel Prize winners. Only women of very high intelligence can use their sperm bank. What do you think is the purpose behind this kind of sperm bank? How do you feel about this? Why?

Modal Perfects

Why have so many planes disappeared in the Bermuda Triangle? (*Bill Jerome*)

Theme: Disasters

Grammar: Modal Perfects: May/Might Have, Must Have,
             Should Have, Could Have

Dialogue

(JACK just got off the telephone.)

MOLLY: Who were you just talking to?

JACK: That was my friend Johnny. You'll never believe what happened to him.

MOLLY: Is that the friend who's been taking skydiving lessons?

JACK: You mean the one who was taking. He'll never take another skydiving lesson again. He made his first and last jump yesterday.

YOLANDA: He **must have been** terrified.

JACK: He was. He looked so terrified that the instructor told him he didn't have to jump. He **could have waited** for two or three more lessons.

YOLANDA: Why didn't he?

JACK: I don't know. He **might not have wanted** to look like a coward. So he jumped.

YOLANDA: What happened?

JACK: Everything went wrong. His parachute **should have opened** automatically at 2,500 feet, but it didn't.

MOLLY: What did he do?

JACK: He didn't do anything. He **should have pulled** the cord and **opened** the parachute manually, but he was too scared to remember where the cord was. He panicked when he realized he was all alone, 2,000 feet above the earth . . . falling.

MOLLY: Then what happened?

JACK: Well, the second parachute **should have opened** when the first one didn't, but something was wrong with it. Johnny didn't pull the cord for another 200 feet. Finally it opened automatically.

YOLANDA: He **must have been** out of his mind[1] until the parachute opened!

MOLLY: He's lucky the second parachute opened.

YOLANDA: I don't understand how anybody could jump out of a plane. He **could have killed** himself.

MOLLY: He **must have been praying** all the way down.

JACK: Wait till you hear the rest of the story. He saw himself floating toward some treetops. He doesn't remember how he did it, but he **must have done** something to change his direction. He landed in a swimming pool on a country estate, in the middle of a big party.

---

1. *out of his mind:* crazy with terror.

MOLLY:	Boy, they **must have gotten** the surprise of their lives.
YOLANDA:	Were they angry that he crashed[2] their party?
JACK:	Well, they **couldn't have been** too angry, because they invited him to stay for dinner.

In this chapter we are going to show you how to use the following modals when you talk about the past: *might, may, must* (of deduction), *should, ought to,* and *could.* For the past form of *have to* and *must* (of necessity), see chapter 12.

Here is how to form a modal perfect:

Subject + *may*   *(not)* + *have* + past participle
           might
           must (of deduction)
           should
           ought to
           could

Johnny's parachute should have opened automatically, but it didn't.

Part 1   May, Might, Must + Have + Past Participle

Explanation
When we use *may* and *might,* we have several possibilities in mind. There is no difference between *may* and *might.* When we use *must,* we usually have only one possibility in mind. In negative statements we usually do not contract *may, might,* and *must* with *not.*

Examples
Amelia Earhart was a famous American pilot. She was the first woman to cross the Atlantic, and she was the first person to fly alone from Honolulu to California. These flights were in the 1930s. She **must have been** very brave to make these flights alone in those early planes. In 1937 she set off with a copilot on a trip around the world. After they left New Guinea, they were never heard of again. The world was saddened at this, and people developed many theories to explain what happened to them. For example, their plane **may have run** out of gas, or they **might have lost** control of the plane in a storm. Some say they **might have landed** on an island and that they **might not have died**. No evidence of a crash was ever found.

---

2. *crashed:* went to a party uninvited. In this case "crashed" is a pun: he literally landed with a crash.

Part 2   _Should, Ought To_ + _Have_ + _Past Participle_

Explanation

We use this pattern when we want to say that something was a good idea or advisable in the past but this action was not done. If we tell someone they shouldn't have done something, we mean that they did something and we think it was a bad idea. Notice that we can contract _should_ with _not_ (_shouldn't_); we rarely use _ought to_ in the negative.

Examples

The _Titanic_ was a magnificent ocean liner which sank on its maiden voyage[3] from England to the United States. Many important and famous passengers who were on board wanted to see icebergs close up, so the captain changed course and went farther north. He **shouldn't have listened** to their request. He **should have followed** the course he had already set, and he **should have paid** closer attention to the warnings about icebergs in that area of the North Atlantic.

Part 3   _Could_ + _Have_ + _Past Participle_

Explanation

When we use the modal perfect of _could_ in affirmative statements, we believe that something was possible in the past but that it wasn't done for some reason. When we say that someone couldn't have done something, we make a strong logical deduction based on what we know about the situation. We believe it was impossible for something to have happened.

Examples

On the night of April 14, 1912, the _Titanic_ struck an iceberg and began to sink. There was a ship fewer than ten miles away that **could have reached** the _Titanic_ in time. Unfortunately, the ship's radio operator was asleep and never heard the S.O.S. from the _Titanic_. The crew on the _Titanic_ also set off distress flares. However, people from other ships thought these flares **couldn't have been** a call for help. They believed that the _Titanic_ was unsinkable, so they thought the flares were just a fireworks display.

---

3. _maiden voyage_: first voyage.

Part 4   Questions and Short Answers

Explanation

We can ask questions by using a modal perfect in this pattern:

> (Question word) + modal (not) + subject + have + past participle?
>
> *Should Johnny have jumped out of the plane?*
>
> Short Answer:
> Subject + modal (not) + have.
>
> *No, he shouldn't have.*
>
> If the main verb is be, the short answer is:
> Subject + modal + have + been.

Examples

Could more people **have survived** the disaster?

Yes, they **could have.** Some of the lifeboats were less than half full.

Was there a lot of confusion after the ship struck the iceberg?

There **must have been.** People probably didn't know exactly what had happened.

Were there enough lifeboats for the passengers of the *Titanic?*

No, there weren't, unfortunately, but there **should have been.**

Part 5   Modal Perfect Continuous

Explanation

We use the continuous form of modal perfects in sentences where we would use a continuous tense about the past.

> Subject + modal (not) + have + been + base form + ing
>
> *Jack's friend must have been praying all the way down.*

Example

The captain didn't slow the *Titanic* down even after he had warnings of icebergs. In fact, the ship **must have been going** very fast when it struck the iceberg because four out of five compartments of the engine room were ripped open.

Exercise 1   *May Have* and *Might Have*

In the late nineteenth century Cuba was a Spanish colony. For a long time the Cubans had been unhappy under Spanish rule. They began to rebel against Spain in the 1890s. The United States did not want the Spanish to control the island of Cuba. They did not want powerful European countries to control territories so near to the United States.

In January 1898 the United States sent a battleship called the *Maine* to Cuba. On February 15, 1898, an explosion in Havana harbor killed 260 men on the *Maine* and sank the battleship. The incident helped to start the Spanish-American War in April 1898.

Most Americans blamed the Spanish for the disaster. There were investigations. Although the U.S. Navy reported that a submarine mine caused the explosion, no one could say exactly who was responsible.

The Spanish blamed the disaster on an explosion that took place inside the *Maine*. They said it had been an accident.

The cause of the accident was never satisfactorily explained.

Directions

People had many theories about what happened to the *Maine*. Complete the following sentences, considering some of the possibilities. Use *may have* or *might have* + past participle.

A. An accident?

1. The explosion _____*might have been*_____ an accident.
        (be)

2. What _____ the accident?
        (cause)

3. A submarine _____ a mine in the harbor.
        (leave)

4. The battleship _____ the mine by accident.
        (strike)

5. Did a terrorist leave the mine close to the battleship deliberately?

    He _____. (short response)

B. The Spanish?

1. The Spanish _____ the *Maine*.
        (blow up)

2. The Spanish _____ a bomb on board the *Maine*.
        (put)

3. They _____ the Americans to go home.
        (want)

4. They _____ the battleship was going to attack them.
        (think)

C. The Cubans?

1. The Cubans _____ the *Maine*.
   (destroy)

2. They _____ to start a war between the Americans
   (want)

   and the Spanish.

3. They _____ the Americans to fight the Spanish
   (want)

   for them.

4. Did they think a war would help them win their independence from

   Spain? They _____. (short response)

D. The Americans?

1. The Americans _____ the bomb on their own
   (plant)

   battleship.

2. They _____ an excuse to begin the fighting.
   (need)

3. They _____ this was a means of getting
   (believe)

   Spain out of Cuba.

4. Did the people who planted the bomb know there were so many

   sailors aboard the *Maine*?

   They _____. (short response)
   (negative)

Exercise 2   *Must Have* and *Might Have/May Have*

There is an area of the West Atlantic Ocean between Miami, Bermuda, and
San Juan, Puerto Rico, known as the Bermuda Triangle. More than 100
planes, ships, and small boats have come into this area and disappeared
without a trace. More than 1,000 people have been lost here in the last
twenty-six years. There has been almost no sign of a plane crash or of a

wreck. Most planes disappeared in perfectly calm weather. Often they radioed that all was well just before they went out of radio contact. There are many theories about what happened to these lost ships and planes.

Directions
Imagine what happened to the missing people, planes, and ships. Use *may* and *might* + *have* + past participle if you are not sure of what happened. Use *must* + *have* + past participle if you are almost sure of what happened.

1. During the nineteenth century many ships disappeared in the area known as the Bermuda Triangle. In 1945 the first planes disappeared. Six navy bombers took off at 2:00 P.M. on December 5, 1945, for routine training exercises. Their commander was Lieutenant Charles Taylor, with 2,500 hours of flying time. All the pilots and crewmen were experienced fliers. They completed their training exercise and were returning to the base. Everything had gone well.

   They ___*mustn't have been expecting*___ trouble.
   (negative, expect)

2. The temperature was 65° and the sun was shining. There was a slight breeze and only a few clouds in the sky.

   It _____ good flying weather.
   (be)

3. At 3:15 P.M., when the bombers were returning to the base, the flight tower received this radio message from Lieutenant Taylor: "This is an emergency. We seem to be off course. We cannot see land. . . . Repeat . . . we cannot see land."

   They expected to be over land, so they _____ lost.
   (get)

4. A little later they radioed again. They said their compasses were "going crazy." Although the planes were all flying in the same direction, their compasses each showed a different reading. Why did this happen? There are several possibilities:

   a. The compasses _____ defective.
      (be)

   b. Something _____ wrong with the bombers.
      (go)

   c. A magnetic field _____ the compass needles.
      (affect)

5. The bombers could not hear the radio tower, but the radio tower could hear them. There was a lot of static. Why was there so much static? (Use the continuous form for (a) and (b).)

a. The U.S. government _____ secret research
   (conduct)
   in that area.

b. Enemy forces of the United States _____ to destroy
   (try)
   the bombers.

c. Creatures from outer space _____ this static.
   (cause)

6. A radio message from the bombers said that winds were as high as 75 miles per hour. The weather had been fine a little earlier. No high winds had been reported until that time. Why did they report such high winds?

Their instruments _____ properly.
   (negative, work)

Some supernatural force _____ nearby.
   (be)

7. At 4:00 P.M. Lieutenant Taylor turned the control of the planes over to a new pilot. Why do you think he did this?

_____

8. Another plane with a crew of thirteen left the base. This plane went to rescue the navy bombers. The rescue plane sent one message about strong winds at 6,000 feet. This was the last message ever received from the rescue plane. What do you think happened to the rescue plane?

_____

9. A great search began. More than 300 planes, submarines, and destroyers searched 380,000 square miles for the six missing planes. They found no sign of a wreck. What do you think happened to the six planes?

_____

10. People learned that before the flight, one of the instructors suddenly said he did not want to go. Why do you think he didn't want to go?

He _____ a premonition.[4]

11. Another story involved the U.S.S. *Cyclops*, which disappeared with 309 people on board. This was on March 4, 1918, during World War I. At first people believed the Germans _____ the ship. But it
(torpedo)
turned out that no submarines had been in the area at the time. People considered other possibilities. A tidal wave _____ the
(strike)
Cyclops, or an old bomb _____ and sunk the *Cyclops*. But
(explode)
no trace was ever found of the *Cyclops*.

12. Some scientists explain the disappearances by magnetic fields. They believe something very powerful _____ the compasses act
(make)
so wildly. According to these scientists, the only thing that could do this is a powerful magnetic field. They insist that these bombers, for example, _____ lost because their compasses didn't work
(get)
properly. Their compasses _____ because of an unknown
(malfunction)
magnetic field.

13. Other people say the planes were not lost through natural causes. They _____ because flying saucers (UFOs) attacked them. These
(disappear)
people point to strange radio reports about "white lights." They say it is impossible that these "white lights" came from earth. They _____ from outer space, and they _____ very
(come)   (be)
powerful.

---

4. *to have a premonition*: to have a feeling that something is going to happen.

14. What do you think?

_____

Exercise 3   _Should Have_

The Salem witchcraft trials began in 1692. Many people believed in the devil at that time. They thought the devil could make a bargain with a person and that this person then belonged to the devil. They thought the devil entered the person and controlled him. This was called "possession." The person had to confess to being "possessed" by the devil in order to be saved. A person who denied being "possessed" was thought to still be under the influence of the devil.

Many women were accused of witchcraft in the Massachusetts town of Salem. Twenty were burned at the stake as witches.

One of the Salem judges, Samuel Sewall (1652–1730), was a member of the council that tried the witches. The council was responsible for the deaths of twenty people. In 1697 Samuel Sewall admitted that he had been in error. He publicly blamed himself for the witch trials. He admitted he and the other judges had done many things that were wrong.

Directions
Read each of the following sentences. Then write a sentence with _should have_ + past participle based on the first sentence.

1. The judges accepted the word of very young children as evidence.

    They should not have accepted the word
    of very young children.

2. They forced innocent people to confess to crimes.

    _____

    _____

3. They did not examine the motives of the people who made the

    accusations.

    _____

    _____

4. The judges weren't objective. They considered people as guilty before they heard any evidence.

_____

_____

5. Some people accused their enemies of witchcraft. They wanted their land, or sometimes they wanted to ruin people because they were envious. The judges did not question the motivation of the accusers.

_____

_____

6. Some actually accused members of their own families. When this began to happen, citizens of Salem did not try to stop the trials.

_____

_____

7. One of the judges, Judge Hathorne, did not admit that he had been in error. He insisted that he was right.

_____

_____

In history, Judge Hathorne is remembered as an evil man.

Exercise 4   _Should Have_

Directions
Jack's mother visited MOLLY last night. MOLLY was very nervous and did everything wrong. Today she feels terrible. She is talking to YOLANDA on the telephone. Complete the sentences with _should have_ + past participle. Make up the sentence that best supplies the meaning.

MOLLY: I didn't get home until late. I wanted to clean the whole house before she got there. When she rang the bell, I was still vacuuming.

I should have vacuumed the day before.

YOLANDA: I'm sure she didn't mind. She knows you have a lot to do.
MOLLY: Then I asked her to come in, and I forgot to take her coat.

I _____

YOLANDA: That's not so bad.
MOLLY: I didn't tell her about the broken couch. She sat down and the seat collapsed.

I _____

YOLANDA: She probably thought it was funny.
MOLLY: I don't think so. Then I offered her a cup of tea, but she wanted coffee. I didn't have any in the kitchen.

I _____

in the afternoon. Then she asked me about my life. I didn't know what to say. I just kept talking on and on. I never asked her about herself.

I _____.
(short form)

YOLANDA: She probably knew you were nervous. Don't worry.
MOLLY: And then I was trying to carry everything at once—the teapot, the cups and saucers, the sugar, and the cream. I dropped the tray because I was trying to balance everything.

I _____ at once.
(negative)

YOLANDA: What a day! What happened then?
MOLLY: She was really very nice. She helped me pick everything up. But I kept apologizing over and over again.

YOLANDA: Oh, you _____.
(negative)

She sounds like a nice woman. I bet she understood.

Exercise 5 _Could Have_ and _Could Not Have_

Shakespeare's famous tragedy _Othello_ is a story of love and death.
Desdemona was a beautiful Italian girl who fell in love with an exotic Moor
named Othello. She loved to listen to his stories of faraway places. She
didn't know him very well, but she decided to marry him against the advice
of others. After the marriage they were only happy for a short time. Iago, a
trusted friend of Othello, told his wife to steal Desdemona's handkerchief.
This handkerchief was a special present from Othello to his wife.
Desdemona knew Othello liked the handkerchief a lot, so she lied to him
about losing it. Iago told Othello that Desdemona had given the handkerchief to another lover. He told Othello that Desdemona was unfaithful. Iago
used the handkerchief as proof. Othello became wildly jealous. He believed
Iago and never questioned Desdemona to find out if Iago was telling the
truth. Othello strangled his wife because he was so jealous that he didn't
want her to love another.

Directions
Read the following sentences about _Othello_. Then write sentences with
could have when you want to say something was possible but wasn't done
and with _could not have_ when you want to say something was impossible.

1. Othello made many mistakes. He didn't have to trust Iago or kill his

   young wife.

   a. He _____could have talked_____ to Desdemona.
   (talk)

   b. _____ to listen to Iago.
   (refuse)

   c. _____ Iago away.
   (send)

   d. _____ Desdemona what Iago had said.
   (tell)

   e. _____

2. Desdemona never overheard the conversations between Othello and

   Iago. Do you think she understood why her husband turned against her?

   _____
   (negative)

3. Iago never told his wife, Emilia, why he wanted her to take the handker-

   chief from Desdemona. Emilia _____ he
   (negative, know)

   planned to use it to trap Othello.

4. Both Desdemona and Othello trusted Iago as their true friend. They believed he had only their best interests in mind. Therefore they never talked directly to each other.

a. They _____ their feelings to each other.
   (express)

b. _____ their doubts.
   (share)

c. _____ Iago's motivation in telling
   (examine)
   them such terrible stories.

Exercise 6 Integration

Two thousand years ago 20,000 people lived in Pompeii, a city in southern Italy off the Bay of Naples. Pompeii was built at the foot of Vesuvius, a volcano 4,000 feet high.

Directions
Select the correct modal perfect form and complete the sentences. Use *may, might, should, must,* and *could.*

1. Pompeii had a lot of ships in its harbor. Many wealthy Romans came to stay in its resorts. Statues and mosaics decorated many of its buildings. What kind of a city was Pompeii?

   Pompeii must have been a rich Roman seaport.

2. For four days before the volcano Vesuvius erupted on August 24, A.D. 79, there were tremors and vibrations under the ground. The volcano was smoking and no one could get water from the wells. How do you think people in Pompeii felt?

   _____

3. Less than twenty years before, there had been a serious earthquake in Pompeii. Some people who felt the earth trembling on August 20, A.D. 79, decided to leave Pompeii right away. Why did they decide to leave?

   _____

4. Many people laughed at those who left. They didn't believe there was any reason to be afraid. This mistake cost many of them their lives.

They _____

5. Many people went to the resorts of Pompeii to relax and have a good time. They refused to believe anything bad could happen to them there. This area was so beautiful that they didn't realize how dangerous the volcano was.

_____

6. When the volcano erupted, it forced a lot of rocks and lava to shoot up-wards. There was also a huge flame that flew up into the sky, and there was a great crash. The earth shook.

Buildings _____

People _____

Did the eruption surprise them? It _____. (short form)

7. People saw a great black cloud in the sky. It was like night even though it was daytime. Then the cloud started raining poisonous material. It rained on the nearby towns. Some people made the mistake of going down into their cellars rather than trying to escape by sea. They got trapped in their cellars.

_____

8. Some time passed between the eruption of the volcano and the rain of poisonous material. Not everyone who died had to die. There was some time to escape.

More people _____,

but they panicked and made foolish mistakes.

9. Pliny the Elder, a famous Roman writer, was across the bay when the volcano erupted. So was his nephew, Pliny the Younger. Pliny the Elder received a note from someone across the bay. It was a call for

help from a close friend. Pliny decided to go across the bay to help people there. His nephew did not go with him. Why not? Give two possibilities.

He _____ (or)

He _____

10. Pliny the Elder took his ship and crew and sailed across the bay. He sailed exactly toward the place of greatest danger. Everyone else was going in the opposite direction. Pliny's men asked him to turn back. He refused. Why?

He _____

11. There was enough room to turn the boat around. There was also enough time, even though some poisonous material was starting to fall from the sky.

Pliny _____,

but he didn't. He went on shore to look for his friend. Later he died on the beach.

12. The city was rediscovered in 1847. At first people were amazed by the gold and treasures of the city. They didn't try to keep everything exactly as it was. They were more interested in stealing the treasures.

_____

It wasn't until the nineteenth century that the city was excavated by responsible archeologists. Now it is preserved almost exactly as it was on the day the volcano erupted in A.D. 79.

Expressing Your Ideas: Speaking and Writing

1. Have you ever done anything you consider dangerous? For example, skydiving, scuba diving, car racing? Or some sport that wasn't very safe? Why did you do it? Was it more exciting because it was dangerous? Why do people do dangerous things? Have you ever made a dangerous mistake? What was it? What happened?

2. People sometimes live in dangerous places—in areas where there are a lot of earthquakes, near active volcanoes, underneath a dam that could burst. Why do you think people live in these areas? How does it

influence their lives? Have you ever lived in a place you considered dangerous? Why did you leave or remain there?

3. Many people put their lives in danger for different reasons. For some, danger is connected to a sport. Others risk their lives in order to help people. Many scientists and explorers have done this. Tell about some famous person or someone you know who has done this. Can you imagine yourself risking your life for others?

4. Have you ever done anything foolish or dangerous because you didn't want to look like a coward or because you were afraid of what other people would think? Tell about it.

5. Discuss some of the mistakes you made in your life, important mistakes. For example, a time you did something and lost a friend, a time you didn't say something you should have said, a time you didn't study for an important exam, a time you didn't make an application for something you really wanted. What prevented you from doing what you should have done?

6. Write about a time when you almost got married, but you didn't. Should you have? Why or why not?

7. Discuss an accident that happened to you or someone you know—a time you were in a car crash, a plane crash, or a time you were in a boat that capsized. What could have prevented these accidents? Should you have done something you didn't do? Should someone else have done something he or she didn't do?

8. Write about a famous mistake in your country's history. What should have happened that didn't happen, or what shouldn't have happened that did? Describe the causes of the mistake. If you don't know, guess about the causes.

9. Write about a famous court case or a famous trial in which some mistake was made. Tell who was tried, whether the person was condemned or freed, and what you think should have happened. Tell why.

10. A serious accident occurred near Harrisburg, Pennsylvania, on March 28, 1979, at the Three Mile Island Nuclear Power Plant. A lot of radiation was released into the environment. A lot of people left the area to avoid the radiation. A lot of people stayed. Many mistakes were made. What could the government and the nuclear industry have done to prevent this accident? What do you think people from Harrisburg should and shouldn't have done at the time? Do you know about any other nuclear accidents around the world?

Simple Passive: Present, Past, and Future

The Jefferson Memorial and the Washington Monument.

Theme: Government

Grammar: Simple Passive: Present, Past, and Future

Dialogue

YOLANDA: What's wrong, Jack? You look ill.

JACK: You know I **was hired** part time at the observatory[1] this semester. I just got my first paycheck.

YOLANDA: So why are you so down?[2] You should be happy.

JACK: I was ... before. But when I looked at my paycheck and saw how much money **was taken** out in taxes, I couldn't believe it.

YOLANDA: I feel the same way. Taxes are already high, and the president wants to raise them next year.

JACK: What! If taxes **are raised** any more, I won't have any salary left. Is he kidding?

YOLANDA: No. You know inflation is skyrocketing.[3] I guess the president hopes that inflation **will be slowed** by increasing taxes. When taxes **are raised**, people have less money to spend.

JACK: Great, but how do I make ends meet?[4] I can't live on my income now.

YOLANDA: Everyone's having the same problem. We **are** all **going to be asked** to sacrifice a little.

JACK: What's it like for you? When **were** you last **given** a raise? **Are** your raises **determined** by the cost of living?

YOLANDA: Not exactly. My salary **is increased** only about 5 percent every year, but the rate of inflation is much higher.

JACK: Why **isn't** something **done** about it? What are those idiots in Washington doing?

YOLANDA: Well, the president doesn't know what to do. If the tax bill **is passed**, he'll be very unpopular. He probably **won't be reelected**. But if it **isn't passed**, the economy will get worse, and he'**ll be blamed**.

JACK: Well, I'm glad I'm not the president.

YOLANDA: Who knows ... you might do a better job.

---

1. *observatory:* a special building where astronomers can observe the stars.
2. *down:* unhappy, depressed (colloquial).
3. *skyrocketing:* going up very fast.
4. *make ends meet:* have enough money to pay all your bills.

Explanation

Up to now we have studied verb tenses only in the *active* voice. The active voice means that the subject of the sentence performs the action of the verb in that sentence.

Examples: Active Voice

1.   In the United States, citizens **elect** the president.
2.   The media **announce** the results the day after the election.

In the passive voice the subject of the sentence does not perform the action of the verb.

Examples: Passive Voice

1.   In the United States, the president **is elected** (by the citizens).
2.   The results of the election **are announced** the day after (by the media).

We use the passive voice when we want to put more emphasis on the person or thing that receives the action than on the person or thing that does the action. In the sentence "In the United States, the president is elected (by the citizens)," the word "citizens" is called the agent. The agent is the person or thing that performs the action of a verb in the passive voice. (The citizens elect the president.)

The passive form of any tense contains two things: the verb *to be* and the past participle.

PAST   subject + *was* (*not*) + past participle
                        were

Jack was hired at the observatory.

PRESENT   subject + *is*   (*not*) + past participle
                        are

Yolanda's salary is increased about 5%0 a year.

FUTURE   subject + *am*   (*not*) + going to be + past participle
                        is
                        are
                        will   be   + past participle

The president will be blamed if the economy gets worse.

Part 2 Use of the Passive Voice

Explanation
We use the passive voice for different reasons:

A. Sometimes we know who did something and we want to talk about who received an action instead. In the sentence "The president is elected" we know he is elected by the people. If the agent is common knowledge, we don't use it. Look at the following examples for this use of the passive:

Examples: Past
George Washington, the first president of the United States, **was elected** in 1789. He served eight years, or two terms, as president. Then he decided not to run again. The custom **was established** at that time for a president to serve no more than two terms. It was not until Franklin D. Roosevelt **was elected** to a third and fourth term that this custom **was broken**.

Examples: Present
Elections **are followed** with great interest in the United States. The president is the head of the political system, and presidential elections **are held** every four years. Many people work under the president. Many of them **are not elected** though. Members of his cabinet **are appointed**.

Examples: Future
Presidents have usually been men who are white, Protestant, and married with families. John F. Kennedy broke one of these traditions. He was a Catholic. But the traditions of race and sex **aren't going to be broken** very easily. Some people are trying to change these traditions though. Shirley Chisholm, a black woman, ran for president in 1972 but was defeated. Some people hope a black or a woman **will be elected** president of the United States someday. However, it seems likely that a person from a minority group **will not be elected** president in the very near future.

B. The following paragraph is about Mount Vernon, the house George Washington lived in. In this paragraph we want to concentrate on Mount Vernon and its history, not on the Washington family. Therefore *Mount Vernon, the furniture,* and *a writing desk* become the subjects of sentences, and the verbs are usually in the passive voice. Sometimes we add the agent (*by the family*) to give additional information.

Examples
Mount Vernon is the name of the estate where George Washington lived. The house **was built** not far from Washington, D.C., on the Potomac River. It is a beautiful house and interesting to visit. No one knows exactly when the main part **was constructed**, but we know that it **was owned** for many generations *by the Washington family* before George inherited it. More sections **were planned** and **added** later *by George Washington* when he lived there. Some of the furniture in the house is original. Upstairs in the

"blue bedroom" is a writing desk that **was imported** from France *by Washington's wife, Martha.* The kitchen contains some original utensils that **were used** *by slaves* to prepare the meals.

C. Often we use the passive voice when we want to describe a process or how something is done. In this case the agent may be completely unknown or not very important.

Examples
One of the duties of government is to mint money. Most coins **are made** in Philadelphia, but some **are also minted** in Denver. Minerals such as copper, zinc, and silver **are delivered** to these mints and **are used** to make coins. Pennies **are made** mostly of copper. Dimes and quarters have no silver, but half dollars contain 40 percent silver. The mottoes "In God We Trust," "E Pluribus Unum," and "Liberty" **are placed** on all coins. The date **is also stamped** on each coin. Gold **isn't used** in coins anymore. Gold which **is owned** by the government **is stored** in Fort Knox.

D. Questions

PAST	(question word) + was/were + subject + past participle?

Was Jack hired full-time?

PRESENT	(question word) + am/is/are + subject + past participle?

How are Yolanda's wages determined?

FUTURE	(question word) + will + subject + be

+ past participle?

Will the President be

reelected?

(question word) + am/is/are + subject + going to be

+ past participle?

Are taxes going to be

raised?

Examples

ARNOLD: Boy, money isn't worth much anymore, is it?

YOLANDA: I know silver dollars aren't made with silver anymore. The price of silver is too high.

ARNOLD: How about pennies? **Are** they still **made** of copper?

YOLANDA: I don't think so. Going back to[5] silver dollars, what ever happened to that Susan B. Anthony coin? **Was** it **taken** out of circulation?

ARNOLD: Yes, it sure was. No one liked it. It was too easy to confuse with a quarter. Hey, *why* **was** Susan B. Anthony **chosen** for that coin?

YOLANDA: She was a famous suffragette. She worked hard to get the vote for women.

ARNOLD: Paper dollars wear out really fast. **Is** a new silver dollar **going to be minted** soon?

YOLANDA: I don't know. It takes a long time to design a coin.

Exercise 1   Passive Voice: Past and Present

A. Fill in the blanks with the correct form of the passive voice. Use the past or present passive.

Monticello is the name of a famous American home. It ___is located___
(locate)
near Charlottesville, Virginia, and looks out over the beautiful hills and

mountains of Virginia. The house _____ in the 1770s by
(build)
Thomas Jefferson, the third president of the United States. It

_____ of red brick and wood, and the construction of the
(make)
house _____ by the slaves of Thomas Jefferson. Most of the
(carry out)
materials, such as bricks and nails, _____ on the plantation.
(produce)
The house _____ by Jefferson himself. It is a beautiful ex-
(design)
ample of Classical Revival architecture. The inside of the house was

also beautiful and very different from other houses of the period. For

example, Jefferson loved space, so he built the beds into the walls.

---

5. *going back to:* I want to return to the subject (of silver dollars).

Storage space _____ under the beds. Jefferson's bed
(build)

_____ between his bedroom and his study. When the bed
(place)

wasn't in use, it _____ by ropes. This home has many
(raise)

interesting inventions of Jefferson's.

Monticello is open to the public and _____ by a great
(visit)

many tourists each summer. The house and the grounds _____
(maintain)

by a group of interested citizens. A small fee _____ to help
(charge)

with the upkeep. Monticello is well worth a visit.

B. Choose a famous building that is important in the history of your
    country. Tell when, how, where, and why it was built. Give a little of its
    history.

Exercise 2   Test Your Knowledge of American History and Politics

Directions

Make questions using the passive voice. The subject and verb that you must
use are given. The question word is given in parentheses. Form the
questions in the passive first. Then write the answers in complete
sentences. Work in groups to make the questions, then see if any of your
classmates know the answers. If no one knows the answer, look at the end of
the exercise.

A. Past

1. (Where)   the first battles of the Revolutionary War   fight

    Where were the first battles of the Revolutionary
    War fought?

2. (When)   the Constitution   write

    _____

3. (How many)   amendments   add at that time

_____

4. (What)   these amendments   call

_____

5. (When)   the South   defeat

_____

6. (Where)   Abraham Lincoln   assassinate

_____

7. (How many times)   Franklin D. Roosevelt   elect

_____

B. Present

1. (How)   a presidential candidate   choose

_____

2. (?)   the presidential finances   make public

_____

3. (How)   the votes   count

_____

4. (How many)   representatives   elect from each state

_____

5. (How many)   senators   elect from each state

_____

6. (How)   federal judges   choose

_____

7. (How long)   Supreme Court judges   permit to stay in their job

_____

C. Future

Directions

Form questions about the future. These are questions that many Americans are asking nowadays.

1. A black woman   elect president

Will a black woman ever be elected president?

2. New political parties   form

_____

3. The voting age   lower from eighteen to sixteen

_____

(Today election campaigns are primarily financed by private donations.)

4. Presidential election campaigns   finance by the government

_____

5. Taxes   raise

_____

6. Social programs such as socialized medicine   enact by Congress

_____

7. A world government   form

_____

D. Ask more questions about American history. Use either the active or the passive voice.

E. Interview a classmate. Find out about how his or her country was founded. Were battles fought? Was a revolution fought? Was your country liberated by a famous person? Was it colonized by another country?

A. 1. Lexington and Concord in Massachusetts
    2. 1789
    3. Ten
    4. Bill of Rights
    5. 1865
    6. In Ford's Theater in Washington, D.C.
    7. Four
B. 1. At national conventions
    2. Yes
    3. Usually by machine
    4. It depends on the population
    5. Two
    6. By appointment
    7. For life

Exercise 3   Active and Passive Voice

A. Fill in the blanks with the correct verb form. Decide between the active
    and the passive voice. The passage describes a process and is mostly in
    the present tense.

Everyone who works in the United States ___*pays*___ an
                                              (pay)
income tax. Every month taxes _are taken out_ of an employee's
                                 (take out)
paycheck. First, the federal tax _____ from the total
                                      (subtract)
amount of the check. Some states _____ an income tax, so
                                      (have)
the state income tax _____ too. In addition, if you live in
                          (take out)
New York City, a city income tax _____. Of course, a large
                                      (take out)
amount _____ of everyone's salary for Social Security.
          (take out)
This means that when a person _____, a certain amount of
                                  (retire)
money _____ to him or her every month by the federal
          (pay)
government.

Every January tax forms _____ to every worker by the
(send out)

federal government. These forms _____ and _____
(fill out)   (return)

before April 15. If a person has paid too much money to the government,

this extra money _____. However, if the taxpayer still
(refund)

_____ money to the government, a check for the difference
(owe)

_____ with the tax forms. If the forms _____
(include)   (negative, mail)

by midnight of April 15, a penalty _____.
(add)

There are more taxes, of course. Americans also _____
(pay)

taxes if they _____ property. These property taxes
(have)

_____ by the city government. They _____ for
(collect)   (use)

public schools, local roads, public hospitals, and many public services,

such as police and fire departments. Finally, almost every time an

American _____ something, he _____ a sales
(buy)   (pay)

tax, which can be anywhere from 2 to 8 percent, depending on the

state. No wonder people say there is no end to taxes.

B. Describe how citizens are taxed in your country.

Exercise 4   Change from Active to Passive

Directions
Look at the following paragraphs. All the sentences are in the active voice.
Rewrite the paragraph, and in every sentence where it is possible, change
the main verb to the passive voice. Decide when it makes sense to add the
agent.

Before a presidential election in the United States, candidates campaign
very hard. They begin their campaigns as much as one year before the
election. Candidates spend a great deal of money. They do this in a number
of different ways. For example, the government allows taxpayers to donate

$1 of their taxes to presidential campaigns. In addition, business corporations and labor unions contribute heavily. They make these contributions public, of course. Finally, private citizens may contribute. Candidates give special fund-raising dinners; at these dinners, people sometimes pay $250 a plate. The government limits the amount anyone can contribute.

One reason that campaigns are so expensive is that candidates often advertise on TV, and television time is expensive. Television is a new element in American political life. Some say political "spots"[6] are like commercials. Because spots are short—usually about thirty seconds—candidates don't discuss the issues. Often cameramen film them with their families or in a local neighborhood talking to voters. Critics of television spots ask these questions: Is a candidate's image becoming more important than the issues? Do the American voters become familiar with the issues?

Before a presidential election in the United States, candidates campaign very hard. Their campaigns are begun as much as one year before the election.

Exercise 5 Future Passive

Directions
Fill in the blanks with the correct verb tense. Choose between the active and the passive voice.

Within the next two weeks, a congressman is going to introduce a bill to lower taxes. This bill will begin in the House of Representatives, because all tax bills must start here. In order for this bill to become a law, it must go through many steps. Here are the steps that this bill will follow.

First this bill _will be sent_ to a committee in the House, where it
        (send)

_____. Experts _____ to testify about the ad-
(debate)   (ask)

vantages and disadvantages of this bill. After the bill _____,
                                    (discuss)

---

6. *spot:* a short television or radio highlighting of a person or product, usually lasting fifteen or thirty seconds.

it _____ on. If it _____ a majority vote, it
    (vote)   (receive)

_____ to the floor of the House. If it _____ a ma-
  (go)   (negative, receive)

jority vote, it _____ . On the floor of the House, it _____
            (die)   (discuss and vote on)

again. If it _____ a majority vote, it _____ to
        (receive)   (send)

a committee in the Senate. Here it _____ , and experts
                      (debate)

_____ again. Once more, if it _____ a majority
  (testify)   (negative, receive)

vote, it _____ . If it _____ by this committee, it
      (die)   (pass)

_____ to the floor of the Senate. After the bill _____
  (go)   (reach)

the floor, it _____ the same process again. If the bill
         (follow)

_____ by the Senate, it _____ to the president. If
  (pass)   (send)

he _____ it, it _____ a law. If he _____ it, it
  (sign)   (become)   (veto)

_____ to the House and the Senate. If it _____ a
  (return)   (receive)

two-thirds majority vote, it _____ a law without the president's
           (become)

signature.

Exercise 6   *Future Passive*

Directions

Americans are naturally mistrustful of government power. They watch as government grows in size and are afraid of the consequences. They fear that their lives will be controlled by "Big Brother"[7] and that they will lose their individuality. Here are some fears and predictions about the future. Read the following predictions and discuss in groups or with a classmate whether or not it is possible for any of these things to happen. Give reasons for your opinions.

1. People's lives will be controlled by the government in the future.
2. People will be told what to study.
3. People will be told what career to enter.

---

7. *Big Brother:* A government that controls all aspects of our lives.

4. People will be told when they can get married.
5. The number of children people can have will be regulated.
6. Only the most intelligent and attractive people will be allowed to have children.
7. Gender, I.Q., and athletic ability will be decided on before birth.
8. The gender of children will be determined by the government.
9. Antisocial people will be reeducated. Prisons will be a thing of the past.
10. People's moods and personalities will be regulated by drugs.

Make some predictions of your own about future developments in government or science.

Exercise 7   Integration

Directions
Look at the following statements. Choose one of them and make a report to your class on the statement.

1. Choose a product and describe the process by which it is made (food products such as cheese or beer, clothing, movies, or any product that your country is famous for or you know about).
2. Tell how a government official is elected in your country: for example, the president or prime minister.
3. Describe how many branches or divisions of government there are in your country. Tell what the functions of each are.
4. Choose a famous person. Tell when he or she was born, where he or she was brought up and educated, and what he or she achieved.

Expressing Your Ideas: Speaking and Writing

1. Are people taxed at a high rate in your country?
2. Are taxes based on how much a person earns? What do you think of this?
3. Do you agree with how the money is spent in your country? In the United States?
4. Can you think of any programs where the tax money was misspent?
5. Do people receive good services for their taxes in your country? In the United States?
6. Are taxes taken out of your paycheck, or do you pay them at the end of the year?

7. Do people pay sales taxes and property taxes in your country? Are they high?

8. Name several items that are taxed in your country and several that are tax-free. In the United States, for example, cigarettes are heavily taxed, but most food isn't taxed. What items do you think should be tax-free? Shouldn't be tax-free? Explain why.

9. Are most people honest when they pay their taxes?

10. People are beginning to protest against the high rate of taxation and are voting for tax reductions. Is this happening in your country?

Perfect Passives, Continuous Passives, Modal Passives

Columbia University Graduation, 1980.

Theme: Education

Grammar: Perfect Passives, Continuous Passives, Modal Passives

---

Dialogue

MOLLY: Yolanda, I have big news to tell you. I've made a very big decision.

YOLANDA: Well, come on. What is it?

MOLLY: I'm going to apply to medical school!

YOLANDA: You're what? But I thought you wanted to teach.

MOLLY: I've decided to give that up.[1] Teaching jobs **are being cut** back now at many universities.

YOLANDA: Yes, and I've read that a number of liberal arts colleges[2] **have been closed**.

MOLLY: I have a friend who finished his Ph.D. in history last year. He's been looking for a teaching position for a year, and he**'s been turned down**[3] by every school so far. He **must have been rejected** by about fifteen colleges.

YOLANDA: I suppose a Ph.D. in the humanities[4] isn't worth very much these days.

MOLLY: No, it isn't. And even if you find a teaching job, the salary is very low.

YOLANDA: Yeah, college teachers **should be paid** more. But Molly, it's very difficult to get into medical school today.

MOLLY: I know. **I've been told** the same thing by everyone.

YOLANDA: How are you going to pay for it? It costs a fortune to go to medical school now.

MOLLY: Maybe I can get a loan from the federal government. I have a friend who is in medical school now, and all his expenses **are being paid** by the government. Some rural areas of the country really need doctors. If you agree to work there for a year for a low salary, one year of your medical school will be paid by the government.

YOLANDA: Really? That's an interesting possibility. Your whole life is changing. I think it's wonderful.

---

1. *to give something up:* to stop.
2. *liberal arts college:* a college that has courses in the humanities—literature, history, philosophy, and the fine arts—but does not emphasize technical and professional fields.
3. *to turn down:* to reject or refuse.
4. *humanities:* courses in literature, philosophy, history, and the fine arts.

In chapter 20 you studied the passive voice of the simple present, simple past, and future tenses. In this chapter we will show you the passive voice of several other tenses and also of modal auxiliary verbs. Review the general explanation of the passive voice before you do this chapter.

Part 1   The Perfect Passives

A. The Passive Voice of the Simple Present Perfect Tense

Explanation

Review the uses of the present perfect tense in chapters 16 and 17. Do not try to use the passive voice with the present perfect continuous tense. We almost never use it. Use the active voice or the simple present perfect passive.

Statements: subject + *have* (not) *been* + past participle
                              has

A number of liberal arts colleges have been closed.

Questions: (Question + *have* + subject + *been* + past
               word   *has*   participle?

Have any colleges been closed?

Examples

Many American universities have serious financial problems today because they are losing students. In the past several years a decrease in the number of students **has been reported** by most universities. Some small universities **have been forced** to close because they don't have enough students. One reason for the decrease in the number of students is that today there are fewer students of college age than in the 1950s and 1960s. There is also another important reason: many students with master's degrees and even Ph.D.s **have been told** that there are no jobs for them, so many students don't go on for advanced degrees.

Have students **been discouraged** by this difficult job situation?
    Yes, they **have been.** They feel that even having a Ph.D. does not guarantee a good job.

Which departments of universities **have been hurt** the most by the decrease in the number of students?
    The humanities departments **have been** because students with degrees in such areas as history, literature, and languages have a harder time finding a job than students with degrees in engineering or business.

Exercise 1   Present Perfect Passive

A.   Fill in the blanks, using the passive voice of the present perfect tense.

Seniors[5] in college have started to think very carefully about the deci-

sion to enter graduate school. At Harvard, 94 percent of the graduating

class of 1978 said that they planned to continue their education in

graduate school, but only 40 percent said that they planned to continue

immediately. This is the lowest proportion in twenty years. This change

has been reported by other colleges around the United States. Medical
 (report)

schools have always had more applicants than any other graduate

school, but even medical schools _____ by this change. In
                                      (affect)

recent years a 10 percent decrease in the number of applications

_____ by the Association of Medical Colleges. Many
     (report)

students _____ to explain their reasons for postponing
              (ask)

graduate studies. Some say that they are sick and tired of going to

school after eight or nine years of elementary school, four years of high

school, and four years of college. They also want to get work

experience before they continue their studies. Also, because tuition

_____ so much in recent years, many students need to
     (raise)

work to save money before they can afford graduate school. This change

_____ by educators. They think postponing graduate work
     (welcome)

is a good idea because the students will have time to mature.

---

5. *seniors:* students in their fourth year of college.

B. Write questions using the passive voice of the present perfect tense.

American high-school students must take a standardized test in mathematics and verbal ability called a Scholastic Aptitude Test (S.A.T.) before they can apply to college. The score on the test is a major factor in a college's decision to accept or reject an applicant. The College Entrance Examination Board has been using these tests for many years.

1. How long *have these tests been used* by the College Entrance
   _____(use)_____
   Examination Board?

   Since 1947, when the Educational Testing Service of Princeton,

   New Jersey, began making such tests.

2. How many students _____ to take these tests since
   _____(require)_____
   1947?

   Millions. About 1,200,000 high-school seniors take the tests each

   year.

3. _____ the questions from one year's test ever

   _____ on another test?
   ____(use)____
   Yes, they have been. In the past all questions and answers were

   kept secret.

4. _____ this system of testing ever _____
   _____(criticize)_____

   or _____?
   ____(question)____
   Yes, in New York State a "truth in testing" law was passed in 1979.

   This law requires manufacturers of standardized tests to publish

   the questions and to let students see their answer sheets.

5. For what other reasons _____ these tests

   _____?
   ____(criticize)____

Some people say there are too many possibilities for error in scoring the tests. Also, some people argue that the tests do not measure imagination, creativity, or motivation—qualities which are also necessary in college work. Others say that the tests are culturally biased.

C. Prepare a brief talk for your class on these subjects.

1. What changes have taken place in recent years in higher education in your country? Have fewer students been admitted to colleges and universities, or has enrollment increased? Why? Have entrance requirements been lowered or raised? Have many new universities been built?

2. What changes have taken place in your country's economy, society, or government in recent years? For example, has production of a particular product been increased or decreased or promoted recently? Has more of a particular product been exported or imported recently? Have taxes been increased? Have new programs been started to help poor people? Have demonstrations or protests been made against the government? Has a new leader recently been elected?

3. Have your country's society and culture been changed by outside influences in the past five or ten years? Has the structure of the family been influenced or weakened by some changes? Have women been influenced by the women's liberation movement? Have divorce laws been liberalized? How has the family been affected by this? Have new programs that affect the family (such as birth control programs) been started by the government?

B. The Passive Voice of the Simple Past Perfect Tense

Explanation
Review the uses of the past perfect in chapter 18. Do not try to use the passive voice with the past perfect continuous. Use the active voice or the simple past perfect passive.

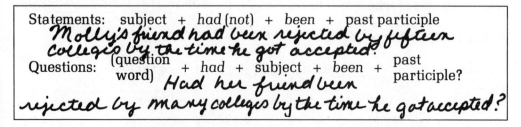

Statements: subject + *had* (not) + *been* + past participle

Molly's friend had been rejected by fifteen colleges by the time he got accepted.

Questions: (question word) + *had* + subject + *been* + past participle?

Had her friend been rejected by many colleges by the time he got accepted?

Examples

The United States has a system of free public education. Thomas Jefferson was president from 1801 to 1809. He was one of the first Americans who believed in free public education, and he fought long and hard for this system. Many other people took up the fight after he died. However, public education did not develop quickly. Between 1800 and 1870, only about 50 percent of school-age children attended school. People who believed in the importance of education for all continued to push for public education, and by 1918 compulsory school attendance laws **had been passed** in all states. Before 1918, the decision to send children to school or keep them at home **had been left** to the parents.

Other changes in education occurred during the nineteenth century. New subjects such as history, English grammar, and music were added. What subjects **had** children **been taught** before? In most cases, they had been taught only reading, writing, and arithmetic.

Special schools for teachers were opened beginning in 1820. How much education **had** teachers **been required** to have before this time? Most had been required to have only an elementary-school education.

Exercise 2 Past Perfect Passive

Directions

Fill in the blanks, using the passive voice of the past perfect tense.

Horace Mann is one of the most famous educators in American history.

He brought about many changes in the field of education. He became the

secretary of the new Massachusetts State Board of Education in 1837, a

time when the public-school system was in very bad condition. Mann fought

long and hard to change it. By the end of his twelve-year period of service,

public interest in the improvement of public education *had been awakened*.
(awaken)

School problems _____ to light and _____. A move-
(bring)   (discuss)

ment for better teaching and better pay for teachers _____, and
(start)

training schools for teachers _____. The curricula of the
(establish)

schools _____ to include history and geography.
(expand)

In Horace Mann's time, most colleges for men and women were separate.

Mann was a strong believer in coeducation.[6] In 1853 he became the first president of Antioch College, one of the first coeducational schools. By the end of Mann's term in office, the practicality of coeducation _____
(demonstrate)
and the academic standards of the college _____.
(raise)

Part 2 The Passive Voice of the Continuous Tenses

Explanation
The only tenses in which we use the continuous passive are present continuous and past continuous. See chapters 1 and 9 for the uses of these tenses.

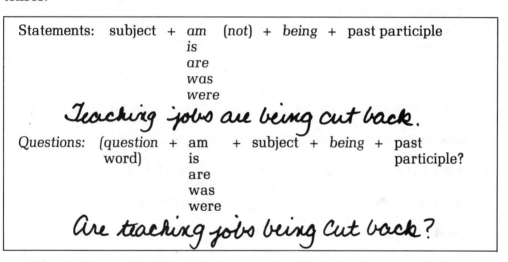

Statements: subject + am (not) + being + past participle
is
are
was
were

Teaching jobs are being cut back.

Questions: (question + am + subject + being + past
word) is participle?
are
was
were

Are teaching jobs being cut back?

Examples: Present Continuous
Many changes are happening in American education today. Developments in technology **are being used** in the classroom. Children **are being taught** mathematics with calculators. Television **is being used** to teach basic reading and mathematics.

Are computers **being experimented** with in the classroom?
Yes, they are.
What subject **are** they **being used** to teach?
At Stanford University in California computers are being used to teach languages.

---

6. *coeducation:* men and women attending the same school.

Examples: Past Continuous

Not all of these new methods are successful. A number of years ago, universities experimented with television in college lectures. Professors recorded their lectures on videotapes, which were later played in class. The professors were not present in the classroom. This new method **was being used** when studies came out showing that students were not learning. One professor received an unpleasant surprise when he entered his classroom. His lecture **was being shown** on the television, but no students were in the room.

Exercise 3   Present Continuous Passive

A.   Fill in the blanks, using the passive voice of the present continuous tense. We can use the simple present passive in several sentences here, but the present continuous passive emphasizes that these changes are happening nowadays.

Here is one of the changes that is happening in education today. In the traditional classroom, the teacher is in complete control. The teacher decides when the class will study which subject, and all students must work on the same subject at the same time. In some schools a new method called "the open classroom" _is being used_ these days. More
(use)

and more students _____ to choose for themselves which
(permit)

subject they want to work on and for how long. Students can work by themselves or in groups. Children are usually enthusiastic about this new method, but some parents are beginning to have doubts. According to these concerned parents, the children _____ too much
(give)

freedom nowadays, not enough time _____ on real work,
(spend)

and the children _____ the subjects which are most impor-
(negative, teach)

tant. In some schools that have experimented with the open classroom in the past, the traditional methods of teaching _____ nowadays.
(reinstate)

B. JACK is talking to ARNOLD on the phone.

JACK: I'm going crazy. I'm trying to type my job résumé and send out applications for jobs, and my apartment is a mess right now. Can I spend the next day or two at your place?

ARNOLD: Sure, but what's happening in your apartment?

JACK: It's *being painted*. All my furniture is in the middle of the
(paint)
room. And that's not all. The landlord decided to make several other repairs at the same time. A new shower_____,
(install)
and a new floor _____ down in the kitchen.
(put)

ARNOLD: _____ anything _____ about that
(do)
prehistoric stove you have?

JACK: Yes, it _____, too.
(replace)

ARNOLD: I suppose this means your rent _____, too.
(raise)

JACK: Yeah. It's going up $50 a month.

C. Prepare a brief talk on the subject of modern education. What new methods and theories are being used in the field of education in your country today? What about public schools and private schools? Are taxes being increased in order to build more public schools?

Part 3 The Passive Voice of Modals

A. Modal Passives: Present and Future

STATEMENTS

subject +
can
should
may
might
could
have/has to*
must (necessity)
would rather
had better
(not) + be + past participle

College teachers should be paid more.

*In American English the negative form is $\begin{Bmatrix} don't \\ doesn't \end{Bmatrix}$ have to.

QUESTIONS

(question word) +
can
should
could
+ subject + be + past participle?

Should teachers be paid more?

(or) (question word) + $\begin{matrix} do \\ does \end{matrix}$ + subject + have to + be

+ past participle? *Do children have to be given shots before they start public school?*

(or) (question word) + would + subject + rather + be

+ past participle? *Would you rather be sent to a private school or a public school?*

Examples

Integration of black and white students in schools is still a major issue in American education today. American law says that all children **must be given** an equal opportunity to get a good education. Before 1954, in many states black children weren't permitted to attend white schools. In 1954 the Supreme Court decided that segregated schools were unconstitutional. The law now says that black children **can't be segregated** in separate schools. It has been difficult to desegregate schools in some areas because black people and white people frequently live in different neighborhoods. Since children usually go to the school closest to their homes, this creates a different form of segregation.

How **can** this problem **be solved**? In some communities the law says that some children from white neighborhoods **have to be taken** by bus to schools in black neighborhoods, and some black children **must be bused** to schools in white neighborhoods. Many parents feel that busing **shouldn't be used** as a solution to the problem. Where **should** children **be sent** to school in these parents' opinion? They believe their children **should be sent** to school in their own neighborhoods.

Exercise 4   Modal Passives: Present and Future

A.   Write questions using the passive voice. If you have an opinion, answer them. Try to use the passive form of a modal auxiliary in your answer.

1.   Some people believe that schools have to be integrated in order for

children to receive an equal education. What's your opinion?

Do *schools have to be integrated* in order for
                (integrate)
children to receive an equal education?

Answer: _____

2.   Some schools have only white children or only black children

because the neighborhood is all white or all black. Many people

believe the problem should be solved by busing children. What's

your opinion?

How _____?
                (solve)

Answer: _____

3. Many parents feel busing should not be used as a solution. What do
    you think?

    Should _____?

    Answer: _____

B. Fill in the blanks with the passive voice.

    The United States has always been a country of immigrants. In the

big cities there are thousands of children in the public schools who

speak little or no English. Many teachers and parents feel that these

students cannot ___*be put*___ in the same class with native
                     (put)
speakers for many reasons. They might _____ by the other
                                            (ridicule)
students. They might _____ by their inability to do the
                          (discourage)
schoolwork and develop a bad attitude toward school. Also, the other

students might _____ back by students who can't speak
                    (hold)
English. Many parents and teachers believe that these children

shouldn't _____ in regular classes, but they don't think
                (place)
they should _____ in classes for slow learners either.
                  (place)
Massachusetts was the first state to pass a bilingual education law to

try to solve this problem. The law says that in schools that have a large

number of students who speak the same language but who can't speak

English, these students must _____ all their subjects in
                                   (teach)
their own native language. They also have to _____
                                                   (give)
classes in English as a second language so that after they learn enough

English, they can _____ in regular classes. Other states
                        (place)

have since passed such laws.

What's your opinion about this law? What do you think should be

done when a school has a large number of students who can't speak the

language of that country?

B. Modal Passives: Past

MODAL PERFECTS

subject +	may might could must should would rather	+ (not) have + been + past participle

More children should have been given an opportunity for education in the nineteenth century.

PAST TENSE OF <u>CAN</u>

subject + could (not) + be + past participle

Many children couldn't be sent to school because they lived on isolated farms far from any school.

PAST TENSE OF <u>HAVE TO</u>

subject +	had to didn't have to	+ be + past participle

Several colleges had to be closed in the 1970s because they ran out of money.

Examples

YOLANDA: There really aren't many women doctors, are there?
MOLLY: No, I've been reading about that. And do you know that there weren't any women doctors in the United States until 1847? Elizabeth Blackwell was the first woman doctor. She was turned down by twenty-eight medical schools before she was finally admitted.

YOLANDA: People **must have been shocked** by the idea of a woman doctor in those days.

MOLLY: They were. Her friends and relatives thought she was crazy when she told them that she wanted to be a doctor, but she **couldn't be persuaded** to change her mind. Also, her male classmates thought she **should not have been admitted** to the medical college. They treated her coldly at first, but finally she **had to be accepted** as an equal because she had the highest marks in the school.

Exercise 5   Modal Passives: Past

Directions

Fill in the blanks, using the past form of the modal auxiliary and verb under the blank in the passive voice. The dialogue continues.

YOLANDA: Any other woman *might have been discouraged* by so
(might/discourage)

much opposition.

MOLLY: Well, her father gave his daughters the same education as he

gave his sons. Everyone thought he was making a mistake. When

Elizabeth announced her decision to become a doctor, they said,

"She _____ all that geometry, Latin, and
(negative, should/teach)

history. She _____ only how to sew, cook,
(should/teach)

and sign her name. That's all a woman needs to know." Also, she

had a lot of responsibility when she was young. Her father died

when she was just eighteen. Something _____
(have to/do)

to support the family, so Elizabeth and her sisters started a

school in their home.

YOLANDA: Where did she get the idea to become a doctor?

MOLLY: She had a friend who was dying of cancer. While Elizabeth was

nursing her, the friend said that Elizabeth should become a

doctor. At first Elizabeth thought the suggestion was ridiculous

because in those days only men _____ to

(can/admit)

medical school, but she _____ by the sug-

(must/influence)

gestion because she later made the decision to study medicine.

YOLANDA: What did she do after she graduated from medical college?

MOLLY: She went to Paris to study surgery, but this dream

_____ because she caught an eye infection

(negative, can/fulfill)

from a sick patient and lost the sight of one eye.

YOLANDA: She _____ by that.

(must/discourage)

MOLLY: I suppose so, but when she went back to New York, she started a

hospital for nurses in America and later a medical school for

women. When she died in 1910, there were 8,000 women

doctors.

Exercise 6   Integration of All Passive Forms and the Active Voice

Directions

Fill in the blanks with the correct tense of the verb under the blank. Most of the blanks will be passive voice, but some are active voice. When you see modal + verb, choose the correct modal auxiliary verb, tense, and voice.

In the United States today there are many difficult problems in the field of education. However, people from all over the world come here to study because the United States has one of the best educational systems in the world. American education is particularly excellent in the field of science. In 1979 Americans won many of the Nobel prizes for science. There were three prizes in physics; Americans won two of them. There were two prizes for medicine, chemistry, and economics; Americans won one in each category.

In this dialogue JACK and ARNOLD are discussing the reasons for this.

ARNOLD: Hey, Jack. Why wasn't your name in the list of Nobel Prize winners in the newspaper today?

JACK: Don't worry. My turn will come. Do you know that since 1946 more than half the science prizes __*have been won*__ by
(win)
Americans?

ARNOLD: That's fantastic! I guess the sciences _____
(teach)
really well in this country. Also, American scientists _____
(give)
_____ more support from the government than scientists
in other countries.

JACK: That's true. I was reading an article about that in a magazine.
The government and the scientific community _____
(become)
_____ partners during World War II, and that special
partnership _____ and _____
(continue)   (encourage)
_____ by the government since then. Millions of dollars
_____ to science since the war. Also, the sit-
(give)
uation in America is different from that in many other countries
because American scientists _____ a great
(always/give)
deal of freedom in their research.

ARNOLD: Many scientists from other countries _____
(modal + attract)
to this country by this freedom.

JACK: Yes. Arno Penzias _____ here from Nazi
(come)
Germany. He _____ the Nobel Prize for
(win)
physics. And Einstein came here too, but he had won his Nobel Prize

before that. I think the government _____ all
(modal + give)

scientists freedom or they will never discover anything really revo-

lutionary. In some countries scientific research _____
(direct)

by a central agency. Scientists who _____
(belong)

to the agency _____, and promotions
(negative, modal + fire)

_____ on seniority instead of achievement.
(base)

ARNOLD: That's not good for research. If you want good scientists,

promotions _____ on the quality of their
(modal + base)

research.

JACK: What do you think about the future? Do you think the United

States will continue to do so well in science?

ARNOLD: Well, the situation might change because a lot of people in this

country think less money _____ on science
(modal + spend)

and more money _____ on helping the poor.
(modal + spend)

If the government _____ back on money for
(cut)

scientific research, who knows what will happen?

Expressing Your Ideas: Speaking and Writing

1. Are colleges and universities having financial problems in your country now? Why or why not? What is the government doing about the problem? Do the colleges get money from the government, from private sources, or from both?
2. If you have a bachelor's degree (four years of college or university) in your country, does it guarantee that you will find a job? If you have a master's degree (usually about two more years after the bachelor's degree), are your chances better? Are they better with a Ph.D.?

3. Which fields are the best to study if you want to be sure of finding a job? Do many professional people with master's degrees and Ph.D.s have trouble finding jobs in your country? Do many professionals leave your country to find better jobs in other countries?

4. Is teaching a respected profession in your country? Is it difficult for teachers to find jobs? Are teachers well paid? Would you like to be a teacher? Why or why not? In your country, how much education do you need to become an elementary-school teacher? A high-school teacher? A university professor?

5. Are there enough colleges and universities in your country, or do many students have to go to other countries to study? How large are the classes? Is anything being done to provide more colleges?

6. Describe the different levels of education in your country.

7. Are boys and girls educated in the same way in your country? Are schools coeducational? Do girls have the same opportunity as boys to go to college or to professional and technical schools?

8. Many people choose not to go to college. Are there good technical or secretarial schools in your country?

9. How do you feel about your education? Are you satisfied with your educational experiences so far?

Wish Clauses and
Present Unreal Conditional

Theme: *Inflation*

Grammar: *Present Unreal Conditional; Wish Clauses*

Dialogue

(YOLANDA is going to have all the people who work in her law office to her apartment for a buffet dinner. Now MOLLY and YOLANDA are in a supermarket.)

YOLANDA: Thanks for helping me with this dinner, Molly. I'm really nervous about it. **I hope it'll be a success. I wish I weren't a nervous wreck.**[1]

MOLLY: **If I were you, I wouldn't worry.** Your parties are always great. Everything will be fine. Wow, I don't believe these prices! They're outrageous.

YOLANDA: Look at this coffee. It costs almost twice as much as it did a month ago.

MOLLY: And it's not going to get any better. Prices are only going to go higher.

YOLANDA: If this keeps up, how on earth are we going to live? Sometimes **I wish we could all go back and live like we did a hundred years ago.**

MOLLY: You mean live without a washing machine? And **what would you do if you didn't have a telephone? I couldn't live the way they did a hundred years ago.**

YOLANDA: Sometimes **I just really wish I were rich.**

MOLLY: Yeah, **I wish someone would give me a million dollars.**

YOLANDA: Then **you could pay for all these groceries.** Seriously though, **would you be any happier if you had that much money?**

MOLLY: Maybe **I wouldn't be any happier if I were rich,** but **life would sure be a lot easier.**

---

1. *a nervous wreck:* an extremely nervous person.

Part 1   *Wish* Clauses: Present

A. Complete Statements

Explanation

When we talk about something that we want but that we don't think is possible to have, we often use *wish* clauses followed by another clause.

---

subject + *wish* + (*that*) + subject + past tense form

Yolanda wishes she weren't so nervous.

NOTES:

1. It's correct but not necessary to use *that*.
2. With the verb *be*, the correct form is *were* with both singular and plural subjects.

Examples

Americans *wish* that inflation **were** less severe.
We *wish* economists **knew** how to stop inflation.
We *wish* we **didn't have** to pay so much for the basic necessities.
Everybody *wishes* that taxes **weren't** so high.
People *wish* there **were** an easy answer to the problem.

B. Short Responses

Explanation

We often ask questions in the present tense which can be answered with a *wish* clause. Notice the short answer form is *did(n't)* or *were(n't)* or *could(n't)* after the *wish* clause.

Examples

Do economists have any real solutions to the inflation problem?
   No, they don't, but **Americans wish they did.**

Can young Americans afford new houses?
   No, they can't, but **they wish they could.**

Is there an easy way for the average person to beat inflation?
   There isn't really, but **we all wish there were.**

Part 2   *Present Unreal Conditionals: If Clauses*

A. Statements

Explanation

We use an unreal conditional pattern when we want to talk about situations that are contrary to existing facts or reality.

$$\text{If} + \text{subject} + \begin{Bmatrix} \text{past} \\ \text{tense} \\ \text{form} \end{Bmatrix} \dots \text{subject} + \begin{Bmatrix} \text{would} \\ \text{could} \\ \text{might} \end{Bmatrix} + \text{base form}$$

If I were rich, life would be a lot easier.

Examples

The United States imports about 8 million barrels of oil a day. Because it imports so much oil, the United States spends more money on imports than it earns on exports. **If the United States imported less oil, we would have a better balance of trade.** Americans sometimes use oil and other energy sources carelessly. **We would suffer less from inflation in the United States if we produced more oil ourselves.**

The United States uses more energy than any other nation on earth. **If Americans didn't use so many electrical appliances** and **if our homes weren't so overheated, we wouldn't consume so much energy.**

NOTES:

1. Notice that the *if* clause can come at the beginning or end of the sentence.
2. We often use a contraction with *would* in spoken English. The contraction is *'d* (*I'd, you'd, she'd, he'd, they'd*).

B. Questions and Short Answers

1. What **would** the United States **do** if the OPEC countries cut our oil supply in half?
   Who knows, but the country *would be* in turmoil.
2. The United States government taxes the interest that people earn on savings accounts. **Would** Americans **save** more money if the government didn't tax this interest?
   Maybe they *would*.
   (or)
   They might.

C. Continuous Form of the Present Unreal Conditional

Explanation

We often use the continuous form in the *if* clause or in the main clause.

Examples

The total amount of goods and services produced in the United States is dropping at the rate of 3.3 percent a year. The economy of the United States is heading for a recession. Our economic strength **wouldn't be declining** if productivity **weren't dropping** so sharply.

Exercise 1 <u>Wish</u> Clauses

A. Using *wish* clauses, make statements about the following situations.

Example

1. Arnold is trying to become a successful rock musician. Right now no one knows his name.

   He wishes *everyone knew his name* .

2. Yolanda's favorite kind of car is a Mercedes. Of course, Yolanda can't afford one now.

   _____ a Mercedes now.

3. Arnold doesn't come to visit his father very often. His father is unhappy about this.

   _____ more often.

4. On many weekends Arnold and Yolanda can't go out together because Arnold works late at the discotheque.

   _____ more often on weekends.

5. Jack is upset because the government takes so much money out of his paycheck every month.

   _____.

6. Molly can't enter medical school until next year because she has to take a lot of basic science courses first. She's very impatient to begin medical school.

   _____ in medical school now.

   _____ these courses first.

B. Respond to the following questions with a short answer. Continue the answer using *wish* followed by a short answer. Look at the example.

Example

1. Molly likes her new apartment but she has some problems. Does Molly have a large kitchen?

   No, she doesn't, but she wishes she did.

2. Can she give large dinner parties?

   No, _____.

3. Molly's apartment is very dark. Is there enough light to grow plants?

   No, _____.

4. Does she have a stereo?

   No, _____.

5. Her neighbor is a musician. Does he practice late at night?

   Yes, _____.

6. Is the superintendent ever in the building when Molly needs him?

   No, he _____ but Molly _____.

C. Write five sentences about things that are wrong with your home or apartment. After each sentence, write what you wish.

   Example

   1. _My apartment doesn't have a view._
      I wish it did.

   2. _____

      _____

   3. _____

      _____

   4. _____

      _____

5. _____

_____

6. _____

_____

Exercise 2   Present Unreal Conditional

Directions
Fill in the blanks with the correct form of the unreal conditional.

1. Inflation makes life especially difficult for the working class. Many

    wives in blue-collar families have to work. If these wives _didn't bring_
    (bring)

    in a second income, many families _would be_ in serious
    (be)

    financial trouble.

2. Many blue-collar workers buy merchandise on credit, so they pay much

    more for the item because of high interest rates. They _____
    (negative, buy)

    so much on credit if they _____ more real income.
    (have)

3. The average income of an American family has doubled in the last ten

    years, but real buying power is up only 11 percent. Americans

    _____ more money if inflation _____ up all
    (save)   (negative, eat)

    their buying power.

4. Americans are eating less beef these days because beef prices are so

    high. If beef prices _____ so high, Americans
    (negative, be)

    _____ more beef.
    (buy)

5. Inflation also makes life very difficult for the elderly, who live on fixed

    incomes for the most part. People over the age of sixty-five receive

    Social Security checks from the government, but the amount they receive doesn't cover the cost of living. Many senior citizens work at

low-paying jobs to supplement their Social Security checks. If Social

Security _____ a lot higher, many of these senior citizens
          (be)

_____ at these low-paying jobs.
   (negative, work)

6.   Many citizens don't vote in elections anymore because they don't think

the government helps them. If the government _____ more
                    (work)

efficiently, more people _____ .
                (vote)

Exercise 3   Present Unreal Conditional and <u>Wish</u> Clauses

Directions
Fill in the blanks with the correct form of the unreal conditional.

(ARNOLD is thinking of buying a new car. He and JACK are in a car showroom
now.)

JACK: Look at all the cars to choose from. Which one of these cars

     would you buy if you ____*had*____ enough money to
       (buy)   (have)

     buy any one that you wanted?

ARNOLD: I _____ that big yellow Mercedes over there.
            (buy)
     But I can't afford it, of course. I wish I _____ .

JACK: I like that convertible over there, but it's as big as a house. I'm

     afraid it uses too much gas.

ARNOLD: If only gas _____ so much, I _____
             (negative, cost)   (consider)
     buying it.

JACK: Look at that antique car. It's a beauty.

ARNOLD: It costs an arm and a leg² when you bring those old cars into a

garage. I wish I _____ how to repair cars.
(know)

JACK: Yeah, too bad. Everybody _____ us if we
(notice)

_____ down the street in that car.
(drive)

ARNOLD: Let's get out of here. Everything in here is too expensive. I only

have about $1,000 to spend on a car.

JACK: Well, if I_____ you, I_____ at their used
(be) (look)

cars. They're outside.

Exercise 4   Present Unreal Conditional

A. In the following sentences, we have given you the *if* clause of an unreal
conditional sentence. Finish the sentence by writing your own main
clause.

1. If OPEC countries lowered the price of oil, *Americans might
start buying big cars again.*

2. If a house in America didn't cost so much money, _____

_____

3. _____

if people understood and respected each other more.

4. If I discovered a cure for cancer, _____

_____

5. _____

if doctors had a cure for every disease.

---

2. *an arm and a leg:* a lot of money.

6. If I didn't have so many things to do, _____

_____

7. If we could travel back in time, _____

_____

8. _____

if I could live any place in the world.

B. In the following sentences we have given you the main clause of an unreal conditional sentence. Finish the sentence by writing your own unreal *if* clause.

1. Molly would buy a small apartment in the city if *she had*

more money.

2. I would be much happier if _____

_____

3. If _____,

I'd be a millionaire.

4. I'd be famous all over the world if _____

_____

5. We wouldn't need to have prisons if _____

_____

6. If _____,

there would be no war.

7. If I could go back and begin my life over again, _____,

_____

8. _____

if I had more American friends.

Exercise 5 Present Unreal Conditional

Directions
Look at the following professions or situations. Use your imagination, and
write some funny or playful statements using the unreal conditional.

1. a secret agent

   If I were a secret agent, I would become 008.

2. on the moon _____

   _____

3. director of the CIA _____

   _____

4. Superman or Wonder Woman _____

   _____

5. on a train next to a beautiful woman or a handsome man _____

   _____

6. on a sinking ship _____

   _____

7. sixteen years old again _____

   _____

8. a teacher of English as a second language _____

   _____

Exercise 6   Practice with the Present Unreal Conditional

A. Ask a classmate questions using the ideas in parentheses. Your class-
    mate will answer the questions.

    Example

    1. (a famous actor or actress)   (what kind of movies) _If you_
        were a famous actor or actress, what kind
        of movies would you make?

    2. (a famous writer)   (what subjects) _____

        _____

    3. (criminal)   (what kind of crimes) _____

        _____

    4. (mad scientist)   (what kind of crazy inventions) _____

        _____

    5. (marry anyone in the world)   (who) _____

        _____

    6. (meet any famous person in the world)   (who) _____

        _____

B. Ask questions that you can answer with *yes* or *no*.

    Example

    1. (marry someone)   (rich but very boring) _Would you marry_
        someone if he or she were rich but very boring?

    2. (skydive)   (someone/you $10,000.) _____

        _____

    3. (make a bargain with the devil)   (eternal life) _____

        _____

4. (tell the teacher)   (a friend/cheat) _____

   _____

5. (have a beautiful sailboat)   (sail around the world alone) _____

   _____

6. (find $1,000 on the street)   (police) _____

   _____

Part 3   <u>Wish</u> Clauses: Future

Explanation
When we know that something is impossible or unlikely to happen in the future, we use this pattern:

> subject + *wish* + (*that*) + subject + *would* + base form
>
> *Molly wishes someone would give her $1,000,000.*

Examples
The OPEC nations will probably never lower the price of oil. The price will probably continue to rise. Americans wish that OPEC nations **would lower** the price of oil. Scientists will probably not be able to develop alternate energy sources fast enough. We all wish they **could develop** them faster.

We often use *would* after a *wish* clause when we don't like someone's behavior. This pattern often has a critical tone to it. We use this pattern to express annoyance.

Example
(MOLLY and YOLANDA are sitting in a movie theater. The couple in front of them is talking and laughing very loudly.)

YOLANDA: Please, I'm trying to watch the movie. I wish you **would stop** talking!

Part 4   Contrast of <u>Hope</u> and <u>Wish</u> and of Real and Unreal Conditionals

A. Contrast of <u>Hope</u> and <u>Wish</u>

Explanation

When we use *hope* followed by a clause, we mean something is possible in the future. We can use either the future tense or the simple present tense in the second clause. When we use *wish* followed by a clause, we mean something is impossible or unlikely in the present or future.

Example

Yolanda's sister, Sandra, and her fiancé will probably get married in a year

or so. They *hope* that the economy **is** / **will be** better by then because they want

to buy a house. It's very difficult for them to save money, so they don't have much money in savings now. Interest rates on savings accounts will go up some, but they will never keep up with inflation. Sandra and Jeff *wish* the interest rate on their savings **would go** up faster.

B. Contrast of Real and Unreal Conditionals

Explanation

When we think something is possible or likely to happen, we use the real conditional. However, when we think something is impossible or unlikely, we use the unreal conditional.

REAL CONDITIONAL

If + subject + simple present ..., subject + *will* + base form
If yolanda's party is a success, she'll be very happy.

UNREAL CONDITIONAL

If + subject + past tense form ..., subject + $\left\{\begin{array}{l}\text{could}\\ \text{would}\\ \text{might}\end{array}\right\}$ + base form
If I were rich, life would be a lot easier.

Examples

Part of the American dream has always been for American families to own their own homes. However, as inflation continues in the United States, this dream becomes more difficult for middle-class families to achieve. Economists feel inflation will continue for a long time. **If inflation continues** at its present rate, no one but the rich will have enough money to buy a home. If the government by some miracle found a way to stop inflation, more families would have enough money to buy their "dream" home.

Exercise 7   _Wish_ Clauses: Future

A. Finish the following sentences. Tell what someone wishes about the future.

1. It's unlikely that Yolanda's boss will be able to give her a big raise next year.

   Yolanda wishes _he would give everyone a raise_.

2. Yolanda loves flowers, but Arnold never thinks of buying them for her. Next week is Yolanda's birthday.

   Yolanda wishes _____,

   but she knows he probably won't remember.

3. Jack and Arnold took their car to a mechanic. He can't have the car ready before next week. They want to go to the country this week-end.

   They wish _____.

4. Arnold, Yolanda, Jack, and Molly want to take a trip around the United States this summer. The price of gas is very high, and it probably won't go down.

   They wish _____.

5. Construction workers are working on a building next to where Jack lives. Jack can't sleep because of the noise.

   Jack wishes _____.

B. In the following situations someone is irritated at another person's behavior. Write sentences with _wish_ expressing that person's irritation.

1. A student is scraping his fingernail on the blackboard. Another student says:

   "I wish _you wouldn't do that_____.
   It hurts my ears."

2. Yolanda's mother is concerned because her husband isn't spending much time with the children nowadays. She says:

"I wish _____."

3. Someone is smoking a cigar at the table next to Molly in a restaurant. The smoke from his cigar is blowing over to her table. Molly says:

"I wish _____."

4. A mother is talking to her child, who never puts his clothes away. The mother says:

"I wish _____."

5. A boss is irritated because one of his employees is always thirty minutes late to work. The boss says:

"I wish _____."

Exercise 8   _Wish_: Present and Future

Directions

Tell what these people wish about present and future situations in the world today.

1. The pope
2. The president of the United States
3. The military leaders in my country
4. The leaders of developing nations
5. Astronauts
6. Psychiatrists
7. Labor leaders
8. Teachers
9. Parents
10. Children

Exercise 9   Real and Unreal Conditionals

Directions
Complete the following sentences with the correct forms of the present *real* conditional or the present *unreal* conditional.

1. It's very difficult for a person to get into medical school, so Molly has applied to ten schools for next September. She hopes that at least one of the schools _will accept_ her. Medical school is also very expen-
   (accept)
   sive. If she _goes_ to medical school in the fall, she
   (go)
   will probably have to take out a student loan.
   (probably, have to)

2. Yolanda's parents want to buy a house in New Jersey, but they can't afford to pay the interest on a bank loan because interest rates are so high. They wish interest rates _____ so high. If they
   (negative, be)
   _____ to buy a new home, they _____ one
   (can, afford)   (buy)
   near the ocean, because they love the water.

3. Molly, Jack, Yolanda, and Arnold are planning to go out for dinner, but there's a problem. They are trying to decide whether to go to a Chinese restaurant or a Mexican restaurant. If they _____ to a
   (go)
   Chinese restaurant, Jack _____ very happy because he ate
   (negative, be)
   Chinese food last night. However, if they _____ a Mexican
   (choose)
   restaurant, Arnold _____ because he doesn't like spicy food.
   (negative, go)
   One thing is certain. They aren't going to a French restaurant. If they

   _____ to a fancy French restaurant, they _____
   (go)   (negative, have)
   any money left for the rest of the month.

4. Molly is going to run in another mini-marathon next week. She hopes

it _____ very hot. If it _____ hot, she
    (negative, be)   (be)

_____ a much harder time finishing the last mile. She
    (have)

wants to run faster than she did in the last mini-marathon. If the

temperature _____ above 90°F, she knows she
              (be)

_____ very good time.
(negative, can/make)

5. JACK: Hey, Arnold. Can you lend me about $50 until the end of the

            week? I have to pay a lab fee for my astronomy course.

    ARNOLD: Gee, I wish I _____. I only have $25 myself. You
                          (can)

            know that I _____ you the money if I
                        (lend)

            _____ it. If I _____ you, I
                (have)   (be)

            _____ the university to wait one more week.
                (ask)

    JACK: Well, I could. I don't know. Maybe I'll ask my parents to lend

            me the money. If I _____ them, I'm sure they
                               (call)

            _____ me to come home for a visit, and they
                (ask)

            _____ about Molly. My mother liked Molly when
                (probably, ask)

            she visited her. If we _____ talking about Molly,
                                   (start)

            my parents _____ that I get married soon and
                       (suggest)

            settle down. I hope I _____ the conversation
                                  (can, make)

            short.

    ARNOLD: I wish my father _____ me about Yolanda when
                             (ask)

I speak to him. All we every talk about is my "future career

plans."

JACK: Yeah, parents are strange! Why can't they let us make our

own decisions? If I _____ a parent, I
                                               (be)

_____ to control my children's lives so much.
  (negative, try)

Exercise 10   Final Integration

1. You are listening to a conversation at Yolanda's party. Arnold's father, a very conservative businessman, is having an argument about the American economy with a radical young lawyer. With a classmate, act out the dialogue that takes place between Arnold's father and the radical young lawyer.
2. Name some of the economic problems in your country. Then discuss how life would be different if these problems didn't exist. How would you change things if you were the leader of your country? What are some things that you wish were true now or that you wish would happen in the future?
3. Write a letter to the mayor of the city or town you are now living in (in your own country or in the United States) and tell how and why you would change things if you were the mayor.
4. Suppose you had the money and opportunity right now to build your "dream" house. Write some sentences about its location, its style, its special features, the interior decoration, and the gardens. What would this house be like if money were of no importance? How many people could live in the house? Who would they be?

Expressing Your Ideas: Speaking and Writing

1. Is inflation a serious problem in your country? If so, what are some possible ways to deal with inflation?
2. Do you think government should control or regulate the economy of a country or should it follow a hands-off policy?[3]

---

3. *a hands-off policy:* This means the government does not control business, industry, or the economy in any way.

3. Who owns the major industries in your country? Are any industries owned and run by the government? Are labor unions strong? Do all unions have the right to strike? Are unions successful in gaining rights and wage increases for their workers?
4. Who are some famous economists? What are their theories?
5. Do people save a lot of money in your country? Why or why not?

Past Unreal Conditional
and Wish Clauses

A reenactment of a Civil War battle.

Theme: The Civil War

Grammar: Past Unreal Conditional and <u>Wish</u> Clauses

Dialogue

YOLANDA: I just saw *Gone with the Wind* for the fifth time last night.

ARNOLD: **I wish you'd told me about it.** It's one of my favorite movies.

MOLLY: Me, too. **If I'd known it was playing, I would have gone with you.**

YOLANDA: I called you, but you weren't home.

MOLLY: I really love that movie. It always makes me cry.

ARNOLD: It's a brilliant movie, but it isn't an accurate portrayal of slavery or the Civil War.

JACK: What do you mean?

ARNOLD: To begin with, it romanticizes[1] slavery. It only shows the slaves as happy and loyal to their masters.

YOLANDA: That's true. It doesn't show anything about how miserable the slaves were.

MOLLY: One thing that I've never understood is why slavery lasted as long as it did. I know there were a few slave revolts, but why weren't there more?

ARNOLD: **There probably would have been more revolts if the slave owners hadn't done a number of things to prevent them.**

MOLLY: Like what?

ARNOLD: They systematically separated families and slaves who spoke the same language. Also, it was against the law for slaves to learn how to read and write.

MOLLY: Why was it against the law? **What would have happened if they'd been able to read and write?**

ARNOLD: **If they'd been able to read, they could have read about blacks in the North who were free, and they might have written an underground newspaper.**[2]

YOLANDA: Then **they might have started a revolution.**

ARNOLD: **They might have,** except that the slave owners made it impossible for them to organize.

---

1. *to romanticize:* to make reality seem prettier than it is.
2. *an underground newspaper:* at the time of the Civil War, an illegal revolutionary newspaper.

Part 1   Past Unreal Conditional: *If* Clauses

A. Statements

Explanation

When we want to talk about situations in the past which are contrary to what actually happened, we use the past unreal conditional pattern:

If + subject + *had* + (*not*) + past participle, + subject +
$\begin{Bmatrix} would \\ could \\ might \end{Bmatrix}$ + (*not*) + *have* + past participle

If Molly had known about the movie, she would have gone with Yolanda.

Examples

The American Civil War was fought from 1861 to 1865 between northern states (the Union) and eleven southern states (the Confederacy). The industrialized Union believed in a strong federal government and the abolition of slavery. The agricultural Confederacy believed in strong state government and wanted to maintain slavery. After Lincoln was elected president in 1860, the South left the Union because Lincoln wanted to stop the spread of slavery. The war began. The war caused more deaths than any other war in American history, cost billions of dollars, ruined the southern economy and land, and increased hatred for seventy to eighty years after the last battle was fought.

Daniel Webster and Henry Clay were two men in Congress who had succeeded in getting the North and South to compromise, but, unfortunately, they died in 1852. No one else was able to take their place.

If the North and South **had solved** more of their difficulties in the Congress, the Civil War **wouldn't have happened.**

If President Lincoln **hadn't won** the election of 1860, the South **wouldn't have left** the Union to form the Confederacy.

NOTE: We often use a contraction with the subject and *had*:
If *I had* known = If *I'd* known
Sometimes we contract the subject with *would*:
I *would have* gone = *I'd have* gone
If *I'd* known it was playing, *I'd* have gone with you.

B. Questions and Short Answers

We can only ask questions in the main clause. In short answers we use

subject + $\begin{Bmatrix} would \\ could \\ might \end{Bmatrix}$ + have.

Examples

Slavery was an issue in American life as early as 1776 during the American Revolution. Many northerners felt that the Constitution should not have allowed slavery.

Would southerners **have abandoned** slavery if northerners **had been** more insistent at the time of the Revolution?
  It's difficult to say, but they might have.

What **would have happened** if more blacks **had revolted** against slavery?
  Some would have escaped, but the rebellions probably would have failed, because all the weapons were in white hands.

One of the few black rebellions was led by Nat Turner in 1831. He and his followers were captured and killed.

Exercise 1   Past Unreal Conditional

A. Fill in the blanks with the correct forms of the past unreal conditional.

The period following the Civil War from 1865 to 1877 is called the Reconstruction Period. It was a time of difficulty and anger between the North and the South. Here is a list of some of the events that happened.

1. Many Confederate soldiers couldn't own land after the war. A

    great deal of good farmland was left without anyone to farm it, so

    there was a severe shortage of food after the war. If the North

    had permitted the soldiers to own and farm the land, there
       (permit)
    wouldn't have been a shortage of food.
       (negative, be)

2. Many northerners, called carpetbaggers, went to the South. They

    often cheated southerners out of their land. The southerners'

    hatred grew, and bad feelings between the North and South lasted

for decades after the war. If these northerners _____
(negative, cheat)

the southern landowners, the bad feelings between the North and

the South _____ so intense.
(negative, become)

3. Northern liberals in the Congress felt that Andrew Johnson, who

became president after Lincoln was shot, was too easy on the

South. They tried to remove him from office. If Johnson's policies

toward the South _____ harsher, northern liberals
(be)

_____ to remove him from office. A vote was taken in
(negative, try)

the Senate to remove Johnson. President Johnson won by one vote

and remained president. If one more senator _____
(vote)

against him, he _____ office.
(have to, leave)

4. Immediately following the war, blacks gained political and

economic freedom. However, some conservative southerners began

to join the Ku Klux Klan, an organization that terrorized blacks and

southern liberals. It became very powerful, and blacks became

afraid to vote. Slowly, conservative southerners gained control of

state governments. If the Ku Klux Klan _____
(negative, be)

so powerful, blacks _____ afraid to vote, and
(negative, be)

conservative southerners _____ so much
(negative, gain)

power.

5. Because the South never developed industry before the Civil War,

it took a long time for the southern states to recover from the war.

If the South _____ so dependent on
(negative, be)
agriculture, it _____ more quickly.
(recover)

6. Many people wonder why the South didn't abandon slavery and

industrialize sooner. The invention of the cotton gin is one factor in

the South's continued dependence on agriculture and slavery. The

institution of slavery was beginning to become unprofitable before

the cotton gin was invented. Too many slaves were needed to

remove the seeds from the cotton after it was picked. In 1793 Eli

Whitney invented a machine which separated the seeds from the

cotton. This machine was known as the cotton gin. It made the

production of cotton profitable and reinforced the need for slavery

since cheap slave labor was needed to plant the land. If Eli

Whitney _____, the production of cotton

_____. If the production of cotton

_____, slavery _____.

Eli Whitney tried but was unable to get a patent on his new

machine. He never made great profits from his invention. If

_____ a patent, he _____.

Cotton growers constantly needed more land. They pushed west to

find this land. They were determined to make slavery legal in the

new states of Mississippi and Louisiana, too. If _____

_____, Mississippi and Louisiana _____

slave states.

B. Prepare a brief talk for your class about these subjects.

1. Think of a famous person who was influential in the history of your country. If this person had not lived, how would the history of your country have been different? How would your country be different today? If you had been this person, would you have done things the same way or differently? Why?

2. Think of some of the great mistakes that have been made throughout history. How might the situation have been different if these mistakes hadn't happened? For example, how would history have been different without Napoleon's invasion of Russia, Mark Antony's blind love for Cleopatra, the Watergate scandal?

Exercise 2 Questions

Directions
In each example, read the first statement. Then write the question: *What would have happened if . . . ?* Then, using the information given in parentheses, answer the question.

1. Lincoln died soon after the war ended.

   What would have happened if Lincoln hadn't died?

   (The bitterness between the North and the South/negative, be/strong)

   The bitterness between the North and South wouldn't have been so strong.

2. England was sympathetic to the South, but England never gave the South much financial aid.

   _____ if England

   _____ the South financial aid?

   (the South/win the war)

   If England _____,

   the South _____.

3. The South lost many of her finest young men in the war.

_____ if _____

_____?

(the South/recover/sooner)

If _____.

4. Andrew Johnson wasn't a very strong president.

_____ if _____ a stronger

president?

(negative, be/so much chaos after the war)

If _____,

there _____.

In this part of the exercise, no information is given for the answer. Use your imagination to supply a logical answer.

5. The South didn't win the war.

_____ if the South _____?

_____

6. Slavery was a terrible institution which caused endless problems for

the United States. One of the biggest mistakes the United States ever

made was to permit slavery.

_____ if _____?

_____.

Would _____ if _____?

_____.

7. Lincoln was in a theater watching a play on the night of his assassination.

_____ if Lincoln _____

to the theater that night?

_____.

8. John Wilkes Booth is the man who shot Lincoln. Booth had made a careful plan with another man, George Atzerodt. Atzerodt was assigned to assassinate Vice-President Andrew Johnson on that same night. However, Atzerodt became afraid and lost his nerve at the last minute.

_____ if Atzerodt _____?

_____.

Part 2   <u>Wish</u> Clauses about a Past Event

Explanation
When we talk about something that we wish about an impossible or contrary to fact event in the past, we use a *wish* clause followed by a clause in the past perfect tense.

| subject + *wish*(es) + (*that*) + subject + *had* + (*not*) + past |
| (ed)   participle |

Arnold wishes that Yolanda had told him that she was going to the movies.

Examples
The South was ruined after the Civil War because most battles were fought in the South. Homes were destroyed; the land was left in ruins; and cities were burned. Many brave men who could have helped the South rebuild itself were killed in the war. After Lincoln's death in 1865, northern politicians passed laws that harmed the South. The "New South" of today has almost recovered from this destruction, but at a terrible cost.

Many southerners *wish that the North and South* **hadn't fought** most of their battles on southern land. They also *wish northerners* **hadn't punished** *the South so severely after the Civil War.*

After the South surrendered in April 1865, President Lincoln wanted to treat the southern states with mercy, and he wanted them to rejoin the Union quickly. Tragically, he was assassinated soon after. Many people *wished that Lincoln* **had lived** *to rebuild the South.*

Part 3 Past Time *If* Clauses with Present Time Main Clauses

Explanation

When we talk about an impossible or contrary to fact event in the past which we relate to the present, we use this pattern:

> If + subject + had (not) + past participle,
>
> *If the North and South hadn't fought the Civil War,*
>
>   + subject + would + (not) + base form
>   could
>   might
>
> *perhaps the United States would be a very different country today.*

Example

In 1863 President Lincoln issued the Emancipation Proclamation. This proclamation abolished slavery. However, for years after the Civil War, many blacks in the South were denied the right to vote, to go to white schools, or to go into white restaurants. After World War II, blacks began to demand their rights vigorously. Today, blacks still insist that there is discrimination against them, and that the battle for equal rights continues.

If the southern states **hadn't denied** *blacks their rights as citizens after the Civil War, there* **might not be** *so much racial tension in the United States today.*

Exercise 3 *Wish* Clauses about the Past

Directions

Read the following information. Then make a sentence using *wish.*

1. Robert E. Lee was the commander of the Confederate troops. He was a

    brilliant soldier. Lincoln had great respect for him. Lincoln

    wished that Lee *had been* a commander for the Union.
                                (be)

2. The Battle of Gettysburg was one of the bloodiest in the Civil War.

    Almost 50,000 young American men lost their lives. After the battle

    Lincoln made a speech at Gettysburg. He was terribly saddened at the

    great loss of human life. He _____ he _____

    (be able)

    to prevent this tragic loss.

3. William Sherman, a Union general, burned Atlanta. Atlanta was a

    beautiful southern city. When General Sherman burned it, he destroyed

    some of the most beautiful architecture of the country. Even many

    northerners _____ Sherman _____ Atlanta.

    (negative, burn)

4. William Faulkner, a famous American writer, often wrote stories about

    the relationship between southern whites and blacks. He

    _____ blacks and whites _____ each other

    (understand)

    better during his lifetime.

5. Martin Luther King, Jr. was a courageous black leader in the 1950s and

    1960s. He was assassinated in 1968. Both black and white Americans

    _____ he _____.

    (negative, die)

Exercise 4   Past Time _If_ Clauses with Present Time Main Clauses

A. Read the following sentences about America. Then change the
    sentences into a sentence with a past unreal _if_ clause and a present
    unreal main clause. Use _would_ or _might_ in the main clause.

1. Texas was once a part of Mexico, but it fought a revolution and

    won. It's a state now. If _Texas hadn't won the revolution_,

    it _might not be part of the United States today_.

2. The American government bought Alaska from Russia in 1867. It paid $7,200,000. Today the United States has important sources of oil there.

If _____ ,

_____ .

3. England didn't win the war with the American colonies. The United States isn't part of the British Empire anymore.

_____ ,

_____ .

4. America became a separate nation. Pronunciation in American English is very different from pronunciation in British English.

_____ ,

_____ .

5. There was a political scandal known as Watergate in the early 1970s. Many Americans do not have much confidence in their elected leaders.

_____ ,

_____ .

B. Think about the following question. Then share your story with your classmates.

1. Think of a mistake you or someone you know made. How would things be different today if you hadn't made this mistake?

Exercise 5   General Review of All Conditionals

A. Fill in the blanks with the correct form of the real conditional, present unreal conditional, past unreal conditional, clauses with *hope* and *wish*.

MOLLY: I'm ready for our vacation next month. I wish we

_____ tomorrow.
     (can, go)

YOLANDA: Why? What's bothering you?

MOLLY: Well, for one thing, New York City is so hot in the summer. I don't have an air conditioner. I wish I _____ .

It's so humid. If it _____ so humid, I

(negative, be)

_____ the heat so much. I hope the rest of the

(negative, mind)

United States _____ as humid as New York.

(negative, be)

YOLANDA: Well, you know you love New York the rest of the year. Any other problems?

MOLLY: Yes. I took an exam yesterday. I didn't do very well on it.

YOLANDA: Didn't you go to a late-night party the night before last?

MOLLY: Yes, and I didn't study for my test. If I _____

(study)

for the test, I _____ better on it.

(do)

YOLANDA: Well, that's not the only test you're going to have all semester, is it? There will always be more tests. If I

_____ you, however, I _____ a lot

(be)   (study)

for my next test. Why did you stay so late at the party?

MOLLY: Jack and I had a lot of fun dancing and talking to people.

We _____ so long if there _____

(negative, stay)   (negative, be)

so many nice people there. I wish I _____ that

(negative, take)

test yesterday. My professor is a nice guy. If I

_____ him, he probably _____ me

(ask)   (let)

take it at a later date. I hope I _____ an F in

(negative, get)

the course.

YOLANDA: Don't worry. You won't fail.

B. Complete each sentence with the correct form of the conditional: real, present unreal, or past unreal.

1. If Cleopatra hadn't fallen in love with Mark Antony, _____

   _____

2. Most Americans wish _____

   _____

3. Most people in my country hope _____

   _____

4. If interest rates on loans go any higher, _____

   _____

5. There wouldn't be so many political refugees in the world today if

   _____

6. American Indians wish _____

   _____

7. If _____,

   Napoleon might have won his war with Russia.

8. If we had peace in the world today, _____

   _____

9. My English will improve if _____

   _____

10. After I _____,

    I wished _____

Expressing Your Ideas: Speaking and Writing

1. Has there ever been a civil war or any kind of rebellion in your country? What were the reasons for it? When did it happen? How long did it last? Who won? What are some of its consequences?

2. What other famous civil wars have happened in history? What caused them? Why are civil wars so tragic for a nation?

3. Most Americans feel ashamed that slavery was ever a part of their country's history. Is there any period or event in your country's history that you or other people feel ashamed about? Explain.

4. How do people in your country feel about the problem of discrimination in the United States? Do you think that Americans are more prejudiced than people from other countries? Explain. Do you think that Americans are honestly trying to do something about racial discrimination? If there were as many racial, religious, or ethnic groups in your country, do you think your country might have the same problems of discrimination as the United States?

Causative

Arnold watching TV.

Theme: Television

Grammar: Causative

Dialogue

(ARNOLD and YOLANDA are watching TV, but the TV set is not working very well, so the picture on the screen is not very clear.)

ARNOLD: This stupid TV! I just **had it fixed** a couple of days ago.

YOLANDA: What **did** you **have done** to it?

ARNOLD: I **had a new picture tube installed.** It cost a lot of money. Not only that, they **made me wait** for two weeks.

YOLANDA: Who **did** you **have fix** it? I won't go to them next time my TV breaks.

ARNOLD: The repair shop around the corner.

YOLANDA: I bet you went crazy without your TV.

ARNOLD: Yeah, I did. I guess I'm a TV addict.[1]

YOLANDA: How can I **get you to turn** this thing **off?** There's nothing but garbage on TV now anyway. Let's go out.

ARNOLD: You're right. Look at that commercial. Stupid commercials like that one **make me want** to throw this set out the window.

YOLANDA: That commercial may be stupid, but it's very persuasive. Even simple-minded commercials **get people to buy** things that they don't really need.

ARNOLD: Yeah, there are too many ads on TV. I think the government should **make the networks reduce** the number of commercials.

YOLANDA: And here's another problem. Most parents **let their kids watch** too much TV. When I was a kid, my parents only **let me watch** one program a night. They **made me turn** it **off** after an hour.

ARNOLD: I know watching TV is really a waste of time. I should **have the garbage men come** and **take** this TV **away.**

YOLANDA: Oh, come on, Arnold. You'll never give up TV.

---

1. *addict:* someone who cannot stop doing something; in this case, watching television.

Part 1   The Active Causative

Explanation

When one person causes or persuades or forces another person to do something, we can use three different causative patterns to express this. These three causative patterns are:

1. have someone do something
2. get someone to do something
3. make someone do something

The first verb in each of these patterns (*have, get, make*) can be used in any tense, but the second verb does not change. Use the base form after *have* and *make* and the infinitive form after *get*.

A. Have Someone Do Something

Explanation

We use *have someone do something* when we ask someone to do something for us, or when we hire someone to work for us, or when we have the position or authority or money to ask others to perform tasks for us. We use this pattern when we want to show that we don't do something ourselves. For example, *Arnold didn't fix his TV himself. He had a TV repairman fix it for him.*

Examples

Many sociologists believe TV has a negative influence on our society. They are especially worried about the effect of violence in TV programs on children. In one study sociologists **had children watch** a violent TV program. After the program, they **had researchers observe** these children playing, and they found an increase in aggressive behavior in the children.

B. Get Someone to Do Something

Explanation

We usually *get someone to do something* instead of *have someone do something* when it is necessary to use psychological persuasion or to offer a reward to cause someone to do something.

Examples

Sociologists also complain that commercials **get people to buy** things that they don't need. Commercials have an especially strong influence on young children. After they watch certain commercials, children want sweet junk food and expensive toys. They try to **get their parents to buy** these things for them.

Concerned parent groups are trying to change television advertising, but they haven't yet **gotten all advertisers to cooperate** with them.

C. Make Someone Do Something

Explanation
We generally use *make someone do something* when we mean that it is necessary to use some force to cause someone to do something.

Examples
The Federal Communications Commission (FCC) is an agency of the federal government which regulates television and radio programs. It **makes television networks follow** certain rules. For example, it **makes the stations show** programs with sex or violence after 9:00 at night when children are in bed. Also, when a movie contains vulgar language, the FCC can **make the networks take** obscene words out before they show it.

NOTE: Sometimes the causative pattern with *make* does not carry the meaning of force. In the following examples, *make* simply means to cause something to happen:

1. Sad movies make me cry.
2. A host should make a guest feel comfortable in his home.
3. Good music makes people want to dance.

Part 2   Let Someone Do Something

Explanation
Let has a different meaning from the preceding three causative verbs. *Let* means permit. It follows the same grammatical structure as *have* or *make someone do something*.

Examples
Concerned parents control the amount of TV that their children watch. They usually **let their children watch** one or two hours of TV a day, but they **don't let them watch** it all day long.

Part 3   The Passive Causative

Explanation
We choose to use the passive causative for the same reasons that we choose to use any other passive. *Have* is used in the following passive causative pattern:

have   something   done

Examples
Advertising is very important to television. Companies **have** *careful studies* **done** by marketing analysts to determine what kind of commercials people respond to. Sometimes they **have** *special pilot commercials* **made** and **shown**

in one or two test areas in the country. Based on the success of these pilot commercials, the companies decide whether or not to **have** *them* **shown** on a national network.

NOTE:

1. *Have* can be used in any tense, but the second verb is always the past participle.
2. *Get* can also be used in the passive causative. When we use *get*, there is no *to* before the second verb. (She *gets* her hair *done* at Richard's.)

Part 4 Summary of Active and Passive Causative Formation with <u>Have</u>

Look at the following sentences and notice the difference in form between the active and passive causative.

Arnold's TV set broke a couple of days ago.

1. A repairman *fixed* it.
2. Arnold *had* a repairman *fix* it.
3. Arnold's TV set *was fixed* a couple of days ago.
4. Arnold *had* his TV set *fixed* a couple of days ago.

Sentence 1 is in the active voice. In the active causative (sentence 2), the verb following the causative verb (*have*) is always the base form. Sentence 3 is in the passive voice. In the passive causative (sentence 4), the verb after the causative verb (*have*) is always the past participle.

When you ask a question about the object and use the active causative, you will see *have* + the base form next to each other:

Who did Arnold **have fix** his TV set?
He *had* a repairman *fix* it.

When you ask a question about the object and use the passive causative, you will see *have* + the past participle next to each other:

What did Arnold **have done** to his TV set?
He *had* a new picture tube *installed*.

Exercise 1 The Active Voice of the Causative

A. Choose the correct tense for the causative verb (*have, make, get, let*) and choose the base form or the infinitive form for the second verb.

There have been more than 2,300 studies and reports on the effects

of television on American society. Most of them show that these effects are mainly negative. Researchers have been especially concerned

about children. In the past decade researchers _have had_
(have)

children _participate_ in numerous studies. A few years ago a
(participate)

University of California research team _____ a group of
(have)

elementary school children _____ a test. From this group
(take)

the researchers selected 250 children who were especially intelligent

and creative. They _____ these children _____
(have) (watch)

television intensively for three weeks. Then they _____
(have)

them _____ a similar test a second time. The results
(take)

showed a drop in the children's creativity. The researchers concluded

that television _____ the children _____ some
(make) (lose)

of their creativity.

Many elementary school teachers agree with the findings of this

study. They believe that TV _____ children
(make)

_____ the ability to concentrate in school. Teachers can't
(lose)

_____ children _____ attention for any length
(get) (pay)

of time because today's children want everything to be as fast and

entertaining as TV. Dr. Benjamin Spock, an expert in child raising,

once complained that he couldn't _____ his grandchildren
(get)

_____ the TV set when he wanted to take them to the zoo.
(leave)

Some of today's children are so addicted to TV that nothing else

interests them. Parents have to _____ them
(make)

_____ off the TV and _____ out to play or
(turn) (go)

read a book. They can't _____ them _____
(get) (do)
these traditional childhood activities without having an argument over

the TV.

   Although most of these studies have shown the negative effects of

television, some sociologists argue that television has become a part of

our lives. They do not think that parents should _____
(make)
their children _____ the amount of TV that they watch to
(limit)
one or two hours a day. They believe that parents should

_____ their children _____ for themselves
(let) (decide)
what and how much they want to watch.

B. Fill in the blank with the correct active causative form: *have, make,* or
    get. There are six sentences. Use each causative twice.

    (eat)   1. Most children do not like vegetables, but parents

                    _____ them _____ vegetables

                    because they are full of vitamins.

    (check)   2. Arnold's father bought some gas the other day, and he

                    _____ the gas station attendant

                    _____ the oil.

    (leave)   3. When Yolanda lived at home, her younger brother

                    always used to bother her when she was studying. She

                    _____ him _____ her alone by

                    giving him some money to go to the candy store.

(answer) 4. Arnold's father is the president of a bank. He never

answers his own phone. He always _____

his secretary _____ it.

(give) 5. Last week there was a robbery in the bank. A man

pointed a gun at the bank teller and _____

her _____ him all the money.

(notice) 6. In the past a woman could _____ a man

_____ her by dropping her handkerchief.

C. Fill in the blanks with the correct tense and the correct active
causative form. Choose from *have, make,* or *get.* For some blanks you
may feel that more than one of these causative forms is correct.

Although most studies show the negative effects of television, there

are also some important positive influences. There are many excellent

educational programs, especially for children. Some schools

_____ children _____ certain programs in
                              (watch)
the classroom. They often _____ them _____
                                                    (watch)
worthwhile programs at home by encouraging them to discuss what

they have seen the next day in class. "Sesame Street" is a program

that is watched by millions of children around the world. It uses bright

colors, fast timing, and humor in order to _____ children

_____ attention. It _____ children
        (pay)
_____ learning about the alphabet, reading, and numbers.
     (enjoy)
Some teachers have even found ways to use television to improve

reading ability. Several years ago teachers in a Philadelphia school

_____ children _____ scripts for TV
         (read)

programs at home, and the next day their teachers _____

them _____ what they had read. By the end of the
  (discuss)

semester some students' reading scores had gone up three grade levels.

  Television also exposes children to different people and places. A

little girl who had never seen a ballet before watched a famous

ballerina on TV. This program _____ her _____
                   (decide)

to become a ballerina herself. TV also increases young people's under-

standing of other people's views of life. Many people feel that "Roots,"

a program on the history of black people in the United States, is an

example of this. Because viewers of this program became emotionally

involved with the characters, "Roots" _____ some people

_____ more compassionately about the difficulties of
  (think)

black people in the United States.

Exercise 2 Questions: Active Causative

Directions
Work with a partner. Ask questions using the active form of the causative.
Your partner will answer them. After you practice this orally, write the
questions and answers for homework.

A. Make Someone Do Something. All parents make their children do
  certain things that the children don't want to do.

  Example

  1. (make/do) What ___*did*___ your parents *make you*

   ___*do*___ that you didn't want to do? _____

   _____

2. (make/eat) _____ they _____

   certain food that you didn't like?

   _____

3. (make/go) _____ to bed early?

   _____

4. (make/do) _____ chores to help around

   the house? _____

   What _____?

5. _____?

   _____

6. _____?

   _____

B. Let Someone Do Something. Most parents do not let their children do
   whatever they want to do.
   Example

   1. (let/stay) When you were seven years old, _____*did*_____

      your parents _*let you stay up*_ until midnight?

      _____

   2. (let/walk) When you were six, _____ your

      mother _____ to school alone or did she take you to

      school?

      _____

3. (let/eat) _____ as much candy as you wanted

   when you were a child?

   _____

4. (let/date) _____ when you were about

   fourteen or fifteen years old?

   _____

   When _____ for the first time?

   _____

5. (let/drink) How old were you when _____

   for the first time?

   _____

6. If you had children, what are some things that you would or would

   not let your children do?

   _____

   _____

   _____

C. Have Someone Do Something
   Example
   1. (have/repair) (your mother) When you were a teenager and you

      tore your clothes, did you repair them yourself or *did you have*

      your mother repair them _____ for you?

      _____

      _____

2. (have/carry) (porter)   When you travel by plane, do you usually

carry your own suitcases into the airport or _____

_____?

_____

3. (have/repair) (the superintendent)   When people rent an apart-

ment, do they usually repair things themselves or _____

_____?

_____

4. (have/type) (someone)   When you have to write a paper for school,

do you type it yourself or _____?

_____

Exercise 3   Get Someone to Do Something

Directions

Complete these questions and answer them. Discuss your answers in class.

In matters of love and relationships between men and women, people often use special persuasive techniques. In most countries there are superstitions about how to get someone to love you.

Example

1. If a woman is interested in a man, but he doesn't pay attention to her,

how can she ___*get him to notice*___ her?
         (get/notice)

_____.

2. How can she _____ her out for a date?
         (get/ask)

_____.

3. If a man is interested in a woman but she doesn't pay any attention to

   him, what can he do to _____ him?

(get/notice)

   _____.

4. If a woman refuses a date with a man, how _____

(get/change)

   _____ her mind?

   _____.

5. If a woman thinks the man she loves doesn't love her enough, what

   should she do to _____ her more?

(get/love)

   _____.

6. What about a man in this same situation? What should he do to

   _____?

(get/love)

   _____.

7. If the person you love isn't interested in marrying you, what can you do

   to _____?

(get/marry)

   A woman can _____

   A man can _____

8. If you don't want to go out with a person, but this person keeps

   bothering you and keeps inviting you out, how can you _____

(get/leave)

   _____ you alone?

   _____.

Exercise 4   Active Causative: <u>Who</u> Questions with <u>Have</u>

Directions
Ask questions and answer them.

Most people love to imagine being rich and the things that they would
have someone do for them if they had enough money.

Example

1. (have/design)   If you were rich, *Would you have someone design*

   the house of your dreams for you?

   Yes, I would.

   (have/design)   There are many famous architects. Who *would you*
   have design your house. ?

   _____

2. (have/entertain)   If you were rich, _____ someone

   _____ at your parties?

   _____?

   (have/entertain)   There are many famous singers and entertainers.

   Who _____?

   _____

3. (have/design)   If you were rich, _____ someone

   _____ your clothes for you?

   _____

   (have/design)   There are many famous designers. Who _____

   _____?

   _____

4. (have/live) If you were rich, _____ your relatives

_____ with you in your big mansion?

_____

(have/live) Who _____ with you?

_____

Exercise 5 The Passive Voice of the Causative

A. Fill in the blanks, using *have something done.*

ARNOLD: I saw a great program on TV last night.

YOLANDA: What was it about?

ARNOLD: It was about a rock star who became a multimillionaire. His

life-style is incredible. He has so many servants that he

never lifts a finger. He never has to do anything. He bought

an island and he _____ a mansion

_____ on it. The gardens were spectacular. He
    (build)

_____ rare trees and flowers _____
                                        (bring)

in from exotic places. In the mansion he _____

a huge bathtub _____ into the natural rock,
                    (carve)

and he _____ gold faucets _____.
                                (install)

He _____ a stereo system _____
                                (design)

for every room in the mansion. His parties are fantastic! He

always serves the best food. He _____ his

meals _____ by the finest chefs of Europe, and
      (prepare)

_____ caviar _____ in anytime
                         (fly)

he wants.

YOLANDA: How do his guests get to the island? Does he _____

them _____ in?
        (fly)

ARNOLD: Yes, he _____ them _____ to the
                                          (fly)

island in his private helicopters. And you should see his

yacht!

YOLANDA: Did he _____ it specially _____?
                                              (build)

ARNOLD: Oh, yes. There's no other one like it in the world. And his

clothes!

YOLANDA: Does he _____ them all _____ to
                                            (make)

order?

ARNOLD: Yes.

YOLANDA: Honestly, Arnold, would you really like to live like that?

ARNOLD: I don't know, but I'd like to try it.

B. Imagine what else this millionaire has done for him by other people.
   Write several more examples.

Exercise 6   Questions with the Passive

A. Use the passive form *have something done* to write questions.
   Example
   1. (clothes) (dry clean) Do you *have your clothes*
      drycleaned or do you wash them yourself?

2. (apartment) (clean)   How do you keep your home or apartment

   clean? Do you _____

   by a professional cleaner or do you clean it yourself?

3. (your hair) (cut)   When did you last _____?

   How often _____?

   Where _____?

4. (your watch) (repair)   When did you last _____

   _____?

5. (your fortune) (tell)   Have you ever _____

   _____ by a gypsy?

6. (your picture) (take)   When was the last time that you _____

   _____?

7. (your back) (scratch)   Do you like to _____

   _____?

8. (your back) (rub)   Do you like to _____

   _____?

B. In the next five questions try to write several sentences to answer the
   questions.
   Example

   1. (dry clean)   What should you *have dry cleaned* ?

      A silk shirt? A cotton shirt? A wool sweater? Wool pants?

      _____

2. (do)   Most people have their hair cut in a beauty parlor or a barber shop. What else can you _____ in a beauty parlor or barber shop?

_____

3. (check)   When people take their cars to a garage, what _____
_____?

_____

4. (make)   When you have your photo taken for a passport, how many copies do you _____
_____?

_____

5. (do)   The president or leader of a country does not have time to do everything for himself or herself. What does he or she _____ by other people?

_____

6. (send)   Many students miss things from their home country when they go abroad to study. What do students _____ from home by friends and family?

_____

Exercise 7 Contrast of Active and Passive Causative

A. Choose between the passive form of the causative and the active form. Also choose the correct tense for the causative verbs. In the active form choose *have, get, make,* or *let.* In the passive form use only *have.*

Many people think the government should pass stronger laws to

_____ companies _____ more truthfully and
                                         (advertise)
responsibly. Some companies have used deceptive advertising to

_____ people _____ their products. In the
                                   (buy)
1960s, for example, some companies experimented in movie theaters

with a new and unusual form of commercial. They _____

an image _____ on the movie screen faster than the eye
               (flash)
could see. The viewer did not even know that he had seen a commercial.

All he knew was that something _____ him _____
                                                             (want)
a particular kind of soda or candy. This subliminal advertising

_____ people _____ certain products without
                                   (buy)
their knowing that they had been influenced by a commercial. Some

people thought that the government shouldn't _____

companies _____ this form of advertising, and they fought
                    (use)
to _____ it _____.
                              (ban)

Many people complain about the number of commercials that

interrupt programs. Most TV networks are supported by advertisers

who want to sell their products. The success of a TV program depends

on the number of viewers. Research companies _____ surveys

_____ to determine the number of viewers that a
         (make)

particular program has. A program may be very good, but if it cannot

attract viewers, it cannot attract advertisers, and the network

_____ it _____ off the air.
(take)

Public television has no commercials. It is supported by the

government and by contributions from private citizens and

corporations. Corporations are motivated to support public TV because

doing so improves their image with the public. They can also

_____ these contributions _____ from their
(deduct)

taxes.

B. Imagine you have just been crowned king or queen of the island
kingdom of Watanango. You have complete power. You can make your
people do anything, and you can have anything done for you. What are
your plans? How are you going to make your people obey you? Will you
make everyone bow to you? Are you going to make people display your
picture in stores and public areas? Will you have your statue erected in
public areas? Will you let newspapers criticize your policies? Will you
try to get other countries to give you economic aid?
(Continue with other examples. Use the causative patterns.)

Expressing Your Ideas: Speaking and Writing

1. What is your opinion about television? Does television make people use
   their minds? Is it only a waste of time? Which programs do you think
   are good? Which are bad? Which do you like? Why? Do people read
   less or talk to each other less when they have television in their homes?
2. Does TV have a negative or bad influence on children? If you think it
   does, tell how. What good or positive influences does TV have on
   children? Should parents let children watch as much TV as they want,
   or should they limit the amount of TV that their children watch? Why?
3. What do you think of TV commercials? Do they ever get you to buy
   things that you don't need? Are there too many commercials? Should
   the government make the networks show fewer commercials? Should
   the government regulate commercials that are directed at children?
   How should the government regulate commercials?

4. Are TV programs better in your country or in the United States? How?

5. Does your country broadcast a lot of American TV programs? Does this affect your culture? How?

6. Do American TV programs realistically reflect American life? What kind of image do American TV programs give you about life in the United States?

7. American television stations are not owned by the government. Are TV stations privately or publicly owned in your country? What dangers or or disadvantages are there when the government owns TV stations? What are the dangers or disadvantages when private companies own TV stations?

8. Should TV programs be censored? By whom? What should be censored? Sex? Violence? News?

Albert Einstein on his seventy-fifth birthday. *(Wide World Photos)*

Theme: *Famous Americans*

Grammar: *Noun Clauses*

Dialogue

(JACK is talking to MOLLY on the telephone.)

JACK: Hi, Molly. What's new?

MOLLY: Hi, Jack. Oh, nothing much.

JACK: What are you doing?

MOLLY: I'm reading an article about Albert Einstein. His life was really fascinating.

JACK: Does the article talk about his childhood? **Does it say if there were any early signs** that he was a genius?

MOLLY: It talks about his childhood, but it says he didn't even begin to talk until he was three.

JACK: I understand that he failed math in school. **I wonder if that story is true.**

MOLLY: This article doesn't mention that, but it says he didn't like school very much. He was rebellious and he cut[1] classes. One of his teachers once called him a lazy dog and said, "You'll never amount to anything."[2]

JACK: **Can you imagine how that teacher felt** when he heard about Einstein's winning the Nobel Prize for physics?

MOLLY: He probably felt like a fool. Here's something interesting. Can you believe that he made his major discoveries when he was working in an office and earning only $675 a year?

JACK: That's amazing. **Do you know how old he was** when he got the Nobel Prize?

MOLLY: That was quite a bit later, in 1922, when he was about forty-three.

JACK: I know Einstein became an American citizen, but he was quite old when he came here, I think. **Does it say when he came here?**

MOLLY: In 1933. He left Germany after Hitler came into power. You know, it's interesting to think that Einstein's Theory of Relativity changed the whole way scientists look at the universe, but **I wonder how many people really understand his theory.**

JACK: Do you?

MOLLY: No, not at all. All I know is $E = mc^2$. But you must understand it since you're an astronomer.

JACK: Well, I'm going to be working in the observatory tonight. Come on over and I'll explain it to you.

---

1. *to cut class:* to be absent from class.
2. *to amount to something:* to achieve something worthwhile or important.

Part 1   Introduction to Noun Clauses

Explanation

The normal word order for a sentence in English is subject + verb + object.

> *Molly is reading an article.*
>
> subject + verb + direct object (noun)

Sometimes the object is a clause that has its own subject and verb.

> *Jack wants to know what she is reading.*
>
> subject + verb + direct object (noun clause)

We often use noun clauses in object position when we ask or answer questions. Many of these noun clauses begin with question words (*where, what, when*). *Do not use the question word order in noun clauses.* In the simple present and simple past tense we need the words *do, does, did* for direct questions, but we do not use them in noun clauses.

Part 2   Indirect Questions

A. Wh Questions

Examples

Muhammad Ali is one of the most famous names in the history of boxing. People all over the world are fascinated by his life. Here is an imaginary interview between Muhammad Ali and a reporter:

REPORTER: Ali, I think our audience *would like to know* **why you decided** to become a boxer.
(DIRECT QUESTION: Why did you decide to become a boxer?)

ALI: When I was a kid, some bigger kids stole my bicycle, and I couldn't do anything about it. I decided then to learn how to defend myself.

REPORTER: Most people probably *don't know how old* **you were** when you began to fight.
(DIRECT QUESTION: How old were you when you began to fight?)

ALI: I fought my first match when I was fifteen.

REPORTER: You started fighting under the name of Cassius Clay. Then you changed your name to Muhammad Ali when you became a Black Muslim in 1964. Many people *don't really understand* **why you changed your name.**
(DIRECT QUESTION: Why did you change your name?)

ALI: *Do you know* **where the names of black people in this country come from?** They are slave names. The slaves often took the last name of their white masters. My religion says we should denounce our slave names and take a new name.
(DIRECT QUESTION: Where do the names of black people in this country come from?)

B. *Yes/No* Questions

Explanation

We use *if* or *whether* to introduce noun clauses that we use in place of questions that we can answer with *yes* or *no*.

Examples

(The interview continues.)

REPORTER: Ali, in 1964 you won the world heavyweight title. Because you refused to go into the army, the boxing commission took that title away from you. *I wonder* **if you still think** that you were right to refuse to join the army.
(DIRECT QUESTION: Do you still think you were right to . . .?)

ALI: Yes, I still think so. As a minister in the Black Muslim Church, I didn't think I should fight in the Vietnam War. And in 1971 the United States Supreme Court upheld my right to make that decision.

REPORTER: Ali, your first defeat was in your fight against Joe Frazier in 1971. That was a close fight. *I wonder* **whether or not you agreed**[3] with the judges' decision on that fight.
(DIRECT QUESTION: Did you agree with the judges' decision?)

ALI: No, I think I won that fight. I was knocked down in the fifteenth round, but I was ahead on points all the way. I didn't have a mark on me after the fight, but Frazier had to go to the hospital.

REPORTER: Ali, to conclude this interview, would you please tell people how you defeat your opponents. Tell us what your secret is.

ALI: It's simple. I'm the greatest. I float like a butterfly and sting like a bee.

---

3. Notice that we can also say, *"I wonder whether you agreed with the judges' decision or not."*

C. Expressions with Noun Clauses

Here is a list of some expressions that we frequently use before noun clauses in direct object questions:

I know....	I don't know....	Do you know....?
I remember....	I don't remember....	Do you remember....?
I'd like to know....	I wonder....	I don't care....
I'd like to find out....	I'm not sure....	
I want to ask....	Are you sure....?	
Can you tell me....?	I won't tell you....	Can you imagine....?
Could anyone	I can't explain....	I can imagine....
explain....?		I can't imagine....
Would someone please		
ask....?		
Ask him....	Does the sign say....?	
Tell me....	Does the article	
Explain....	say....?	
	It doesn't say....	
Try to guess....		
Try to understand....		
Try to find out....		

We often use indirect questions to ask for information from people we don't know, for example, in stores, restaurants, train stations, because such questions are generally more polite. In these situations we use:

I'd like to know . . .   (or)   Can / Could / Would you tell me. . . ?

Example
Could you tell me when the next train leaves?

D. Punctuation

Be careful with the punctuation of sentences with noun clauses. If the main clause is a question (*could you tell me . . . ? do you know . . . ?*, etc.), use a question mark. If the main clause is not a question (*I'd like to know . . . , I wonder . . .*), use a period.

Examples
I wonder if that story is true.
Do you know how old he was when he got the Nobel Prize?

Exercise 1   Noun Clauses

A.   Here is information about another famous American. Look at the information in the answer first. Use a noun clause to ask for the information.

JACK: What are you reading now, Molly?

MOLLY: The biography of Susan B. Anthony.

JACK: I don't know very much about her. Can you tell me what
Susan B. Anthony did ?

MOLLY: She did many things. First she fought against slavery. Then, later, for women's right to vote.

JACK: I guess that was a really hard fight in those days. I know a lot of women were thrown in jail. Do you know if

_____?

MOLLY: Yes. She was arrested when she tried to vote in 1872.

JACK: In those days it was unusual for a woman to take part in political protests, speak in public, and be arrested. I wonder how

_____.

MOLLY: Oh, I think her family felt that she was doing the right thing. Her father had taught her to be very independent and strong when she was a child. He taught her to read and write when she was only three years old.

JACK: Do you know if _____

before she died?

MOLLY: Well, women got the right to vote in four states before she

died.

JACK: Do you remember when _____?

MOLLY: She died in 1906.

B. Martin Luther King, Jr. is another famous name in American history. In this dialogue imagine that the host of a television talk show is interviewing the author of a biography about Dr. King. Ask for information, using noun clauses.

HOST: Today we are celebrating Martin Luther King's birthday, and

I would like to review a few important events from his life.

Martin Luther King received the Nobel Peace Prize in 1964.

Would you tell us _____

_____?

AUTHOR: He was the most important leader in the nonviolent fight for

racial equality.

HOST: And would you tell us _____?

AUTHOR: He was born in Georgia on January 15, 1929.

HOST: Our audience would probably like to know _____

before he became involved in the fight for racial equality.

AUTHOR: He was a minister.

HOST: Do you know _____?

AUTHOR: Yes, he came from a family of ministers. Both his father and

grandfather were ministers.

HOST: I'm not sure exactly _____.

AUTHOR: He first came to national attention in 1956. In that year a black woman named Rosa Parks got on a bus in Montgomery, Alabama. In the southern part of the country at that time, all black people had to sit in the black section at the back of the bus. Rosa Parks was tired from working all day, and the black section of the bus was full, so she sat in the white section. The driver stopped the bus, and she was arrested. Dr. King was the leader of a boycott of the buses. Black people refused to ride the buses for many months.

HOST: Do you know _____?

AUTHOR: Yes, one year later the United States Supreme Court ruled that racial segregation was illegal in transportation.

HOST: Would you please tell us _____.

AUTHOR: He led a civil rights march on Washington in 1963. At that time in the South, blacks couldn't vote. He led the fight to give his people the right to vote.

HOST: I don't remember exactly _____.

AUTHOR: The federal government passed the Civil Rights Act in 1964 and the Voting Rights Act in 1965.

HOST: Please tell us how many times _____.

AUTHOR: I don't remember exactly, but he was arrested and put in jail several times for his part in protest marches and demonstrations.

Noun Clauses in Object Position: Indirect Questions **429**

HOST: Would you tell us _____?

AUTHOR: He was shot in Memphis, Tennessee, by James Earl Ray.

HOST: That was a tragic moment in the history of the United States.

Exercise 2   Direct and Indirect Questions

Directions

In normal conversation we generally mix direct and indirect questions. In the following dialogue there are both kinds of questions. If a question is direct, change it to the indirect form. If a question is indirect, change it to the direct form.

Walt Disney is another American whose name is famous all over the world. Even people who have never heard his name know his cartoon characters, Mickey Mouse and Donald Duck. Here is an imaginary dialogue between a magazine writer and the author of a biography of Walt Disney.

WRITER: I suppose Walt Disney is a name that people all over the world

know. I wonder how popular Disney's movies are around the world.

How popular are Disney's movies around the world?

AUTHOR: Well, in 1966 Walt Disney Productions estimated that around the

world 240,000,000 people had seen a Disney movie, 100,000,000

watched a Disney TV show every week, and 6.7 million had made

the trip to Disneyland.

WRITER: When was Walt Disney born?

Do you know _____?

AUTHOR: He was born in Chicago on December 5, 1901.

WRITER: I wonder how he got his start in the cartoon business.

_____

Did he go to art school?

Do you know _____?

AUTHOR: When he was a child, he loved to draw, so he took a course in cartoon art through the mail.

WRITER: Could you tell us if his parents encouraged his interest in art?

_____

AUTHOR: His father let him attend an art class on Saturday mornings, but they didn't really give him any other encouragement.

WRITER: What was his first job?

Tell us _____

AUTHOR: He worked in a commercial art studio for $50 a month. Of course, he didn't have much money; when he needed a haircut, he gave the barber some of his cartoons instead of money.

WRITER: When did he make his first cartoon with Mickey Mouse?

Can you tell us _____

AUTHOR: In 1927, but the first name he gave his character was Mortimer Mouse.

WRITER: Do you know if those first cartoons made him rich?

_____

AUTHOR: Not really. He used all the money to make more cartoons.

WRITER: And do you know what his first movie-length cartoon was?

_____

AUTHOR: It was *Snow White.* It came out in 1938. Later he made others: *Cinderella, Pinocchio, Bambi, Dumbo.*

WRITER: When did he open Disneyland?

I can't remember _____.

AUTHOR: That was in 1955.

WRITER: Do you know how old Disney was when he died?

_____

AUTHOR: He died in 1966 at the age of sixty-five.

WRITER: Why do people all over the world love Mickey Mouse and Donald
Duck?

I'd like to know _____

AUTHOR: I suppose it's because there is a little bit of all of us in those
characters. Mickey is good and sweet and happy. Donald gets
angry and insults people. I don't know the reason exactly, but
people all over the world love Walt Disney's movies.

Exercise 3   Noun Clauses: Asking for Information and Directions
Directions
Here are some typical questions that travelers ask in a train station or an
airport. Rewrite the questions using noun clauses.

1.   What's the price of a ticket to Washington?

Could you please tell me what _the price of a ticket to Washington is?_

2.   How long is the flight from New York to Washington?

Do you know _____

3.   Do they serve dinner on that flight?

I'd like to know _____

4. What's the platform number for the train to Boston?

    Can you tell me what _____

5. What's the arrival time for this flight?

    Please tell me what _____

6. What's the difference in price between economy class and first class?

    I'd like to know what _____

7. Is flight 109 on time?

    Do you know _____

8. What time is it now?

    Can you tell me _____

9. Which gate does the flight depart from?

    I'd like to know which gate _____

10. Is the flight to Washington full tomorrow?

    I'd like to know _____

11. Is there any other flight to California on this date?

    Can you tell me _____

Exercise 4   Direct and Indirect Questions: Role Playing

Directions
Choose a famous person from your country or any other famous person that you know a lot about. Imagine that you have written a biography of this person. Your classmate will pretend to be a reporter or talk-show host who is interviewing you about this famous person. The interviewer will ask for information by using both direct and indirect questions.

Exercise 5   Noun Clauses: Writing a Dialogue

Directions

Write a dialogue for each of the following situations. Use questions with noun clauses and direct questions.

1. You and a friend are looking at a menu in a foreign restaurant. The menu is in a language that you don't understand very well. You are asking your friend and the waiter for help because you don't know what to order.
2. You are asking for information in a train station or airport.
3. You are in a store and you see a sweater that you want to buy, but you can't find your size or the color that you want. You are speaking to the salesperson.
4. You and a friend are talking about another friend whom you haven't seen for several years.
5. You are a witness to a car accident or a crime and the police are asking you questions about what you saw.

Expressing Your Ideas: Speaking and Writing

1. What other facts do you know about Einstein's life? Why were his discoveries so important? Describe some of his ideas or theories. Do you agree that he was a genius? Some people question the importance of his contributions to physics. Why?
2. Name some other major discoveries in physics and mathematics. Why are they significant?
3. Einstein's theories opened the door to the atomic age. If you were Einstein, how would you feel about this now? Why? Name the ways atomic power has changed our lives. What are some of the problems atomic power has created?
4. Many people say Einstein's theories changed our world, but many of us don't understand or can't explain his ideas. Name some other scientific theories and laws that have a major effect on our lives but that you don't understand.
5. Germany lost a great scientist when Einstein left. Why do scientists and other scholars sometimes choose to leave their native countries? Does this happen in your country? Do many professionals or highly educated people go to other countries to work and live?

Adjective Clauses

The Grand Canyon.

Theme: *National Parks*
Grammar: *Adjective Clauses*

Dialogue

ARNOLD: How are we ever going to make up our minds? There are hundreds of parks and monuments **that we can choose from.**

MOLLY: We can't visit every one of them. We have to agree on the ones **which we all really want to visit.**

JACK: Well, I'd like to visit parks **that have a lot of wildlife.** Yellowstone is the park **that is famous for its grizzly bears.** I'd love to see one.

YOLANDA: Grizzlies? I think I'll take a nature walk while you stalk a grizzly. Yellowstone itself sounds wonderful. According to the book **I took out of the library,** Yellowstone is the oldest park in the country and one of the most beautiful.

MOLLY: Yes, I want to visit Yosemite. I read that it has sequoias **which are 2,000 years old.**

ARNOLD: Sequoias? Are they the same as redwoods?

MOLLY: I think so. I've just been reading about them. They are evergreens. It says here that sequoias are trees **whose height can reach four hundred feet** and **whose diameter is sometimes thirty feet.** Isn't that amazing?

ARNOLD: Didn't I see a picture once of a tree **that you could drive through?**

MOLLY: That was a giant sequoia. It's in Yosemite National Park.

JACK: Wasn't it Yosemite **that Ansel Adams photographed?**

MOLLY: Who is Ansel Adams?

YOLANDA: He's an American photographer **who's been taking pictures of Yosemite and the surrounding area all his life.** Since the 1920s, I think.

JACK: A book of his photographs was published not too many years ago. His landscape pictures are fantastic.

YOLANDA: Molly, he's the photographer **whose book I showed you last week.**

MOLLY: Oh, yeah. Let's take the book with us and try to find the same landscapes when we get there.

JACK: That's a great idea. We could see the Grand Canyon, Yellowstone, and Yosemite.

ARNOLD: What about visiting the Petrified Forest and maybe the Navajo National Monument after that?

YOLANDA:	That sounds so exciting. The Navajo are Indians **I've always been interested in.**
MOLLY:	Me too. Let's make some definite plans.
JACK:	Who knows a good travel agent? I'll make reservations.
ARNOLD:	I do. Go to the travel agency around the corner and ask for George. He's the agent **that I used for my trip to Mexico.**

Part 1   Restrictive Adjective Clauses

We use adjective clauses when we want to describe or define more fully a noun in a sentence. The adjective clause must contain its own subject and verb. The first word of an adjective clause is usually a relative pronoun: *who, whom, which, that, whose, where, when.* This relative pronoun always refers to a specific noun in the sentence. This noun is called an antecedent. It should come as close to the adjective clause as possible.

Examples

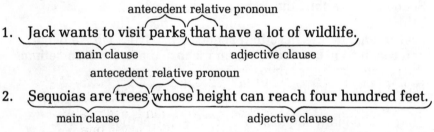

1.   Jack wants to visit parks that have a lot of wildlife.

    main clause   adjective clause

2.   Sequoias are trees whose height can reach four hundred feet.

    main clause   adjective clause

A. The Relative Pronoun in Subject Position

Examples
Yellowstone National Park was established in 1872 by the Congress of the United States. It is a park **which has many natural wonders.** For example, there are two hundred geysers **that erupt and shoot hot water many feet into the air.** The most famous geyser is called Old Faithful. Most of the park is covered by vast evergreen forests. Yellowstone has many park rangers **who are in charge of protecting the park and helping the visitors.** A tourist **that visits the park in the summer** can go on guided hikes or can go backpacking, boating, and fishing. If he goes in the winter, he can take snowmobile trips into the forests.

Explanation
When the relative pronoun is the subject of the adjective clause, we use *who, which,* or *that* to refer to a noun in the main clause. *Who* or *that* can be used when the antecedent is a person.

A tourist *who* visits the park in the summer can go on guided hikes.
A tourist *that* visits the park in the winter can take snowmobile trips
    into the forests.

Which or *that* can be used when the antecedent is a thing.

It is a park *which* has many natural wonders.
It is a park *that* has many natural wonders.

Notice that the verb in the adjective clause must agree in number with the
antecedent. If the antecedent is plural, then the verb in the adjective clause
is plural. If the antecedent is singular, then the verb in the adjective clause
is singular.

It is a *park which has* many natural wonders.
It has *geysers that erupt.*

NOTE: A common mistake which students make is to add an additional
subject after the relative pronoun.

It is a park which ✗ has many natural wonders.

B. The Relative Pronoun in Object Position

Examples

Mount Rushmore, a famous national monument, is located in the Black Hills
of South Dakota. A sculptor named Borglum carved the faces of famous
presidents here. The cliff **which he chose for this project** is made of granite
and is 6,000 feet high. The presidents **whom he selected to be sculpted**
were George Washington, Thomas Jefferson, Abraham Lincoln, and
Theodore Roosevelt. Of these four, Theodore Roosevelt is the one **we
associate with parks and conservation.**

Each face is about sixty feet in length. The models **that Borglum made
first** were only five feet high. So he had to multiply the measurements by
twelve when he worked on the actual faces on the cliff. Of course, he had to
have help on the project. The miners **that he hired** used dynamite and drills
to carve out the features on each face. The entire project took fourteen
years to finish. The money **Borglum used to pay for the project** came from
the federal government for the most part. The total cost was about
$1,000,000.

Explanation

When the relative pronoun is the object of the relative clause, we use
whom, which, or *that* to refer to a noun in the main clause. Notice that we
can omit the relative pronoun.

We use *whom* or *that* if the antecedent is a person.

The miners *whom he hired* used dynamite.
The miners *that he hired* used dynamite.
The miners *he hired* used dynamite.

We use *which* or *that* if the antecedent is a thing.

The cliff *which he chose* is made of granite.
The cliff *that he chose* is made of granite.
The cliff *he chose* is made of granite.

NOTES:

1. In spoken English many Americans don't use *whom*. Many use *who* even through it is not technically correct. In written English, *whom* is the correct form.
2. Be careful not to repeat the direct object in the adjective clause since the relative pronoun has replaced the direct object.

   The models that Borglum made ~~them~~ first were only five feet high.

C. The Relative Pronoun as the Object of a Preposition

Examples

Casa Grande, a national monument in Arizona, is an archeological site. Around A.D. 700, Indians were able to farm this desert area by using irrigation canals. Here are a few facts about these early Indians and their life-style.

The canals **from which water was taken** were sometimes fifteen miles long.

The crops **which the Indians depended on for food** were corn, beans, and pumpkins.

The plant **that they made cloth from** was cotton.

The houses **they lived in** were made of baked mud and dried plants.

Later, around A.D. 1150, other Indians came to this area and mixed with the first inhabitants. They are called the Pueblo. The Pueblo built Casa Grande, a large four-story building, which served as a watchtower and place of residence. The Pueblo were Indians **for whom agriculture was a way of life.** The people **that this tower was built for** were probably the leaders of the tribe and their families. This area ceased to be inhabited around 1450, probably because the land became waterlogged as a result of too much irrigation.

Explanation

Notice that adjective clauses can be written in several different ways when the relative pronoun is the object of a preposition. Look at these sentences, where the antecedent is a person.

The people *for whom* this tower was built were the leaders.
The people *whom* this tower was built *for* were the leaders.
The people *that* this tower was built *for* were the leaders.
The people this tower was built *for* were the leaders.

Now look at these sentences where the antecedent is a thing.

The houses *in which* they lived were made of mud and dried plants.
The houses *which* they lived *in* were made of mud and dried plants.
The houses *that* they lived *in* were made of mud and dried plants.
The houses they lived *in* were made of mud and dried plants.

In spoken English we usually begin the adjective clause with the relative pronoun and place the preposition at the end of the clause. If the preposition comes at the end of the clause, we can omit the relative pronoun. In written English and in more formal usage, we use *whom* or *which* after the preposition at the beginning of the adjective clause. *That* cannot be used after a preposition.

D. <u>Whose</u> in Adjective Clauses

Explanation
For people and for things, the relative pronoun which designates the possessive is *whose*.

Examples
The Grand Canyon is one of the most famous sites in the United States. This is a canyon **whose walls were created by eight million years of erosion and geological change.** The rock formations are of many different and beautiful colors. In addition, Indians lived there for many centuries. They were an ancient people **whose houses were built into the stone walls of the canyon.** These dwellings can still be seen today.

E. <u>Where</u> and <u>When</u> in Adjective Clauses

Explanation
Where and when can also be used to introduce adjective clauses. Since where and when cannot be the subject, the adjective clause must have a subject and a verb.

Examples
1872 was the year **when the National Park Act was passed.** Since then, a large number of parks have been added to the park system. There is a great deal of variety in these parks. There are parks **where volcanoes still erupt;** there are parks **where you can still see cliff dwellings of primitive people;** there are parks **where you can go for miles and miles without seeing another living person.**

Exercise 1 Definitions

Directions

Answer these questions with a definition. Write adjective clauses using *which, who,* or *that* in your sentences.

Example

1. What's a geyser? *A geyser is a fountain of hot water which shoots high into the air.*

2. What's a snowmobile? _____

   _____

3. What's a park ranger? _____

   _____

4. What's a travel agent? _____

   _____

5. What are evergreens? _____

   _____

6. What are backpackers? _____

   _____

7. What are conservationists? _____

   _____

8. What's a volcano? _____

   _____

9. What are grizzly bears? _____

   _____

10. What is a desert? _____

_____

11. What is a bird watcher? _____

_____

Exercise 2 Adjective Clauses with
Which, Who, Whom, That, and Whose

Directions

Finish these sentences by using adjective clauses.

When I go on vacation,

I like to visit places which *I've never been to before.*_____

I like to visit places where _____

I like to eat food that _____

I like to stay in hotels whose prices _____

I like to travel with people who _____

I detest tourists that _____

I like to meet people with whom _____

I don't like tourists whose attitudes _____

I don't like tourists whose behavior _____

I don't like tourists whose manners _____

Exercise 3 Free Practice

Directions

Ask a classmate the following questions and discuss your answers.

1. What kind of person makes a good friend?

A person who is honest and loyal makes a good friend.

2. What kind of person is impolite?
3. What kind of person annoys you?
4. What kind of person bores you?
5. What kind of person makes a good teacher?
6. What kind of person makes a good language learner?
7. What kind of person succeeds in business?
8. What kind of person succeeds as a politician? An artist? A doctor?
9. What kind of person would you like to marry?
10. What kind of country do you like to travel to?
11. What kind of town or city would you like to live in?
12. What kind of school would you want to send your child to?
13. What kind of car would you like to own?
14. What kind of restaurant do you like to eat in?
15. What kinds of clothes do you like to wear?

Exercise 4 Free Practice and Discussion

A. Make sentences in which you define certain things which are true about your country. For example: "The United States is a country which is composed of many different ethnic groups." Then choose several of your sentences; give examples or specific information to explain and expand your ideas. Discuss your ideas in class.

B. Make sentences in which you define the national character of the people of your country. For example: "Americans are people who are always on the move." Then choose several of your sentences; give examples or specific information to explain and expand your ideas. Discuss your ideas in class.

Exercise 5 Test Your Memory

Directions
This exercise is based on the information in the first part of the chapter. The numbered phrases are the first part of sentences. Choose the correct ending of each sentence from the lettered items (a through j) below. Put the sentences together by using adjective clauses. You will have to change some of the sentences slightly. This exercise can be done in groups.

A. Use *which* or *that.*

1. Yosemite is the national park _which is located in central California._

2. The Grand Canyon is the park _____

   _____

3. Yosemite is the park _____

   _____

4. Yellowstone and Yosemite are parks _____

   _____

5. The Grand Canyon is the park _____

   _____

6. Yellowstone is the park _____

   _____

7. Mount Rushmore is the name of the cliff _____

   _____

8. Mount Rushmore is the monument _____

   _____

9. Casa Grande is the monument _____

   _____

10. Yellowstone is the park _____

   _____

   a. It is located in central California.
   b. They are covered by forests of evergreens.
   c. There are many geysers there.
   d. The government paid almost $1 million for this monument.
   e. Roosevelt visited it in 1903.
   f. It was formed by centuries of erosion.
   g. Its history dates back to A.D. 700.

h. Its grizzlies have been known to be dangerous.

i. Borglum chose to sculpt the faces of four presidents on this cliff.

j. People visit it to see beautiful rock formations of many colors.

B. Use *who, whom,* or *that.*

1. Ulysses S. Grant was the president *who dedicated the first national park.*

2. A forest ranger is a person _____

   _____

3. The Pueblo were native Americans _____

   _____

4. Washington, Jefferson, Lincoln, and Roosevelt were the presidents

   _____

5. Borglum was the sculptor _____

   _____

6. Theodore Roosevelt was the president _____

   _____

7. Ansel Adams is the photographer _____

   _____

8. The Navajo are Indians _____

   _____

9. Theodore Roosevelt was the president _____

   _____

10. The Pueblo were people _____

   _____

a. He dedicated the first national park.
b. Borglum sculpted them at Mount Rushmore.
c. His picture was taken in front of a giant sequoia.
d. Conservationists looked to him for leadership.
e. He watches out for forest fires.
f. Their houses were several stories high and were built of mud and clay.
g. They were able to farm the desert of Arizona.
h. Yolanda has always been interested in them.
i. Yosemite has always been important to him.
j. The federal government paid him to sculpt the faces on Mount Rushmore.

C. Use *when* or *where.*

1. Summer is the season _____

   _____

2. Winter is the season _____

   _____

3. Yellowstone is the park _____

   _____

4. Yellowstone and Yosemite are parks _____

   _____

a. Visitors can see Old Faithful.
b. Visitors can go camping then.
c. Visitors can see giant sequoias.
d. Visitors can take snowmobile trips.

Exercise 6 Sentence Combining

Directions

Combine the following groups of sentences by using adjective clauses. Some of the sentences are incomplete without the adjective clause.

Example

A. The Everglades.

1. The Everglades is a national park . . . it is the third largest park in the country.

The Everglades is the national park which is the third largest in the country.

2. The Everglades is a national park . . . it is located in southern Florida.

3. It is unique because it is the only park . . . it is mostly covered by water.

4. It is a vast area . . . its fresh water supply comes from lakes and rivers farther north.

Hunters came to this area around the turn of the century.

5. Some birds almost became extinct at this time . . . the feathers of these birds were used to decorate women's hats.

6. The Everglades is a park . . . many rare birds and animals are protected here.

_____

_____

7. There are also Indians . . . they live in the Everglades.

_____

_____

8. Before Europeans came to this area, there were Indians here . . . the rich resources of the Everglades had attracted them.

_____

_____

9. In the nineteenth century, other Indians arrived . . . white settlers and the American Army had pushed them south to the Everglades.

_____

_____

Later white settlers came to this area.

10. They were hunters and traders . . . the Indians sold them beautiful bird feathers and alligator hides.

_____

_____

Many people were concerned about protecting these animals.

11. Theodore Roosevelt was one . . . he was concerned about the preservation of these rare and beautiful birds.

_____

_____

12. The Audubon Society[1] sent a warden . . . his duty was to protect the wildlife.

_____

_____

13. In a tragic incident, the person . . . was shot . . . the Society had sent him.

_____

_____

Not long after this incident, the Everglades was made into a national park.

B. The Navajo

1. The Navajo are Indians . . . they live at the Navajo National Reservation in Arizona.

_____

_____

2. Basically, the Navajo have been a tribe . . . this tribe has depended on ranching and farming for their livelihood.

_____

_____

3. They live on a reservation . . . oil and gas reserves were found here.

_____

_____

---

1. _the Audubon Society:_ an organization interested in protecting and studying wild birds.

4. They are Indians . . . their tribal income has been steadily increasing because of the oil deposits on their land.

   _____

   _____

5. They are people . . . their religion is highly complex with many ceremonies.

   _____

   _____

6. They settled in the same area . . . the Pueblo had lived here.

   _____

   _____

7. The Navajo are Indians . . . the Pueblo taught them to weave.

   _____

   _____

8. The Navajo are Indians . . . the Mexicans showed them how to work with metal, especially in jewelry making.

   _____

   _____

9. The Navajo are Indians . . . their silver and turquoise jewelry has always been popular.

   _____

   _____

Part 2   Nonrestrictive Adjective Clauses

Explanation

Nonrestrictive (or nonessential) adjective clauses have a different function in the sentence from that of restrictive adjective clauses. Restrictive adjective clauses supply information essential to the meaning of the whole sentence; a nonrestrictive clause gives extra or additional information about the noun it modifies. This information is not essential to the meaning of the main clause.

Look at the following examples.

Trees that are used to make paper are fast-growing.

The main clause in this sentence is: Trees are fast-growing. This sentence is not true. It means that all trees grow fast. However, some trees grow very slowly. The adjective clause is essential to make the sentence accurate; it identifies particular trees. This adjective clause is restrictive (or essential).

Sequoias, which originated in China, are found in great abundance in California.

The main clause of this sentence is: Sequoias are found in great abundance in California. This sentence is a statement about sequoias in general. The adjective clause is not essential to the meaning of the sentence. It only gives extra information.

Nonrestrictive adjective clauses are formed in the same way as restrictive adjective clauses except for these three differences:

1.   *That* is never used in nonrestrictive clauses.
2.   The relative pronoun can never be omitted in nonrestrictive adjective clauses.
3.   Commas are always placed at the beginning and end of the nonrestrictive adjective clause.

Examples

Theodore Roosevelt, **who was an active conservationist**, established five new parks and set aside about 150,000,000 acres of forest reserves during his presidency. He also expanded Yosemite, **which he visited in 1903**. While he was there, he had his photograph taken in front of the Wawona Tunnel Tree. This tree, **whose tunnel was carved out in 1881**, finally fell in a storm in 1969. It was calculated to be 2,200 years old.

In this paragraph, the main clause of each sentence with an adjective clause can stand alone as a meaningful sentence. In the first sentence, we learn that Theodore Roosevelt established five new parks. This is a true statement. The fact that he was also an active conservationist does not change the meaning of the sentence.

Now look at the following sentences that have restrictive adjective clauses.

One president *who was very famous as a conservationist* was Theodore Roosevelt.

The famous sequoia *which fell in 1969* was called the Wawona Tunnel Tree.

Roosevelt disliked people *who had no appreciation of nature and wildlife.*

In these sentences the adjective clauses are necessary (restrictive) because they define or tell *which* president, *which* tree, or *which* people.

NOTE: It is often difficult to decide whether an adjective clause should be restrictive or nonrestrictive. However, there is one rule which will always hold true. If the adjective clause modifies a proper noun (the name of a person, place, or thing), the adjective clause must be nonrestrictive. These clauses are generally more common in writing than in speaking.

Exercise 7   Restrictive and Nonrestrictive Clauses

Directions
Read the following paragraphs. Decide which relative pronoun is correct and fill in the blanks. Then decide which clauses are restrictive and which are nonrestrictive. Add commas where necessary. If there are two blanks, add the necessary preposition.

Hawaii is a state _____ is composed of many islands in the

middle of the Pacific Ocean. Some of these islands still have volcanoes

_____ erupt from time to time. A spectacular eruption began in

November 1961. Lava _____ is liquid or molten rock began to

flow from Kilauea volcano. At one point, lava _____ was

forced up by pressure and steam reached a height of 1,800 feet above the

top of Kilauea. This period of activity lasted for five years, until July 1966.

In 1977 there were more eruptions. The inhabitants _____

the authorities had warned of the danger refused to leave their villages.

They believed the fire goddess Pele _____ they worshiped

would not harm them. The lava flow didn't reach their village, and no one

was hurt.

Kilauea and Mauna Loa _____ are both active volcanoes are

located within the boundaries of a national park. In this park is the

Hawaiian Volcano Observatory _____ was established in

1911. This agency studies volcanoes and tries to predict eruptions. Whenever an eruption occurs, many sightseers rush to see it. Some even fly in small planes in order to get a closer view of the eruption.

Another unusual park is Hot Springs National Park _____ is located in the state of Arkansas. The park has forty-seven hot springs _____ _____ water emerges from a break in the earth's crust. The water _____ is 143°F is channeled into reservoirs _____ bathers can go swimming. Generally, only people _____ _____ doctors have prescribed these waters come to bathe. However, a doctor's recommendation is not necessary. A person _____ obtains a permit at the park may use the facilities.

Hot springs have long been popular all over the world. The water _____ contains different minerals is thought to help cure certain illnesses. Bath, England _____ the Romans built an elaborate system of baths has long been famous for its hot springs. All the baths _____ the Romans built had a heating and a cooling system. In the eighteenth century, wealthy people again came to "take the waters" and relax in Bath _____ the facilities had been rebuilt. Until recently in this country, also, hot springs were for the wealthy _____ visited them for their healing qualities.

Expressing Your Ideas: Speaking and Writing

1. What is the most famous park you have ever visited? Describe it.
2. Does your country have a system of national parks? What is the concept of a park in your country? What activities are provided for visitors to parks?
3. In your opinion, what function should parks serve? What do you expect from a park when you visit one?
4. How would you compare the parks in your country to those in the United States? Do thousands of people travel to these parks to camp, hike, backpack, see the wonders of nature?
5. There are many different kinds of gardens around the world. France is famous for its very formal gardens, while English gardens appear to be more natural. The Japanese have their own style of garden; one well-known type of Japanese garden is the rock garden. Ask different members of your class if they can describe any of these gardens or a typical garden from their country.
6. What are some of the natural wonders that a tourist might visit in your country? Are these places protected by the government?
7. In the United States about 2 percent of the land area is set aside as national parks. Should the government set aside a certain percentage of land for use as parks? Should wildlife also be protected in parks?

Chapter 27

Final Integration of Verb Tenses: Active and Passive and Modal Auxiliaries

Directions

Fill in the blanks with one of the tenses that you have studied in this book. Choose between active and passive voice. When you see *modal* + *verb*, choose the correct modal auxiliary verb, tense, and voice. When you see two verbs next to each other under the line, put the second verb in the infinitive or gerund form.

(YOLANDA, ARNOLD, JACK, and MOLLY are still on vacation. They are around a campfire in Yellowstone Park. It is midnight.)

YOLANDA: This _____ a really super trip so far. I
           (be)

_____ anything so much in my life.
(never/enjoy)

ARNOLD: Yeah. We _____ for three weeks. We only
         (travel)

_____ one week left. I wish we _____
(have)   (negative, be)

so near the end.

MOLLY: You know what my favorite part of the trip _____
              (be)

so far? Remember the beach in Florida? We _____
(swim)

in the Gulf of Mexico at night, when all of a sudden the moon

_____ out from behind a cloud and _____
(come)   (make)

our bodies _____ like silver.
(shine)

JACK: That's because there are tiny phosphorescent organisms that

_____ in the ocean. Every once in a while the tide
(live)

_____ them in to shore.
(bring)

MOLLY: Oh, Jack. You always _____ like a scientist. You
                                        (think)
_____ very romantic.
(negative, be)

YOLANDA: It's too bad that we _____ any pictures that night. I
                                        (negative, take)
wish we _____ our cameras to the beach that night.
                (take)

YOLANDA: That was probably the most beautiful moment of the trip. We

_____ some really funny moments on this trip, too.
        (have)

ARNOLD: I think the funniest thing that _____ so far was
                                                (happen)
when I _____ _____ the suitcases on
                (forget)   (tie)
top of the car after we _____ out of the motel one
                                        (check)
morning. We _____ about ten miles down the road
                (already/drive)
by the time Molly _____ that the rope
                                (notice)
_____ down from the roof and that the suitcases
        (dangle)
weren't there. We _____ all the way back to the
                        (modal + drive)
motel to get them. Luckily, by the time we _____
                                                        (get)
there, the motel owner _____ our suitcases all over
                                (find)
the parking lot and _____ them up.
                        (already/pick)

YOLANDA: Arnold, look at the fire. It _____ a few minutes ago,
                                        (blaze)
but now it _____ low. We _____
                (get)   (need)
_____ some more wood on.
        (put)

ARNOLD: Okay. I _____ some.
                        (get)

JACK: Speaking of the most beautiful moment and the funniest moment

of the trip, what about the most frightening moment? I think we

all _____ that the most frightening moment was
      (agree)

when our canoe _____ on the Colorado River.
                  (capsize)

ARNOLD: We _____ a canoe on that river. It's much too
          (negative, modal + take)

dangerous.

JACK: Yes, we _____. Luckily we're all good swimmers,
           (modal + kill)

and we _____ our life jackets on at the time.
          (have)

YOLANDA: At first I thought I was drowning, but finally I _____
                                                          (be able/swim)

to shore. That water was really cold. It _____
                                          (modal + be)

about 45°.

ARNOLD: It was cold. It's too bad that some of our equipment

_____ when the canoe capsized.
   (lose)

JACK: Yes, but fortunately our canoe _____ by that fisher-
                                         (save)

man who was down the river.

MOLLY: Yolanda and I will never forget how we _____ by
                                                  (rescue)

that cute forest ranger.

YOLANDA: He certainly was attractive. If I _____ with you,
                                            (negative, be)

Arnold, I _____ _____ to know him
             (enjoy)   (get)

better.

ARNOLD: _____ you _____ _____
                                 (try)   (make)

me jealous?

YOLANDA: I _____.
            (joke)

MOLLY: You know Yolanda always _____ _____
                                     (enjoy)   (tease)

you, Arnold. You know she _____ you. It
                              (love)

_____ late. Let's talk about what we (get)

_____ next week. We _____ much (see) (negative, have)

time left. I'm concerned that we _____ everything (negative, be able/see)

that's on our itinerary.

JACK: I just hope that the rest of the trip _____ as (be)

beautiful as what we _____ so far. (see)

ARNOLD: Nothing could be as beautiful as the Painted Desert and the

Grand Canyon.

JACK: Or the Everglades, in my opinion. I wish everyone in the U.S.

_____ the opportunity to travel across our (have)

country. It's breathtakingly beautiful.

YOLANDA: What _____ we _____ next? (see)

ARNOLD: Because we _____ out of time, we _____ (run) (modal + drive)

straight to Yosemite.

JACK: I agree. We _____ _____ everything (negative, modal + try) (see)

else on the way. We really don't have time.

YOLANDA: How long _____ it _____ us to get to (take)

Yosemite from here? I _____ forward to (negative, look)

_____ in the car again. I _____ a little (ride) (get)

tired of _____ . I wish we _____ a van (sit) (have)

instead of a car.

JACK: Yeah. If we _____ a van, we _____ (have) (lie)

down in the back when we got tired.

MOLLY: After we _____ Yosemite, how much time
(visit)

_____ we _____ left to spend in San
(have)

Francisco?

ARNOLD: Just a few days. And don't forget that we _____
(modal + sell)

the car before we _____ home.
(fly)

YOLANDA: Where _____ we _____ in San
(stay)

Francisco?

ARNOLD: Our hotel reservations _____ at the Hilton by our
(already/make)

travel agent in New York.

YOLANDA: Oh, yeah. Now I _____.
(remember)

MOLLY: What time is it?

JACK: It's almost 1:00 A.M. We _____ to sleep or we
(modal + go)

_____ exhausted tomorrow.
(be)

ARNOLD: Wait a minute. Before we _____ to sleep, Yolanda
(go)

and I have something we _____ _____
(want)   (tell)

you. We _____ _____ married.
(decide)   (get)

MOLLY: Congratulations! That's wonderful! I'm so happy for you two.

JACK: That's great news. When _____ you

_____ married?
(get)

YOLANDA: As soon as we _____ back to New York.
(get)

JACK: We _____ when we _____ in San
           (celebrate)   (arrive)

Francisco. Molly and I _____ you out to one of the
                               (take)

best restaurants there. If we _____ a bottle of
                               (have)

champagne, we _____ right now.
             (celebrate)

Do you think Yolanda and Arnold's decision to get married is realistic? Is it a good decision? Do you think they are well matched? Do you think they will be happy? What do you think will happen?

Appendix: Irregular Verbs in English

Here is an alphabetical list of most of the irregular verbs in English. Some of the less common verbs are not included in this list

BASE FORM	PAST	PAST PARTICIPLE
be (am, is, are)	was, were	been
bear	bore	born
beat	beat	beat
become	became	become
begin	began	begun
bend	bent	bent
bet	bet	bet
bite	bit	bitten
bleed	bled	bled
blow	blew	blown
break	broke	broken
bring	brought	brought
build	built	built
burst	burst	burst
buy	bought	bought
catch	caught	caught
choose	chose	chosen
come	came	come
cost	cost	cost
cut	cut	cut
deal	dealt	dealt
do	did	done
dig	dug	dug
draw	drew	drawn
drink	drank	drunk
drive	drove	driven
eat	ate	eaten
fall	fell	fallen
feed	fed	fed
feel	felt	felt
fight	fought	fought
find	found	found

fit	fit	fit
fly	flew	flown
forbid	forbade	forbidden
forget	forgot	forgotten
forgive	forgave	forgiven
freeze	froze	frozen
get	got	got (or) gotten
give	gave	given
go	went	gone
grow	grew	grown
hang	hung	hung
have	had	had
hear	heard	heard
hide	hid	hidden
hit	hit	hit
hold	held	held
hurt	hurt	hurt
keep	kept	kept
kneel	knelt	knelt
know	knew	known
lay	laid	laid
lead	led	led
leave	left	left
lend	lent	lent
let	let	let
light	lit	lit
lose	lost	lost
lie	lay	lain
make	made	made
mean	meant	meant
meet	met	met
pay	paid	paid
put	put	put
quit	quit	quit
read	read[1]	read
ride	rode	ridden
ring	rang	rung
rise	rose	risen
run	ran	run
say	said	said
see	saw	seen
sell	sold	sold
send	sent	sent
set	set	set

---

1. Pronunciation change.

shake	shook	shaken
shine	shone	shone
shoot	shot	shot
shut	shut	shut
sing	sang	sung
sink	sank	sunk
sit	sat	sat
sleep	slept	slept
speak	spoke	spoken
speed	sped	sped
spend	spent	spent
split	split	split
spread	spread	spread
stand	stood	stood
steal	stole	stolen
stick	stuck	stuck
sting	stung	stung
strike	struck	struck
swear	swore	sworn
sweep	swept	swept
swim	swam	swum
swing	swung	swung
take	took	taken
teach	taught	taught
tear	tore	torn
tell	told	told
think	thought	thought
throw	threw	thrown
understand	understood	understood
wake	woke	woken
wear	wore	worn
win	won	won
wind	wound	wound
write	write	written

In the following section, the verbs from the alphabetical list are grouped into different categories. Some of the verbs in the alphabetical list do not fall into a special category, and therefore do not appear in this section.

begin	began	begun		bleed	bled	bled
run	ran	run		feed	fed	fed
sing	sang	sung		lead	led	led
ring	rang	rung		speed	sped	sped
sink	sank	sunk		read	read	read
swim	swam	swum		feel	felt	felt
drink	drank	drunk		keep	kept	kept
				leave	left	left
				mean	meant	meant
bring	brought	brought		sleep	slept	slept
buy	bought	bought		sweep	swept	swept
catch	caught	caught		meet	met	met
fight	fought	fought		deal	dealt	dealt
teach	taught	taught		kneel	knelt	knelt
think	thought	thought				
grow	grew	grown		break	broke	broken
know	knew	known		choose	chose	chosen
throw	threw	thrown		freeze	froze	frozen
blow	blew	blown		speak	spoke	spoken
draw	drew	drawn		steal	stole	stolen
fly	flew	flown		wake	woke	woken
				bear	bore	born
				swear	swore	sworn
drive	drove	driven		tear	tore	torn
rise	rose	risen		wear	wore	worn
ride	rode	ridden				
write	wrote	written				
				pay	paid	paid
				say	said	said
shake	shook	shaken		lay	laid	laid
take	took	taken				
hide	hid	hidden		sell	sold	sold
bite	bit	bitten		tell	told	told
sting	stung	stung				
swing	swung	swung		find	found	found
hang	hung	hung		wind	wound	wound
stick	stuck	stuck				
strike	struck	struck (or) stricken				
dig	dug	dug				

Ability, expression of, 123, 124–125
Active voice, 330
   vs. passive, 337–338
   using, 337–338
Adjective clauses, 437
   nonrestrictive, 451–454
   restrictive, 438–450, 453–454
   sentence combining with, 448–451
   when in, 441
   where in, 441
   whose in, 441
Adjectives, comparison of, 145
   in affirmative statements, 150–151
   expressing equality or near
      equality, 148
   expressing less, 147–148
   expressing more, 146–147
   integration of, 154–155, 161–164
   in negative statements, 151
   in paired questions, 152
   parallelism expressed by, 149
   in questions, 148
Adjectives, superlative of, 167–168,
     170–173, 174–175
Adverbs
   comparison of, 145, 156, 157–159,
     161–164
   definition of, 155
   forming, 156–157
   frequency, 49
   exercises for, 62–63
     position of, 59
     in questions, 60
Advice
   with *had better*, 215, 219–220,
     223–224, 231–234
   with *ought to*, 215, 216, 217,
     218–219, 231–234
Affirmative statements
   in past tense, 36–37
   and past tense of *to be*, 41
   in simple present tense, 50, 52
   verb and infinitive in, 92–93

A lot, use of, 246
Already, present perfect with, 266,
    269–270
Always
   answers with, 261–262
   questions with, 264–265
As of now, present perfect with, 266

Be
   past tense of, 41
   there and, 71, 72–77
Be able to, 123
   affirmative vs. negative form of, 130
   in past tense, 128–129
   in present tense, 124–125, 128–129
Be supposed to, using, 215, 226–229,
    233–234
Best and worst, 167–168
By
   future perfect with, 302
   simple past perfect with, 294–295
By the time
   future perfect with, 302
   simple past perfect with, 294–295

Can, 123
   with future tense, 126
   with past tense, 128–129, 357
   in present tense, 124–125, 128–129
Cannot, impossibility with, 207
Causatives, 401
   active, 402–403, 404–408
     formation with *have*, 404
     vs. passive, 418
     in questions, 408–412
     who questions with *have*, 413–414
   passive, 403–404, 414–415
     formation with *have*, 404
     questions with, 415–417

Changes, 277–291
Cities, 145–164
Civil War, 385–398
Commas, and time clauses, 112
Comparative, integrated with
    superlative, 175
Conditionals
    general review of, 395–397
    past unreal, 385, 386–392
    present unreal, 365, 366–367,
        370–376
        continuous form of, 367
        contrasted with real, 377–378
        integration of, 382
    real, 109, 111–112, 116–117, 377
    real and unreal, 380–382
    time clauses integrated with,
        119–120
Continuous tenses, passive voice of,
    351–353
Could, 123, 195
    affirmative vs. negative form of, 130
    alternative solutions with, 205–206,
        208–209
    + *have* + past participle, 313
    integration of, 210–212
    in past tense, 125–126, 129–130
    possibility with, 206–207
    in present tense, 124–125
Could have, + past participle, 323
Could not have, + past participle, 323
Couldn't, impossibility with, 209–210

Dating, 3–27
Deduction
    with *must*, 195, 199–205, 212
    with *probably*, 199
Direction, noun clauses for asking,
    432–433
Disasters, 311–327
Doesn't have to, using, 189–191
Don't have to, using, 189–191

Education, 345–362
Energy, 49–69
Enough
    with adjectives, 237, 240, 243–245
    with nouns, 237, 240–241, 243–245
Equality, adjectives expressing, 148
Ever, questions with, 60, 260–265
Ever since
    clauses with, 279
    present perfect continuous with,
        285–286
Expectation, with *be supposed to*, 215,
    226–229, 233–234
Exploration and achievement,
    237–256
Extended present, 5, 8–10

Famous Americans, 423–434
Few, as count noun, 83–84
For, present perfect continuous with,
    283
Future. *See* simple future
Future perfect, 293
    with certain adverbs, 303
    integration of, 305–308
    in questions, 303–304
    use of, 302–303, 304–305

Going to, future with, 15, 16, 17–18,
    23–24
Government, 329–342

Had better
    with advice or warning, 214,
        219–220, 223–224, 231–234
    continuous form of 224–226
Had to, to express necessity, 183–186,
    189–191
Have
    with active causative, 413–414
    and causative formation, 404

Have to, 181
  in affirmative statements, 182, 183
  integration of, 186–187, 191–192
  in negative statements, 182, 183
  past tense of, 357
  in questions, 182–183
  using, 183–186, 189–191
Hope clauses, vs. wish clauses, 377
How long, present perfect continuous
    with, 283
How often, questions with, 60, 63–65
How many times, questions with,
    260–265

If clauses, 111–112, 366–376
  past time, with present time main
    clauses, 393, 394–395
  time clauses with, 111–118
  use of, 386
Immigrants, 71–89
Impossibility, with could not, 207,
    209–210
Infinitives
  reduced, 92
  verb + object +, 93–98
Inflation, 365–383
Information, noun clauses for asking,
    432–433
Interrupted action, past continuous
    tense with, 134–138
Irregular verbs, 30, 462–465

Leisure time, 195–212
Less, adjectives expressing, 147
Little, as count noun, 83–84
Logical assumption, with must, 195,
    199–205, 212
Love and marriage, 259–275

May
  + have + past participle, 312
  with present continuous tense,
    203–205
  to show possibility, 195, 196–199,
    201–205, 210–212
May have, + past participle, 315,
    316–320
Medicine, 293–308
Might, + have + past participle, 312
  with present continuous tense,
    203–205
  to show possibility, 195, 196–199,
    210–212
Might have, + past participle, 315,
    316–320
Military, 181–192
Modal auxiliaries
  Be supposed to, 215, 226–229,
    233–234
  continuous forms of, 224–226
  could, 195, 205–212
  in future, 126–128
had better, 215, 219–220, 223–224,
    231–234
  have to, 229–233
  integration of, 231–233
  may, 195, 196–199, 201–205, 210–212
  might, 195, 196–199, 201–205,
    210–212
  must, 195, 199–205, 212
  ought to, 215, 216–217, 218–219,
    231–234
  with past tense, 125–126, 128–129
  in present tense, 124–125, 128–129
  in questions, 126–128
  should, 215, 216, 217–219, 224–225,
    229–234
  would rather, 215, 221–226, 231–234
Modal perfects, 311
  continuous, 314–324
  integration of, 324–326
More, adjectives expressing, 146–147

Must, 181
  in affirmative statements, 187
  + *have* + past participle, 312
  integration of, 191–192
  with logical assumption or
      deduction, 195, 199–205, 212
  in negative statements, 187–188
  with present continuous tense,
      203–205
  in questions, 188
  using, 168–191
Must have, + past participle, 316–320
Must not, using, 189–191

National parks, 437–455
Native Americans, 71–89
Negative questions, in past tense,
      37–38
Negative statements
  in past tense, 36–37
  and past tense of *to be*, 41
  in simple present tense, 50, 52,
      55–56
  verb + gerund in, 100
  verb + infinitive in, 92–93
Never
  answers with, 161–162
  questions with, 264–265
Noun clauses, 423
  asking for information and
      directions, 432–433
  expressions with, 426
  introduction to, 424
  and punctuation, 426
  using, 427–430
  writing dialogue with, 434
Nouns
  comparison of. 145, 159–164
  count, 71–72
    examples of, 78
    few, 83–84
    integration of, 85–88
    introduction to, 77
    large quantities with, 80–81

plural, 169
  in questions, 79, 81–83
  small quantity with, 81
non-count, 71–72
  examples of, 78
  integration of, 85–88
  introduction to, 77
  large quantities with, 80–81
  in questions, 79, 81–83
  small quantity with, 81
  using countable expressions with,
      84–85
  ways to count, 80
superlative of, 167, 168–169, 173–174

Object position, in *who/what*
      questions, 40
One of the, 169
Ought to
  with advice or moral belief, 215,
      216, 217, 218–219, 231–234
  + *have* + past participle, 313

Parellelism, adjectives expressing, 149,
      152–154
Passives
  with active voice, 359–361
  continuous, 345, 351–353
  modal, 345
    past, 357–359
    present and future, 354–357
  perfect, 345, 346–351
  simple, 329
    changing from active to, 338–339
    in future, 336–337, 339–341
    integration of, 341–342
    introduction to, 330
    in past and present, 333–336
    in questions, 332
    using, 331–332, 337–338
Past. *See* Simple past

Past continuous, 113
    integration of, 143
    with interrupted actions, 134–138
    vs. simple past, 138–139
    with simultaneous actions in past, 142
Past perfect, 293
    integration of, 305–308
    with *when* clauses, 300–302
Past perfect continuous, 293
    personal questions in, 297–298
    simple past vs., 298–300
    use of, 295–296
Permission, expression of, 123, 125
Personal problems, 215–234
Physical fitness, 109–120
Possibility, 123
    with *can*, 125
    with *could*, 195, 206–207, 209, 210–212
    with *may* or *might*, 195, 196–199, 201–205, 210–212
Preference, with *would rather*, 215, 221–226, 231–234
Preposition, + gerund, 99–100
Present. *See* Simple present
Present, extended, 5, 8–10
Present continuous, 3–4
    extended present, 5, 8
    and future, 6, 10, 25–26
    integrated with simple past, 44–45
    integrated with simple present, 67–69
    with *may*, 203–205
    with *might*, 203–205
    with *must*, 203–205
    and present moment, 5, 6, 8
    spelling problems for, 7
    using, 3–4
Present moment, 5, 6, 8–10
Present perfect, 259
    with *ever*, 260–265
    with *how many times*, 260–266
    integration of, 305–308
    with simple past, 270–273
    with superlative, 273–275

with unstated past, 266–270
Present perfect continuous, 277
    with *ever since*, 285–286
    integration of, 287–291
    with little difference in meaning, 280
    with meaning changing, 280–282
    vs. simple present perfect, 278, 286
    stative verbs, 284–285
    time expressions with, 278–279, 282
    use of, 278, 283
Probably, to indicate future deduction, 199
Problem solving, 119
Prohibition, expression of, 125
Pronoun, relative
    in object position, 439–440
    as object of preposition, 440–441
    in subject position, 438–439

Questions
    comparisons expressed in, 148
    direct, 430–432
    frequency adverbs in, 60
    indirect, 424–434, 430–432
    modal auxiliaries in, 126–128
    in simple past, 35–36
    in simple present, 52, 56–57
    time clauses in, 111
    wh-, 424
    with *who*, 11, 12, 57–58
    who/what object in, 39
    who/what subject in, 38–39
    word order for, 31
    yes/no, 425

Regular verbs, 30, 34
Requirement, with *be supposed to*, 215, 226–229, 233–234
Rock music, 91–106
Role playing, 186
    direct and indirect questions, 433
    with future tense, 24

Sentences, scrambled, 43
Should
  continuous form of, 224–226
  expectation, 216
  + *have* + past participle, 313
  to offer advice or express moral
      belief, 215, 216, 217–219,
      224–225, 229–234
Should have, + past participle,
      320–323
Simple future
  going to, 15, 16–18
  integration of, 305–308
  in passive voice, 339–341
  and present continuous, 6, 10,
      25–26
  will, 15, 19–23
Simple past
  in affirmative statements, 30, 36–37
  chart for, 31
  dialogue using, 29
  explanation of, 30
  integrated with present continuous,
      44–45
  integration of, 305–308
  negative questions in, 37–38
  in negative statements, 30, 36–37
  with present perfect, 270–273
  pronunciation of regular verbs in, 34
  question formation in, 31, 35–36
  spelling problems for, 33
  with *when* clauses, 300–302
Simple past perfect
  with certain adverbs, 295
  passive voice of, 349–351
  use of, 294, 296–297
Simple present, 49
  charts for, 52
  exercises for, 53–54
  integrated with present continuous,
      67–69
  integration of, 65–67, 305–308
  introduction to, 50–58
  questions in, 51, 56–57
  who/what questions in, 51–52

Simple present perfect, 277
  integration of, 287–291
  with little difference in meaning, 280
  with meaning changing, 280–281
  passive voice of, 346–349
  with present perfect continuous,
      286–287
  with stative verbs, 284–285
  verbs requiring, 281
Since
  clauses with, 279
  with present perfect continuous, 283
So far, present perfect with, 266,
      269–270
So much that, 246, 247–250, 252–254,
      255
So that
  with adjectives and adverbs, 237,
      247–250, 252–254
  with quantifiers, 237, 247–250,
      252–254, 255
Space program, 29–47
Sports, 109–131
Still, present perfect with, 266,
      269–270
Subject position, *who/what* questions
      in, 40
Such that, 237, 250–254
Superlative
  of adjectives, 168, 170–173, 174–175
  integration of comparative with,
      175–178
  of nouns, 168–169, 173–174
  present perfect with, 169–170,
      273–275

Television, 401–420
Tenses
  continuous, 351–353
  final integration of, 456–461
  future perfect, 293
    with certain adverbs, 303

integration of, 305–308
  in questions, 303–304
  use of, 302–303, 304–305
past continuous, 133
  integration of, 143
  interrupted actions, 134–138
  vs. simple past, 138–139
  with simultaneous actions in past, 142
  with specific time, 140
past perfect, 293
  integration of, 305–308
  with *when* clauses, 300–302
past perfect continuous, 293
  personal questions in, 297–298
  simple past vs. 298–300
  use of, 295–296
present continuous, 3–4
present perfect, 259
  with *ever*, 260–265
  with *how many times*, 260–266
  integration of, 305–308
  with simple past, 270–273
  with superlative, 273–275
  with unstated past, 266–270
present perfect continuous, 277
  with *ever since*, 285–286
  with little difference in meaning, 280
  with meaning changing, 280–282
  vs. simple present perfect, 278, 286
  time expressions with, 278–279, 282
  use of, 278, 283
simple future
  going to, 15, 16–18
  integration of, 305–308
  in passive voice, 339–341
  and present continuous, 6, 10, 25–26
  will, 15, 19–23

simple past
  in affirmative statements, 30, 36–37
  chart for, 31
  dialogue using, 29
  explanation of, 30
  integrated with present continuous, 44–45
  integration of, 305–308
  negative questions in, 37–38
  in negative statements, 30, 36–37
  with present perfect, 270–273
  pronunciation of regular verbs in, 34
  question formation in, 31, 35–36
  spelling problems for, 33
  with *when* clauses, 300–302
simple past perfect
  with certain adverbs, 295
  passive voice of, 349–351
  use of, 294, 296–297
simple present, 49
  charts for, 52
  exercises for, 53–54
  integration of, 65–67, 305–308
  introduction to, 50–58
  question in, 51, 56–57
  who/what questions in, 51–52
simple present perfect, 277
  with little difference in meaning, 280
  with meaning changing, 280–281
  passive voice of, 346–349
  with present perfect continuous, 286–287
That, adjective clauses with, 443–447
There, and *be*, 71–72, 72–77
Three of the, as count noun, 169
Time clauses, 109
  exercises for, 113–116
  about future, 110–111

integrated with real conditional, 119–120
about past, 110
about present, 110
in questions, 111
Too, to indicate excess, 237, 238, 241
Too . . . to
   with adjective + *for*, 237, 239
   with adjectives and adverbs, 238, 242
   with quantifiers, 239, 242
Two of the, as count noun, 169

UFO's and other unexplained phenomena, 133–143
Unless
   clauses with, 111–112
   time clauses with, 117–118
Up to now, present perfect with, 266
Used to, 45–46

Verbs
   to change meaning, 61
   + gerund, 91, 98, 99, 101, 102–103, 104–106
   and infinitive, 91, 92–93, 94–95, 103, 104–106
   irregular, 30, 462–465
   + object + infinitive, 91, 93–98, 104–106
   regular, 30, 34
   requiring simple present perfect, 281
   stative, 49, 61
Very, to indicate intense quality, 238, 241
Voice. *See also* Passives
   active, 330
   active vs. passive, 330, 337–338

Warning, with *had better*, 215, 219–220, 223–224, 231–234
Was
   in dialogue, 42
   in past tense, 129–130
Was able to, in past tense, 125–126
Were, in dialogue, 42
Were able to, in past tense, 125–126, 129–130
What
   as object in questions, 39
   and past tense, 31
   as subject in questions, 38–39
   as subject of sentence, 6
When clauses
   in adjective clauses, 441
   future perfect tense with, 303
   with past perfect tense, 300–302
   with simple past, 300–302
   simple past perfect with, 294–295
Where, in adjective clauses, 441
Which, adjective clauses with, 443–447
Who
   adjective clauses with, 443–447
   as object in questions, 39
   and past tense, 31
   questions with, 57–58
   as subject in questions, 38–39
   as subject of sentence, 6, 7
Whom
   adjective clauses with, 443–447
   questions with, 11, 12
Who questions, with active causative, 413–414
Whose, in adjective clauses, 441, 443–447
Will
   in dialogue, 15, 19, 23–24
   explanation of, 19
   negative of, 20, 22
   to predict, 20, 22
   to promise, 21

Will be able to, with future tense, 126
Wish clauses, 365, 368–369, 371–372
  with future, 376, 378–379
  vs. *hope* clause, 377
  about past, 392, 393–394
  past unreal, 385
  with present, 366, 379
Won't
  dialogue using, 20
  explanation of, 20

Won't be able to, with future tense, 126
Would rather
  continuous form of, 224–226
  to indicate preference, 215, 221–226, 231–234

Yet, present perfect with, 266, 269–270